interactive

Fender® Bible

FENDER FACTS

Jawbone

An imprint of Outline Press Ltd

2A Union Court, 20–22 Union Road,

London SW4 6JP, England

www.jawbonepress.com

Fender Facts book: © 2007 Outline Press (Book Publishers) Ltd.

DVD: © 2007 Outline Press (Book Publishers) Ltd.

ISBN: 978-1-906002-06-0

TEXT: Paul Day, Dave Hunter

EDITOR: Tony Bacon

DESIGN: Paul Cooper Design, Balley Design Limited

Origination and print by Colorprint (Hong Kong)

1 2 3 4 5 11 10 09 08 07

contents

HOW TO USE THIS BOOK

The *Fender Facts* guidebook provides two sets of listings of all the electric guitars and amplifiers to have carried the Fender logo. The first set – pages 8 to 17 – is an A-to-Z listing of all models, from the American Vintage '62 Jaguar guitar to the 300PS amplifier. The second and main set of listings later in the book – pages 20 to 120 – organizes the models by year of introduction and offers detailed information.

To cross-reference a model in the A-to-Z listing with the later year-by-year listing, look up the first year of production and go to the relevant year.

In the A-to-Z listings, the two most popular guitar types, Stratocaster and Telecaster, have been issued in more variations and spin-offs than any other Fender products, and so they have been separated and given their own headings. Within these, further headings indicate instruments manufactured in the U.S.A., in Japan, in Mexico, or in Korea.

Other model listings in the A-to-Z also indicate country of origin, with special abbreviations when guitars or amps are manufactured outside the U.S.A.: these are MIJ (for manufactured in Japan), MIM (in Mexico), MIK (in Korea), and MII for the small number of amplifiers manufactured in Indonesia. The word *amp* in italics indicates an amplifier; all other listings are guitars.

The later main model listing has a separate explanatory introduction.

A note about Japanese models

This guidebook lists only the models marketed outside of Japan, all of which usually have 'Made In Japan' or 'Crafted in Japan' somewhere on them. It does not cover the models produced solely for the Japanese market, which include numerous interpretations of Fender's established designs and many combinations of construction, components, and cosmetics.

The periods of availability for models sold in Japan often differ to those of the same models officially sold in export markets. These export models, listed here, often appear to come and go, usually because demand from a particular distributor fluctuates. For that reason, certain Japanese models are irregularly removed from and then returned to Fender's various catalogues in the U.S.A. and Europe – while manufacture of the model in Japan might well remain continuous. This interrupted availability is confusing from a Western point of view and makes it difficult to accurately pin down the true periods of production. We have reflected this in the listing by simply showing a start date followed by 'onward'.

A note about Korean models

Many guitars made in Korea for Fender bear the Squier brandname and so are outside the scope of this Facts guide. However, a few have prominently featured the Fender logo, and so these are listed here. All have 'Made in Korea' somewhere on the instrument.

models:
a–z

A–Z Listing

A

AMERICAN VINTAGE '62 JAGUAR
1999–current
AMERICAN VINTAGE '62 JAZZMASTER
1999–current

B

BANDMASTER (tweed) *amp* 1952–60
BANDMASTER (brown Tolex) *amp*
1960–61
BANDMASTER (piggy–back) *amp*
1961–74
BANDMASTER REVERB *amp* 1970–81

BASSMAN (tweed) *amp* 1952–60
BASSMAN (Tolex piggy–back) *amp*
1961–79
BASSMAN 10 *amp* 1972–82
BASSMAN 50 *amp* 1972–76

BLUES DELUXE *amp* 1993–current
BLUES DE VILLE *amp* 1993–current
BLUES JUNIOR *amp* 1995–current

BROADCASTER 1950–51

BRONCO 1967–80
BRONCO *amp* 1968–74
BRONCO (solid state) *amp*
1993–current

BULLET first version 1981–83
BULLET second version 1983
BULLET DELUXE 1981–83
BULLET H1 1983

BULLET H2 1983
BULLET S2 1983
BULLET S3 1983
BULLET *amp* 1993–current

C

CAPRICORN *amp* 1970–72

CHAMP (tweed) *amp* 1953–64
CHAMP (Tolex) *amp* 1964–79
CHAMP II *amp* 1982–85
CHAMP 12 *amp* 1986–92
CHAMP 25 *amp* 1992–94

CHAMPION 30 (MII) *amp*
1999–current
CHAMPION 110 *amp* 1993–1999
CHAMPION 800 *amp* 1948
CHAMPION 600 *amp* 1949–52
CHAMPION 600 *amp* 2007–current

CLASSIC ROCKER 2000–02

COMPETITION MUSTANG 1968–73

CONCERT *amp* 1960–65, 1992–1996
CONCERT 112 *amp* 1982–85
CONCERT 210 *amp* 1982–85
CONCERT 410 *amps* 1982–85

CORONADO I 1966–69
CORONADO II 1966–69
CORONADO II ANTIGUA 1967–1971
CORONADO II WILDWOOD 1967–69
CORONADO XII 12-string 1966–69
CORONADO XII ANTIGUA 12-string
1967–71
CORONADO XII WILDWOOD 12-string
1967–69

CUSTOM 1969–70

CUSTOM ESQUIRE 1959–69
CUSTOM TELECASTER 1959–72

'CUSTOM' VIBROLUX REVERB *amp*
1995–current

CYBER-CHAMP (MIM) *amp* 2003–2006
CYBER-DELUXE (MIM) *amp*
2002–2006
CYBER-TWIN (MIM) *amp*
2001–current

CYCLONE (MIM) 1998–2006

CYCLONE HH (MIM) 2003–05

CYCLONE II (MIM) 2002–2006

D

D'AQUISTO DELUXE 1995–2001
D'AQUISTO ELITE 1994–95, 2000–01
D'AQUISTO ELITE (MIJ) 1984, 1989–94
D'AQUISTO STANDARD (MIJ) 1984

DELUXE (tweed) *amp* 1949–60
DELUXE (brown Tolex) *amp* 1960–63
DELUXE REVERB *amp* 1963–82
DELUXE REVERB II *amp* 1982–85
DELUXE 90 (MII) *amp* 1999–current

DUAL PROFESSIONAL *amp*
1994–current

DUAL SHOWMAN *amp* 1962–69,
1987–94
DUAL SHOWMAN REVERB *amp*
1969–79

DUO-SONIC first version 1956–64
DUO-SONIC second version 1964–69
DUO-SONIC II 1964–69
DUO-SONIC (MIM) 1993–97

E

ELAN I (MIM) 1993

ELECTRIC XII 12-string 1965–69

ESPRIT STANDARD (MIJ) 1984
ESPRIT ELITE (MIJ) 1984
ESPRIT ULTRA (MIJ) 1984

ESQUIRE 1950–69
ESQUIRE (MIJ) 1986–onward
'59 ESQUIRE 2003–06
CLASSIC 50s ESQUIRE (MIM)
    2005–current
CUSTOM ESQUIRE (MIJ) 1986–onward
ESQUIRE CUSTOM CELTIC (MIK) 2003
ESQUIRE CUSTOM GT (MIK) 2003
ESQUIRE CUSTOM SCORPION (MIK)
    2003

F

FLAME STANDARD (MIJ) 1984
FLAME ELITE (MIJ) 1984
FLAME ULTRA (MIJ) 1984

FLAT HEAD SHOWMASTER 2003–04
FLAT HEAD SHOWMASTER HH
    2004–06

FRONTMAN 15G (MII) *amp*
    1997–current
FRONTMAN 15R (MII) *amp*
    1997–current

FRONTMAN 25R (MII) *amp*
    1997–current

G

G-DEC (MII) *amp* 2005–current
G-DEC EXEC (MII) *amp* 2006–current
G-DEC JUNIOR (MII) *amp*
    2006–current
G-DEC 30 (MII) *amp* 2005–current

H

HARVARD *amp* 1956–61
HARVARD (solid state) *amp* 1979–82
HARVARD REVERB II *amp* 1982–85

HIGHWAY ONE SHOWMASTER HH
    2003–04
HIGHWAY ONE SHOWMASTER HSS
    2003–04
HIGHWAY ONE TORONADO 2003–04

H.O.T. *amp* 1990–95

JAG-STANG (MIJ) 1996–onward

JAGUAR 1962–75
JAGUAR (MIJ) 1986–onward
JAGUAR BARITONE CUSTOM (MIJ)
    2004–06
JAGUAR BARITONE HH (MIJ)
    2005–current
JAGUAR HH (MIJ) 2005–current

J.A.M. *amp* 1990–95

JAZZ KING (MIM) *amp* 2005–current

JAZZMASTER 1958–80

JAZZMASTER (MIJ)
    1986–onward

K

KATANA (MIJ) 1985–86

L

LEAD I 1979–82
LEAD II 1979–82
LEAD III 1981–82

LIBRA *amp* 1970–72

LONDON REVERB *amp* 1983–85
LONDON 185 *amp* 1988–92

LTD 1968–74

M

MAVERICK 1969–70

METALHEAD (MIM) *amp* 2005–current

MODEL 26 *amp* 1946–48

MONTEGO I 1968–74
MONTEGO II 1968–74

MUSICMASTER first version 1956–64
MUSICMASTER second version
    1964–75
MUSICMASTER third version 1975–80
MUSICMASTER II 1964–69
MUSTANG 1964–81
MUSTANG (MIJ) 1986–onward

M-80 *amp* 1990–95

N

NOCASTER 1951

P

PERFORMER (MIJ) 1985–86
PERFORMER 1000 *amp* 1993–96

POWER CHORUS *amp* 1991–93

PRINCETON (tweed) *amp* 1946–60
PRINCETON (Tolex) *amp* 1961–79
PRINCETON CHORUS *amp* 1989–2001
PRINCETON RECORDING-AMP *amp*
  2006–current
PRINCETON REVERB *amp* 1963–79
PRINCETON REVERB II *amp* 1982–85
PRINCETON 65 (MII) *amp*
  1999–current
PRINCETON 112 *amp* 1993–95

PRO AMP *amp* 1960–65
PRO JUNIOR *amp*
  1994–current
PRO REVERB *amp* 1965–82
PRO 185 *amp* 1989–92

PRODIGY 1991–93
PRODIGY II 1991–92

PROSONIC *amp* 1995–2001

Q

QUAD REVERB *amp* 1970–79

R

R.A.D. *amp* 1990–95

ROBBEN FORD ELITE 1994–2001
ROBBEN FORD ULTRA FM 1994–2001
ROBBEN FORD ULTRA SP 1994–2001
ROBBEN FORD (MIJ) 1989–94

RR-58 (MIJ) 1993

S

SCORPIO *amp* 1970–72

SEYMOUR DUNCAN SIGNATURE
  ESQUIRE 2003–current

SHOWMAN *amp* 1961–69
SHOWMAN 112 *amp* 1983–85
SHOWMAN 115 *amp* 1983–85
SHOWMAN 210 *amp* 1983–85
SHOWMAN 212 *amp* 1983–85

SHOWMASTER BLACKOUT (MIK)
  2004–05
SHOWMASTER CELTIC H (MIK) 2003
SHOWMASTER DELUXE HH WITH
  TREMOLO (MIK) 2003
SHOWMASTER ELITE 2004–current
SHOWMASTER ELITE HARD-TAIL
  2004–current
SHOWMASTER FAT-HH (MIK) 2004–05
SHOWMASTER FAT-SSS (MIK)
  2004–05
SHOWMASTER FMT 1998–2005
SHOWMASTER FMT-HH (MIK)
  2005–current
SHOWMASTER H WITH TREMOLO
  (MIK) 2003
SHOWMASTER HH WITH TREMOLO
  (MIK) 2003
SHOWMASTER QBT-HH (MIK)
  2004–current

SHOWMASTER QBT-SSS (MIK)
  2004–05
SHOWMASTER QMT-HH (MIK)
  2005–current
SHOWMASTER SCORPION HH (MIK)
  2003
SHOWMASTER SET NECK FMT
  1999–2005
SHOWMASTER SET NECK FMT HARD-
  TAIL 1999–2005
SHOWMASTER STANDARD 1999–2005
SHOWMASTER 7-STRING 2000–01
SHOWMASTER 7-STRING HARD-TAIL
  2000–01

SIDEKICK REVERB 20 (MIJ) *amp*
  1983–85
SIDEKICK REVERB 30 (MIJ) *amp*
  1983–85
SIDEKICK 10 (MIJ) *amp* 1983–85
SIDEKICK 35 REVERB (MIJ) *amp*
  1986–90
SIDEKICK 65 REVERB (MIJ) *amp*
  1986–90

SK CHORUS 20 (MIJ) *amp* 1991–92

SO-CAL SPEED SHOP (MIK) 2005

SOLID STATE BASSMAN *amp* 1968–70
SOLID STATE DELUXE REVERB *amp*
  1968–70
SOLID STATE PRO REVERB *amp*
  1968–70
SOLID STATE SUPER REVERB *amp*
  1968–70
SOLID STATE VIBROLUX REVERB *amp*
  1968–70

STAGE LEAD *amp* 1983–85

STAGE LEAD 212 *amp* 1983–85
STAGE 100 (MII) *amp* 1999–current
STAGE 112SE *amp* 1992–99
STAGE 160 (MII) *amp* 1999–current
STAGE 185 *amp* 1989–92

STARCASTER 1976–80

STEEL KING (MIM) *amp*
　2004–current

STRATOCASTER

STRATOCASTERS MANUFACTURED IN U.S.A.
ALUMINUM-BODY STRATOCASTER
　1994–95
AMERICAN CLASSIC STRATOCASTER
　1992–99
AMERICAN DELUXE ASH
　STRATOCASTER 2004–current
AMERICAN DELUXE FAT STRAT
　1998–2003
AMERICAN DELUXE FAT
　STRAT/LOCKING TREM 1998–2003
AMERICAN DELUXE STRATOCASTER
　first version 1998–2003
AMERICAN DELUXE STRATOCASTER
　second version 2004–current
AMERICAN DELUXE STRATOCASTER
　FMT HSS 2004–current
AMERICAN DELUXE STRATOCASTER
　QMT HSS 2004–current
AMERICAN DELUXE STRATOCASTER
　HSS 2004–current
AMERICAN DELUXE STRATOCASTER
　HSS LT 2004–06
AMERICAN DELUXE STRATOCASTER
　'V' NECK 2004–current

AMERICAN DELUXE 50th
　ANNIVERSARY STRATOCASTER
　2004
AMERICAN DOUBLE FAT STRAT
　2000–03
AMERICAN DOUBLE FAT STRAT HARD-
　TAIL 2000–03
AMERICAN FAT STRAT TEXAS SPECIAL
　2000–03
AMERICAN STANDARD DELUXE
　STRATOCASTER 1989–90
AMERICAN STANDARD ROLAND GR-
　READY STRATOCASTER 1995–98
AMERICAN STANDARD
　STRATOCASTER 1986–2000
AMERICAN STANDARD
　STRATOCASTER HARD-TAIL
　1998–2000
AMERICAN STRAT TEXAS SPECIAL
　2000–03
AMERICAN STRATOCASTER
　2000–current
AMERICAN STRATOCASTER HARD-
　TAIL 2000–06
AMERICAN STRATOCASTER HH
　2003–06
AMERICAN STRATOCASTER HH HARD-
　TAIL 2003–05
AMERICAN STRATOCASTER HSS
　2003–current
AMERICAN VG STRATOCASTER
　2007–current
AMERICAN VINTAGE '57
　STRATOCASTER 1998–current
AMERICAN VINTAGE '62
　STRATOCASTER 1998–current
AMERICAN VINTAGE 70s
　STRATOCASTER 2006–current
AMERICAN 50th ANNIVERSARY
　STRATOCASTER 2004

AMERICAN 60th ANNIVERSARY
　STRATOCASTER 2006
ANTIGUA STRATOCASTER 1977–79

BIG APPLE STRAT 1997–2000
BIG APPLE STRAT HARD-TAIL
　1998–2000
BONNIE RAITT STRATOCASTER
　1995–2001
BOWLING BALL STRATOCASTER 1984
BUDDY GUY STRATOCASTER
　1995–current

CALIFORNIA FAT STRAT 1997–98
CALIFORNIA STRAT 1997–current
CARVED TOP STRAT 1995–98
CARVED TOP STRAT HH 1998
CARVED TOP STRAT HSS 1998
CLASSIC PLAYER STRAT 1998–2005
COLLECTORS EDITION STRAT 1997
CONTEMPORARY STRAT 1995–98
CONTEMPORARY STRAT FMT 1995–98
CUSTOM CLASSIC STRAT
　1999–current

DICK DALE STRATOCASTER
　1994–current

ELITE STRATOCASTER 1983–84
ERIC CLAPTON STRATOCASTER first
　version 1988–2001
ERIC CLAPTON STRATOCASTER
　second version 2001–current
ERIC CLAPTON STRATOCASTER third
　version 2004–current
ERIC JOHNSON STRATOCASTER
　2005–current

FLOYD ROSE CLASSIC STRAT HH
　1998–2002

FLOYD ROSE CLASSIC STRAT HSS
1998–2002
FLOYD ROSE CLASSIC STRATOCASTER
1992–98

GOLD ELITE STRATOCASTER 1983–84
GOLD/GOLD STRATOCASTER 1981–83

HENDRIX STRATOCASTER 1980
HIGHWAY ONE STRATOCASTER first
version 2002–06
HIGHWAY ONE STRATOCASTER second
version 2006–current
HIGHWAY ONE STRATOCASTER HSS
first version 2003–06
HIGHWAY ONE STRATOCASTER HSS
second version 2006–current
HM STRAT (three types) 1989–90
HM STRAT ULTRA 1990–92

INTERNATIONAL COLOR
STRATOCASTER 1981

JEFF BECK STRATOCASTER first
version 1991–2001
JEFF BECK STRATOCASTER second
version 2001–current
JEFF BECK SIGNATURE
STRATOCASTER 2004–current
JIMI HENDRIX STRATOCASTER
1997–2000
JOHN MAYER STRATOCASTER
2005–current

LONE STAR STRAT 1996–2000

MARK KNOPFLER STRATOCASTER
2003–current

N.O.S. STRAT 1998

RELIC 50s STRATOCASTER 1996–98
RELIC 60s STRATOCASTER 1996–98
RELIC FLOYD ROSE STRATOCASTER
1998
RHINESTONE STRATOCASTER 1975
RICHIE SAMBORA STRATOCASTER
first version 1993–99
RICHIE SAMBORA STRATOCASTER
second version 1999–2002
RITCHIE BLACKMORE STRATOCASTER
1999–2005
ROADHOUSE STRAT 1997–2000
ROBERT CRAY STRATOCASTER
1992–current
ROBIN TROWER STRATOCASTER
2005–current
RORY GALLAGHER STRATOCASTER
2004–current

SET NECK STRATOCASTER first
version 1992–1995
SET NECK STRATOCASTER second
version 1995–98
SET NECK FLOYD ROSE
STRATOCASTER 1992–95
SPECIAL EDITION 1993
STRATOCASTER 1993
SPECIAL EDITION 1994
STRATOCASTER 1994
STEVIE RAY VAUGHAN STRATOCASTER
1992–current
STRAT 1980–83
STRAT-O-SONIC DVI 2003–04
STRAT-O-SONIC DVII 2003–06
STRAT-O-SONIC HH 2005–06
STRAT PLUS 1987–98
STRAT PLUS DELUXE 1989–98
STRAT PRO 2006–current
STRAT SPECIAL WITH LOCKING
TREMOLO HH 2002

STRAT SPECIAL WITH LOCKING
TREMOLO HSS 2002
STRAT ULTRA 1990–98
STRATOCASTER 'pre-CBS'
1954–65
STRATOCASTER 'CBS Sixties'
1965–71
STRATOCASTER 'CBS Seventies'
1971–81
STRATOCASTER STANDARD first
version 1981–83
STRATOCASTER STANDARD second
version 1983–84
SUB-SONIC STRATOCASTER HSS
baritone first version 2000–01
SUB-SONIC STRATOCASTER HSS
baritone second version 2001
SUB-SONIC STRATOCASTER HH
baritone 2000–01

U.S. CONTEMPORARY STRATOCASTER
1989–91

VINTAGE HOT ROD '57 STRAT
2007–current
VINTAGE HOT ROD '62 STRAT
2007–current

VOODOO STRATOCASTER 1998–2000

WALNUT ELITE STRATOCASTER
1983–84
WALNUT STRAT 1981–83

YNGWIE MALMSTEEN STRATOCASTER
first version 1988–98
YNGWIE MALMSTEEN STRATOCASTER
second version 1998–2006
YNGWIE MALMSTEEN STRATOCASTER
third version 2007–current

a-z

25th ANNIVERSARY STRATOCASTER
1979–80
40th ANNIVERSARY 1954
STRATOCASTER 1994
50th ANNIVERSARY STRATOCASTER
1996
'54 STRATOCASTER 1992–98
'54 STRATOCASTER FMT 1995–98
'56 STRATOCASTER 1999–current
'57 STRATOCASTER 1983–85, 1986–98
'58 STRATOCASTER 1996–98
'60 STRATOCASTER first version
1992–98
'60 STRATOCASTER second version
1999–current
'60 STRATOCASTER FMT 1995–98
'62 STRATOCASTER 1983–85,
1986–98
'65 STRATOCASTER 2003–06
'66 STRATOCASTER 2004–current
'68 REVERSE STRAT SPECIAL 2002
'69 STRATOCASTER first version
1996–98
'69 STRATOCASTER second version
1999–current

**STRATOCASTERS
MANUFACTURED IN JAPAN**
AERODYNE CLASSIC STRATOCASTER
2006–current
AERODYNE STRATOCASTER first
version 2004
AERODYNE STRATOCASTER second
version 2005–06
ANTIGUA STRATOCASTER 2004

BLUE FLOWER STRATOCASTER first
version 1988–93
BLUE FLOWER STRATOCASTER
second version 2003

CONTEMPORARY STRATOCASTER four
variations 1985–87
CONTEMPORARY STRATOCASTER
DELUXE two variations 1985–87

FLOYD ROSE HRR STRATOCASTER
1992–94
FLOYD ROSE STANDARD
STRATOCASTER 1994–96
FOTO FLAME STRATOCASTER
1995–96

HANK MARVIN STRATOCASTER
1996–97
HM POWER STRAT first type 1988–89
HM POWER STRAT second type
1988–89
HM STRAT two types 1991–92
HRR STRATOCASTER 1990–94

IRON MAIDEN SIGNATURE
STRATOCASTER 2001–02

JERRY DONAHUE HELLECASTERS
STRATOCASTER 1997–98
JOHN JORGENSON HELLECASTER
1997–98

MATTHIAS JABS STRATOCASTER 1998

PAISLEY STRATOCASTER
1988–onward

RICHIE SAMBORA PAISLEY
STRATOCASTER 1996
RITCHIE BLACKMORE STRATOCASTER
1997–98

SHORT-SCALE STRATOCASTER
1989–95

SQUIER SERIES FLOYD ROSE
STANDARD STRATOCASTER
1992–96
SQUIER SERIES '57 STRATOCASTER
1982–83
SQUIER SERIES '62 STRATOCASTER
1982–83
STANDARD STRATOCASTER first
version 1985–89
STANDARD STRATOCASTER second
version 1988–91
STRAT XII 12-string 1988–onward
STRATOCASTER '68 1988–onward
STRATOCASTER '72 1985–onward

THE VENTURES STRATOCASTER 1996

YNGWIE MALMSTEEN STANDARD
STRATOCASTER 1991–94

50s STRATOCASTER 1985–onward
60s STRATOCASTER 1985–onward

**STRATOCASTERS
MANUFACTURED IN MEXICO**
BUDDY GUY POLKA DOT STRAT
2002–current

CLASSIC 50s STRATOCASTER
1999–current
CLASSIC 60s STRATOCASTER
1999–current
CLASSIC 70s STRATOCASTER
1999–current
CHRIS REA CLASSIC STRATOCASTER
1999
CLASSIC PLAYER 50s STRATOCASTER
2006–current
CLASSIC PLAYER 60s STRATOCASTER
2006–current

a-z

DELUXE BIG BLOCK STRATOCASTER
2005–06.
DELUXE DOUBLE FAT STRAT
1999–2004
DELUXE DOUBLE FAT STRAT FLOYD
ROSE 1998–2004
DELUXE DOUBLE FAT STRAT HH WITH
LOCKING TREMOLO 2002–03
DELUXE FAT STRAT
1999–2006
DELUXE FAT STRAT FLOYD ROSE
1998–2005
DELUXE FAT STRAT HSS WITH
LOCKING TREMOLO 2002–03
DELUXE PLAYER'S STRAT
2004–current
DELUXE POWER STRATOCASTER
2006–current
DELUXE POWERHOUSE STRAT
1997–current
DELUXE STRAT HH 2004
DELUXE STRAT HH WITH LOCKING
TREMOLO 2004
DELUXE STRAT HSS 2004–06
DELUXE STRAT HSS WITH LOCKING
TREMOLO 2004–05
DELUXE SUPER STRAT 1997–2004

FLOYD ROSE STANDARD
STRATOCASTER 1994–98

HANK MARVIN CLASSIC
STRATOCASTER 2000
HANK MARVIN STRATOCASTER 1997

JIMMIE VAUGHAN TEX-MEX
STRATOCASTER 1997–current

RICHIE SAMBORA STANDARD
STRATOCASTER 1994–2002

ROBERT CRAY STRATOCASTER
2003–current

SPLATTER STRATOCASTER 2003
SQUIER SERIES FLOYD ROSE
STANDARD STRATOCASTER
1994–96
SQUIER SERIES STANDARD
STRATOCASTER 1994–96
STANDARD FAT STRAT 1999–current
STANDARD FAT STRAT FLOYD ROSE
1999–current
STANDARD FAT STRAT WITH LOCKING
TREMOLO 2002–03
STANDARD ROLAND READY STRAT
1998–current
STANDARD SATIN STRATOCASTER
2003–06
STANDARD STRATOCASTER
1991–current
STANDARD STRATOCASTER FMT
2005–06
STANDARD STRATOCASTER HH
2004–06
STANDARD STRATOCASTER HSS
2004–current
STANDARD STRATOCASTER HSS WITH
LOCKING TREMOLO 2004–current
STANDARD 60th ANNIVERSARY
STRATOCASTER 2006
STRAT SPECIAL 1994–96

TEX-MEX STRAT 1996–97
TEX-MEX STRAT SPECIAL 1997
TOM DELONGE STRAT 2001–03
TRADITIONAL STRATOCASTER
1996–98
TRADITIONAL FAT STRAT 1996–98
50th ANNIVERSARY GOLDEN
STRATOCASTER 2004

**STRATOCASTERS
MANUFACTURED IN KOREA**
KOA STRATOCASTER 2006–current
LITE ASH STRATOCASTER
2004–current
SQUIER SERIES STANDARD
STRATOCASTER 1992–94
TIE-DYE STRAT HS 2005

STUDIO LEAD *amp* 1983–85
STUDIO 85 *amp* 1988

SUPER (tweed) *amp* 1946–60
SUPER (brown Tolex) *amp* 1960–63
SUPER AMP *amp* 1992–96
SUPER CHAMP *amp* 1982–85
SUPER REVERB *amp* 1963–82
SUPER SHOWMAN *amp* 1970–72
SUPER SIX REVERB *amp* 1970–79
SUPER 60 *amp* 1989–93
SUPER 112 *amp* 1988–93
SUPER 210 *amp* 1988–93
SUPER-SONIC *amp* 2006–current
SUPER TWIN *amp* 1976–81

SWINGER 1969

T

TAURUS *amp* 1970–72

TC-90 THINLINE (MIK) 2004–current

TELECASTER

**TELECASTERS MANUFACTURED
IN U.S.A.**
ALBERT COLLINS TELECASTER
1990–current

ALUMINUM-BODY TELECASTER
   1994–95
AMERICAN ASH TELECASTER
   2003–current
AMERICAN CLASSIC TELECASTER first
   version 1995–99
AMERICAN CLASSIC TELECASTER
   second version 1999–2000
AMERICAN DELUXE ASH TELECASTER
   2004–current
AMERICAN DELUXE POWER TELE
   1999–2001
AMERICAN DELUXE TELECASTER first
   version 1998–99
AMERICAN DELUXE TELECASTER
   second version 1999–2003
AMERICAN DELUXE TELECASTER third
   version 2004–current
AMERICAN DELUXE TELECASTER FMT
   2004–06
AMERICAN DELUXE TELECASTER QMT
   2004–06
AMERICAN FAT TELE 2001–03
AMERICAN NASHVILLE B-BENDER
   TELE 2000–current
AMERICAN STANDARD B-BENDER
   TELECASTER 1995–97
AMERICAN STANDARD TELECASTER
   1988–2000
AMERICAN TELECASTER 2000–current
AMERICAN TELECASTER HH first
   version 2003–04
AMERICAN TELECASTER HH second
   version 2004–06
AMERICAN TELECASTER HS first
   version 2003–04
AMERICAN TELECASTER HS second
   version 2004–06
AMERICAN VINTAGE '52 TELECASTER
   1998–current

AMERICAN VINTAGE '52 TELE SPECIAL
   1999–2001
AMERICAN VINTAGE '62 CUSTOM
   TELECASTER 1999–current
AMERICAN 60th ANNIVERSARY
   TELECASTER 2006
ANTIGUA TELECASTER 1977–79
ANTIGUA TELECASTER CUSTOM 1977-
   79
ANTIGUA TELECASTER DELUXE
   1977–79

BAJO SEXTO TELECASTER baritone
   1992–98
BLACK & GOLD TELECASTER
   1981–83
BLUE FLOWER TELECASTER 1968–69
BOWLING BALL TELECASTER 1984
BROADCASTER 1950–51

CALIFORNIA FAT TELE 1997–98
CALIFORNIA TELE 1997–current
CLARENCE WHITE TELECASTER
   1993–2001
CUSTOM CLASSIC TELECASTER
   2000–06
CUSTOM ESQUIRE 1959–69
CUSTOM TELECASTER 1959–72

DANNY GATTON TELECASTER
   1990–current

ELITE TELECASTER 1983–84
ESQUIRE 1950–69

FLAT HEAD TELECASTER 2003–04
FLAT HEAD TELECASTER HH 2004–06

G.E. SMITH TELECASTER
   2007–current

GOLD ELITE TELECASTER *See*
   previous listing.
HIGHWAY ONE TELECASTER first
   version 2002–06
HIGHWAY ONE TELECASTER second
   version 2006–current
HIGHWAY ONE TEXAS TELECASTER
   2003–current

INTERNATIONAL COLOR TELECASTER
   1981

JAMES BURTON TELECASTER first
   version 1990–2005
JAMES BURTON TELECASTER second
   version 2006–current
JERRY DONAHUE TELECASTER
   1992–2001
JIMMY BRYANT TELECASTER 2003–05
JOHN JORGENSON TELECASTER
   1998–2001
J5:BIGSBY 2003–current
J5:HB TELECASTER 2003–current

MERLE HAGGARD TELE 1997–current

NASHVILLE B-BENDER TELE
   1998–current
NOCASTER 1951

PAISLEY RED TELECASTER 1968–69

RELIC 50s NOCASTER 1996–98
ROSEWOOD TELECASTER 1969–72

SET NECK TELECASTER 1991–95
SET NECK TELECASTER COUNTRY
   ARTIST 1992–95
SET NECK TELECASTER FLOYD ROSE
   1991–92

SET NECK TELECASTER PLUS
   1991–92
SEYMOUR DUNCAN SIGNATURE
   ESQUIRE 2003–current
SPARKLE TELECASTER 1992–95
SPECIAL EDITION 1994 TELECASTER
   1994
SUB-SONIC TELE baritone 2001–05

TELE JNR 1995–2000
TELE PLUS first version 1990–95
TELE PLUS second version 1995–98
TELE PLUS DELUXE 1991–92
TELE PRO 2007–current
TELE-SONIC 1998–2004
TELE THINLINE 2006–current
TELECASTER 1951–83
TELECASTER CUSTOM 1972–81
TELECASTER DELUXE 1972–81
TELECASTER STANDARD 1983–84
TELECASTER XII 12-string 1995–98
THINLINE TELECASTER first version
   1968–71
THINLINE TELECASTER second
   version 1971–79

U.S. FAT TELE 1998–2000

VINTAGE HOT ROD '52 TELE
   2007–current

WALNUT ELITE TELECASTER 1983–84
WAYLON JENNINGS TRIBUTE
   TELECASTER 1995–2003
WILL RAY TELECASTER 1998–2001

50s TELECASTER 1996–98
50th ANNIVERSARY TELECASTER 1996
'51 NOCASTER 1999–current
'52 TELECASTER 1983–84, 1986–98

'59 ESQUIRE 2003–06
'60 TELECASTER CUSTOM 2003–04
60s TELECASTER CUSTOM 1996–98
'63 TELECASTER 1999–current
'67 TELECASTER 2005–current
90s TELE THINLINE 1997–2001
1998 COLLECTORS EDITION
   TELECASTER 1998

**TELECASTERS MANUFACTURED
IN JAPAN**
AERODYNE TELE 2004–06
ANTIGUA TELECASTER 2004

BLUE FLOWER TELECASTER
   1986–onward
BUCK OWENS TELECASTER 1998

CONTEMPORARY TELECASTER two
   variations 1985–87
CUSTOM ESQUIRE 1986–onward
CUSTOM TELECASTER '62
   1985–onward

ESQUIRE 1986–onward

FOTO FLAME TELECASTER
   1995–96
FRANCIS ROSSI SIGNATURE
   TELECASTER 2003–04

HMT ACOUSTIC-ELECTRIC first version
   1991–94
HMT ACOUSTIC-ELECTRIC second
   version 1995–97
HMT TELECASTER first version
   1991–92
HMT TELECASTER second version
   1991–92
JD TELECASTER 1992–99

NOKIE EDWARDS TELECASTER 1996
PAISLEY TELECASTER 1986–onward

RICHIE KOTZEN SIGNATURE
   TELECASTER 2005–06
RICK PARFITT SIGNATURE
   TELECASTER 2003–04
ROSEWOOD TELECASTER
   1986–onward

SQUIER SERIES '52 TELECASTER
   1982–83
STANDARD TELECASTER 1988–91

TELECASTER CUSTOM '72
   1986–onward
THINLINE TELECASTER '69
   1986–onward
THINLINE TELECASTER '72
   1986–onward

WILL RAY JAZZ-A-CASTER 1997–98

50s TELECASTER 1990–onward
50s TELECASTER WITH BIGSBY
   2005–06
60s TELECASTER 1994
60s TELECASTER WITH BIGSBY
   2005–current
90s TELECASTER CUSTOM 1995–98
90s TELECASTER DELUXE 1995–98

**TELECASTERS MANUFACTURED
IN MEXICO**
CLASSIC PLAYER BAJA TELECASTER
   2006–current
CLASSIC 50s ESQUIRE
   2005–current
CLASSIC 50s TELECASTER
   1999–2006

CLASSIC 60s TELECASTER
2001–current
CLASSIC '69 TELECASTER THINLINE
1998–current
CLASSIC '72 TELECASTER CUSTOM
1999–current
CLASSIC '72 TELECASTER DELUXE
2004–current
CLASSIC '72 TELECASTER THINLINE
1999–current

DELUXE BIG BLOCK TELECASTER
2005–06
DELUXE NASHVILLE TELE 1997–current
DELUXE NASHVILLE POWER TELE
1999–current

JAMES BURTON STANDARD
TELECASTER 1995–current
JOHN 5 TELECASTER 2004–current
J5 TRIPLE TELE DELUXE 2007–current

MUDDY WATERS TELE 2001–current

SQUIER SERIES STANDARD
TELECASTER 1992–94
STANDARD TELECASTER
1991–current

TELE SPECIAL 1994–96
TEX-MEX TELE SPECIAL 1997
TRADITIONAL TELECASTER 1996–98

**TELECASTERS MANUFACTURED
IN KOREA**
BLACKOUT TELECASTER HH 2004
CUSTOM TELECASTER FMT HH
2003–04
KOA TELECASTER 2006–current
LITE ASH TELECASTER 2004–current

SQUIER SERIES STANDARD
TELECASTER 1992–94

TONE-MASTER *amp* 1993–2003

TORONADO DVII 2002–04
TORONADO HH 2002–04
TORONADO (MIM) 1998–2004
TORONADO HH (MIM) 2005–06
TORONADO GT HH (MIK) 2005–06

TRANSISTOR BASSMAN *amp*
1970–72

TREMOLUX (tweed) *amp* 1955–60
TREMOLUX (Tolex piggy-back) *amp*
1960–66

TWIN (tweed) *amp* 1953–60
TWIN (white Tolex) *amp* 1960–62
TWIN-AMP *amp* 2006–current
TWIN REVERB *amp* 1963–82
TWIN REVERB II amp 1982–85
THE TWIN *amp* 1987–94

U

ULTRA CHORUS *amp* 1993–95

THE VENTURES JAZZMASTER (MIJ)
1996

V

VIBRASONIC *amp* 1959–63
VIBRASONIC REVERB *amp* 1972–79

VIBRO CHAMP *amp* 1964–79
VIBRO-KING *amp* 1993–current
VIBROLUX (tweed) *amp* 1956–60

VIBROLUX (Tolex) *amp* 1961–65
VIBROLUX REVERB *amp* 1964–79

W

WOODY JUNIOR amp 1999–2001
WOODY PRO *amp* 1999–2001

Y

YALE REVERB *amp* 1982–85

30 *amp* 1979–82
'57 AMP *amp* 2007
'57 DELUXE AMP *amp* 2007–current
'57 TWIN-AMP *amp* 2004–current
'59 BASSMAN LTD *amp* 2004–current
'59 BASSMAN VINTAGE REISSUE *amp*
1990–2004
'63 VIBROVERB VINTAGE REISSUE *amp*
1990–96
'65 DELUXE REVERB *amp*
1993–current
'65 MUSTANG REISSUE (MIJ)
2006–current
'65 SUPER REVERB *amp*
2001–current
'65 TWIN CUSTOM *amp* 15
2004–current
'65 TWIN REVERB VINTAGE REISSUE
amp 1992–current
75 *amp* 1979–83
85 *amp* 1988–92
140 *amp* 1980–81
300PS *amp* 1976–79

models: year-by-year

This listing shows in chronological order the production-model electric guitars and amplifiers that have featured 'Fender' (or 'K&F') as their main logo or brandname and that have been manufactured in the U.S.A., Japan, Korea, and Mexico between 1945 and early 2007.

Basic specifications and identifiers are included for each model. The start date shown is the year that production commenced for each model in the country of manufacture, regardless of different start dates elsewhere. The finish date is the final year that each model was available in the U.S.A. and/or Europe.

KEY

a.k.a. means also known as

–current indicates a model still in production at the time of writing

–onward indicates a Japanese-made model with fluctuating availability outside Japan

1x10 etc (speaker configuration): figure before x is number of speakers; figure after x is diameter of speaker in inches; so 1x10 = one 10-inch speaker, 4x12 = four 12-inch speakers, etc.

For guitars, unless stated:
- metal tuner buttons
- regular Fender headstock shapes
- four-screw neckplate
- bolt-on neck
- 25.5-inch scale and 21 frets
- dot markers on fingerboard
- solid, contoured, offset-double-cutaway body
- single-coil pickup(s)
- nickel- or chrome-plated hardware

U.S. manufacture unless noted:
(MII) indicates manufactured in Indonesia
(MIJ) indicates manufactured in Japan
(MIK) indicates manufactured in Korea
(MIM) indicates manufactured in Mexico

1940s

AMPLIFIERS

The earliest Fender amps were in the Model 26 line – often referred to today as 'woodies' for their varnished hardwood cabinets. These first gave us the names Deluxe and Pro (originally Professional) that have remained with the company in one form or another virtually ever since.

The bigger Dual Professional amp of 1946 would soon be renamed the Super, another enduring Fender model. This 2x10 combo, the first twin-speaker guitar amp, was introduced to capitalize on a surplus of 10-inch speakers, and Fender mounted the amp's two alnico Jensens on an angled baffle that led to the models 'angle-front' and 'V-front' nicknames. This was also Fender's first tweed-covered amp, and it established a format for the company that would carry on through the 1950s.

Other longtime classic amps with roots in the late '40s are the little Champion 800, Champion 600, and Princeton models, all born in 1948. The former would evolve into the Champ, one of the most beloved student, practice and recording amps of all time.

The listing of these amps that follows is arranged in chronological order of introduction.

K&F 1945

Leo Fender's first amplifiers, built in conjunction with Doc Kauffman under the K&F logo. Small, single-ended amps with outputs of roughly 4W, available only as part of a set with the K&F lap-steel guitars.
- **Cabinet:** gray crinkle finish, rear-mounted control panel.
- **Controls:** Volume only on smaller model, Volume & Tone on larger.
- **Speakers:** 8-inch in smaller, 10-inch in larger.
- **Tubes:** 6SC7, 6F6 (or 6V6), 5Y3 rectifier.
- **Output:** 4 watts.

MODEL 26 1946–48

These are the earliest of the Fender amplifiers and

THE BIRTH OF FENDER

Many Fender histories written from the perspective of the electric guitar begin with the birth of the Telecaster model (originally Esquire, then Broadcaster) in 1950 and 1951, but the company's roots in the electric musical instruments business go back a few years further than that.

Leo Fender had established a record store and radio repair business in 1939 in the Fullerton district of Los Angeles, where he quickly developed a devoted clientele among the local musicians in this booming California city. It was no great leap for Fender to begin to rent PA systems and repair instruments and, eventually, to make amplifiers and lap-steel guitars himself.

In 1945, Fender teamed up with local musician Doc Kauffman to establish the short-lived K&F company (Kauffman and Fender) to produce a limited line of electric steel-guitar and amp sets. After Kauffman's departure in 1946, Fender set up a new operation as Fender Manufacturing, renamed Fender Electric Instrument Company in the following year.

At the time, the 'lead players' of the guitar world were the lap-steel and console-steel (or table-steel) guitarists. Fender catered to many such artists on the country and the western swing scenes of Southern California at the time. Steel guitars remained Fender's main stock-in-trade in stringed instruments for the first few years after the arrival of his revolutionary Spanish-electric guitar, but they are all but forgotten today in the majority of discussions of Fender's history.

Many amplifier models established at the same time, however, have endured through the years – albeit in a range of modified and evolved forms – and therefore it seems fair to say that Fender established a precedent for itself as an amp-maker even before it started plotting in 1949 to turn the electric guitar world on its head.

are frequently referred to by collectors as 'woodies' because they were manufactured with natural or stained hardwood cabinets.

- **Cabinet:** varnished hardwood, rear-mounted control panel.
- **Controls:** Mic Volume, Inst Volume, Tone (none on

8-inch Princeton).
- **Speakers:** 10-inch in Deluxe, 15-inch in Professional.
- **Tubes:** 6SC7, 6N7, 2x6F6 (later 6V6), 5Y3 rectifier.
- **Output:** 10 watts.

STEEL GUITARS

Fender's electric guitar lines included electric steel and pedal steel guitars from the 1940s to the early 1980s. In those earlier years, along with amplifiers, they were of great importance to the Fender business, but they gradually faded from the catalogue listings.

Non-pedal steels included: **CHAMP** (1955–81); **CHAMPION** (1949–52); **CUSTOM** (1949–58); **DELUXE** (1946–49); **DELUXE 6 / DELUXE 8** (1950–81); **DUAL 6 PROFESSIONAL** (1950–81); **DUAL 8 PROFESSIONAL** (1946–57); **ORGAN BUTTON** (1946–48); **PRINCETON** (1946–49); **STRINGMASTER** (1953–81); **STUDENT** (1952–55); **STUDIO DELUXE** (1956–81).

Pedal steels included: **ARTIST DUAL 10 / SINGLE 10** (1976–81); **STUDENT SINGLE 10** (1976–81); **400** (1958–76); **800** (1964–76); **1000** (1957–76); **2000** (1964–76).

THE PLANK THAT ROCKED THE WORLD

By the late 1940s, Leo Fender saw the need for an entirely new breed of electric guitar. He was intimately acquainted with the requirements of the professional musicians he served and knew that the hollowbody archtops with added pickups played by most country and dance-band guitarists weren't right for the job. The problems with these instruments kept many players at the back of the stage, while the singers, fiddle players, and more recently steel-guitar players were in the spotlight.

Of course, even these hollowbody electrics had been a revelation just a little over a decade before, enabling players of Spanish-style guitars to be heard amid a big-band at least, but they were boomy sounding, prone to feedback, and didn't maximize the potential of the available amplification.

Leo Fender devised a plan for a solidbody electric guitar that, as he saw it, needed to satisfy a number of performance criteria. It should have a bright, cutting, sustaining sound; be resistant to feedback; be relatively simple and economical to manufacture; and should be easy for a player or repairer to fix on the road. To achieve these goals, Fender totally redrew the blueprint for the six-string. The guitar that we now know as the Telecaster – first named the Esquire, and then the Broadcaster – lived up to its billing so successfully that it has remained a staple of rock, pop, and country music for nearly 60 years.

The sound of the Telecaster's twangy, fat, well-defined single-coil bridge pickup has virtually single-handedly defined the sound of country lead guitar, while the guitar's alluring simplicity and fast-playing neck have remained eternally appealing to a diverse camp of players.

Rickenbacker and Bigsby had some years before developed solidbody guitars, which they built in limited numbers, but Fender's successful effort would become the first mass-produced solidbody electric guitar. Many musical instrument retailers and others in the industry derided the Fender electric guitar as a 'plank' and a 'canoe paddle', but hey – they began selling in decent numbers nevertheless.

In early 1951, Fender removed the Broadcaster name from the guitar's decal after Gretsch objected to the use of a name too similar to its established 'Broadkaster' drums. For a few months, the Fender model became what is now known as the Nocaster, before the Telecaster name hit the headstock in the early months of 1951. The Esquire name, which had briefly designated both the early one-pickup and two-pickup guitars, now became the name of the standard one-pickup model.

PRINCETON 1946–48

The little Princeton had no controls whatsoever. Volume was controlled from the lap-steel guitar itself, and you plugged it in to switch on the power.

- **Cabinet:** varnished hardwood, rear-mounted panel.
- **Speakers:** 8-inch in Deluxe, 15-inch in Professional.
- **Tubes:** 6SC7, 6F6 (later 6V6), 5Y3 rectifier.
- **Output:** 4 watts.

SUPER 1946–60

This was the first twin-speaker amplifier and became one of the most popular and enduring of the tweed models.

- **Cabinet:** V-front, then wide-panel tweed, then narrow-panel tweed.
- **Controls:** mic volume, inst volume, tone; 5E4 and 5F4 had bass, treble, and presence.
- **Speakers:** two Jensen 10-inch.
- **Tubes:** 3x6SC7, 2x6L6, 5U4 rectifier in V-front;

then 2x12AY7, 12AX7, 2x6L6GC (briefly
2x6V6GC), 5U4G rectifier.
- **Output:** early models around 18 watts; later
models around 28 watts.

CHAMPION 800 / CHAMPION 600 1948–52

This year marked the introduction of the long-
running, single-ended classic small amp from the
Fender factory, and it became better known through
the years as the Champ.
- **Cabinet:** gray-brown tweed, then two-tone
Naugahyde (1949 onward).
- **Controls:** volume.
- **Speakers:** 8-inch, then 6-inch (1949 onward).
- **Tubes:** 6SJ7, 6V6, 5Y3 rectifier.
- **Output:** 4 watts.

PRINCETON 1948–60

The enduring student amp is moved into a tweed
cabinet and given its own controls.
- **Cabinet:** TV-front, wide-panel tweed, then
narrow-panel tweed.
- **Controls:** volume, tone.
- **Speakers:** 8-inch.
- **Tubes:** 6SL7 (12AX7 post-54), 6V6GC, 5Y3 rectifier.
- **Output:** 4 watts.

DELUXE 1949–60

The early Model 26 evolves into one of the most
popular small blues and rock'n'roll amps of all time.
- **Cabinet:** TV-front, then wide-panel tweed, then
narrow-panel tweed,
- **Controls:** volume, volume, tone.
- **Speakers:** 12-inch Jensen P12R.
- **Tubes:** 2x6SL7 (12AY7 & 12AX7 after 1954),
12AX7, 2x6V6GC, 5Y3 rectifier.
- **Output:** 15 watts.

1950

GUITARS

BROADCASTER 1950–51

Model name on headstock, 21 frets, slab single-
cutaway body, two single-coils, three-saddle bridge.
- **Neck:** fretted maple; truss-rod adjuster at body
end; one string-guide.
- **Body:** slab single-cutaway; originally blond only,
later sunburst or colors.
- **Electronics:** one plain metal-cover pickup (at
neck) and one black six-polepiece pickup (angled
in bridgeplate); two controls (volume, pickup
blender) and three-way selector, all situated on the
metal plate that adjoins the pickguard; side-
mounted jack.
- **Hardware:** five-screw black fiber pickguard; three-
saddle raised-sides bridge with through-body
stringing (strings anchored at bridgeplate and not
through body 1958–60).

BROADCASTER became TELECASTER in 1951, but some
transitional examples have no model name on the
headstock and are unofficially known as NOCASTERS
(see 1951 listing).

ESQUIRE 1950–69

Model name on headstock, 21 frets, slab single-
cutaway body, one pickup.
- **Neck:** fretted maple (1950–59 and 1969), maple
with rosewood fingerboard (1959–69), maple
fingerboard official option (1967–69); truss-rod
adjuster at body end; one string-guide.
- **Body:** slab single-cutaway; originally blond only,
later sunburst or colors.
- **Electronics:** one black six-polepiece pickup
(angled in bridgeplate); two controls (volume, tone)
and three-way selector, all situated on the metal
plate that adjoins the pickguard; side-mounted
jack.
- **Hardware:** five-screw (eight-screw from 1959)
black plastic pickguard (white plastic from 1954;
white laminated plastic from 1963); three-saddle
bridge with through-body stringing (strings
anchored at bridgeplate, not through body,
1958–60).

Very few of the earliest 'pre-production' examples
were without a truss-rod, and some have a second
pickup at the neck.

1951

GUITARS
NOCASTER 1951
See 1950 listing for BROADCASTER and following listing for TELECASTER.

TELECASTER 1951–83
Model name on headstock, 21 frets, slab single-cutaway body, two single-coils, three-saddle bridge.
- **Neck:** fretted maple (1951–59 and 1969–83), maple with rosewood fingerboard (1959–83), maple fingerboard official option (1967–69); truss-rod adjuster at body end; one string-guide (two from 1972).
- **Body:** slab single-cutaway; originally blond only, later sunburst or colors.
- **Electronics:** one plain metal-cover pickup (at neck) and one black six-polepiece pickup (angled in bridgeplate); two controls (volume, tone; but originally volume, pickup blender) and three-way selector, all on metal plate adjoining pickguard; side-mounted jack.
- **Hardware:** five-screw (eight-screw from 1959) black plastic pickguard (white plastic from 1954; white laminated plastic 1963–75 and 1981–83; black laminated plastic 1975–81); three-saddle raised-sides bridge with through-body stringing (strings anchored at bridgeplate and not through body 1958–60).

Previously known as BROADCASTER (1950–51), but some transitional examples have no model name on the headstock and are unofficially known as NOCASTERS (see previous listing).
Fender Bigsby bridge and vibrato tailpiece option (1967–74); no through-body string holes if unit factory-fitted.

1952

AMPLIFIERS
BANDMASTER 1952–60
Somewhat redundant as a 15-inch combo, the Bandmaster evolved into the odd but very collectible 3x10 format in narrow-panel tweed cab.
- **Cabinet:** TV-front, then wide-panel tweed, then narrow-panel tweed.
- **Controls:** volume, tone; from 1954 mic volume, inst volume, treble, bass, presence (narrow panel).
- **Speakers:** 15-inch Jensen; from 1954 3x10 Jensen.
- **Tubes:** 6SC7, 6SL7 (later 12AY7, 2x12AX7), 2x6L6GC (briefly 6V6GC), 5U4 rectifier.
- **Output:** originally 18 watts, later 28 watts.

BASSMAN 1952–53
This early incarnation of Fender's bass amp is an entirely different beast from the great guitar amp it would become (see 1954 listing).
- **Cabinet:** TV-front, then wide-panel tweed.
- **Controls:** volume, tone.
- **Speakers:** 15-inch Jensen.
- **Tubes:** 6SC7, 6SL7, 2x6L6GC, 5U4 rectifier.
- **Output:** 26 watts.

1953

AMPLIFIERS
CHAMP 1953–64
The Champion 600 gets a tweed cabinet to look like a real baby Fender.
- **Cabinet:** wide-panel tweed, then narrow-panel tweed.
- **Controls:** volume.
- **Speakers:** 6-inch, then 8-inch from 1955.
- **Tubes:** 6SL7 (12AX7 after 1955), 6V6GC, 5Y3 rectifier.
- **Output:** 4 watts.

TWIN 1953–60
Originally named the Twin 12 Artist's Model Amp, the Twin was billed by Fender as the finest amplifier available anywhere – and at the time that probably wasn't far from the truth.
- **Cabinet:** wide-panel tweed, then narrow-panel tweed.

THE WORLD'S MOST INFLUENTIAL ELECTRIC GUITAR

The Telecaster had barely become established in the guitar world when Fender began to plan a new, more versatile design. The Fender Stratocaster has become known particularly as a prime choice of rock and blues players, but it's the world's most imitated electric guitar design, and arguably the most popular.

The instrument has been used for every conceivable style of amplified music. That said, Leo Fender was still catering primarily to the country, western swing, and dance-band scenes in the early 1950s, and his revolutionary three-pickup model was still aimed squarely at the requirements of these players. Fender had apparently recognized the need for a guitar with a vibrato tailpiece back in 1952 or even 1951. Many local guitarists, Bill Carson included, had consulted with Fender regarding a solidbody electric with more versatile pickup selections and, it seems, a more comfortable, form-fitting body.

The Stratocaster hit the market in the spring of 1954, embodying all of these advances and more. It had an extremely well-engineered vibrato tailpiece that allowed greater pitch-bend than the popular Bigsby unit while also permitting individual intonation of the strings. Its three pickups provided three very different but usable sounds, from bright and twangy to warm and throaty, yet all with good clarity and definition. Finally, it had heavily contoured curves at the body edges that usually dug into a player's right forearm and ribcage on other guitars but here offered a more comfortable playing experience.

Ironically, although the Stratocaster was taken up by a number of country players, it never became the staple of the genre that the Telecaster continued to dominate. The Strat did, however, receive a more immediate and resounding welcome than its older sibling four years before and, with rock'n'roll waiting in the wings, the new guitar blazed forward to enormous success.

- **Controls:** mic volume, inst volume, bass, treble; presence added in 1955; middle added to high-powered version in 1956.
- **Speakers:** two Jensen P12N.
- **Tubes:** originally 3x6SC7, 6J5, 2x6L6G and 5U4 rectifier; then 3x12AY7, 12AX7, 2x6L6G and 2x5U4GA rectifiers, then 12AY7, 2x12AX7, 4x5881 and GZ34 rectifier.
- **Output:** early models around 25W, then 45W, and 85W for 4x5881s.

1954

GUITARS

STRATOCASTER (pre-CBS) 1954–65

21 frets, small headstock, one string guide, four-screw neckplate, three controls.

- **Neck:** fretted maple (maple with rosewood fingerboard from 1959); truss-rod adjuster at body end; one string-guide.
- **Body:** sunburst or colors.
- **Electronics:** three white six-polepiece pickups (bridge pickup angled). Three controls (volume, two tone) and three-way selector, all on pickguard; jack in body face.
- **Hardware:** eight-screw white plastic or anodized metal pickguard (11-screw white or tortoiseshell laminated plastic from 1959). Six-saddle bridge with through-body stringing or six-pivot bridge/vibrato unit.

Some examples were fitted with gold-plated hardware. (This gold-plated hardware option coupled with a blond-finish body became unofficially known as the Mary Kaye model.)

THE SOUND OF ROCK'N'ROLL

The amplifiers produced by Fender in the 1950s, usually referred to collectively as the 'tweed' amps, are some of the most beloved guitar amplifiers of all time. The first tweed amp of the '50s actually arrived in the late '40s, when toward the end of 1948 the Deluxe model moved from the lacquered hardwood cabinet of the Model 26 series to a light tweed-covered, TV-front cabinet.

The tweed years encompass three main cabinet styles: the early TV-front, so-called because its 'wrapover' design gave it the look of an early television; the wide-panel, which had – yes – wide cabinet panels at the top and bottom of its front face, to which the speaker baffle was internally mounted; and the narrow-panel, similar to the former but with narrower panels. The latter cabinets housed the most desirable of the tweed amps in almost all cases, because the circuits put into these between late 1955 and 1960 had evolved considerably from their origins earlier in the decade. All tweed amps are prized today by players and collectors; variations from each era have their fans.

Effectively one of Fender's earliest models, the Deluxe is also one of the company's most popular amps of all time. TV-front and early wide-panel tweed Deluxes have a smooth, fat, compressed sound that complements many blues styles in particular, thanks in part to the use of octal preamp tubes and a paraphase inverter stage. The arrival of a nine-pin 12AY7 tube in the preamp and a split-load phase inverter helped to give the narrow-panel models a somewhat broader soundstage and better definition, but these amps still don't have a lot of headroom, and they are beloved for the way they transition smoothly into overdrive at relatively low volume levels.

Medium-sized tweed amps like the 2x10 Super and 1x15 Pro are also the stuff that tone dreams are made of, but the Bassman of the late 1950s is really the granddaddy of electric blues and rock'n'roll amps and remains one of the most desirable vintage amps of all time. The most famous bass amp ever adopted wholesale by guitarists, the 4x10 tweed Bassman – especially with its final 5F6-A circuit derivation of 1959–60 – is widely considered by players and collectors alike to be one of the best sounding larger tube amps ever designed.

Leo Fender found that a cab with four 10-inch speakers wired in parallel withstood the rumbling fundamental notes of the electric bass better than the single 15-inch in the first Bassman models of 1952–53, and he added other upgrades along with the smaller speakers when he moved the design into the new narrow-panel tweed cabinet. At this time, the amp was given individual bass and treble controls and an efficient long-tailed-pair phase inverter as well as other ingredients that all helped to make it a tighter, more powerful bass amp. Show a Bassman a Stratocaster or Telecaster and crank it up, and it proves an amazingly toneful and responsive blues and rock'n'roll amp, or keep the volume reined in for sparkling clean country or jazz.

By the end of the decade, the Bassman's cathode-follower tone stack had picked up a middle control and a presence control, a second channel, and a few more upgrades to the circuit besides. This is the vintage Fender amp that gets more guitarists drooling than any other.

To ratchet the volume up even further, Fender developed the mammoth high-powered tweed Twin model toward the end of 1958. The redesigned circuit, designated 5F8-A, doubled its predecessor's output tube complement to carry four 5881s; these, along with a larger output transformer and a more refined long-tailed-pair phase inverter like the Bassman's, enabled it to produce between 80 watts and 100 watts of power.

'54

AMPLIFIERS
BASSMAN 1954–60

The most famous bass amp ever adopted wholesale
by guitarists, the 4x10 tweed Bassman – especially
with its final 5F6A circuit of 1959–60 – is widely
considered by players and collectors alike to be one
of the best sounding larger tube amps ever
designed.

- **Cabinet:** narrow-panel tweed.
- **Controls:** first just volume, treble, bass, presence;
  later (by 5F6) added bright volume and middle
  controls.
- **Speakers:** four 10-inch Jensen P12R or P12Q.
- **Tubes:** 12AY7, 2x12AX7, 2x5881s (or 6L6GCs),
  5AR4 rectifier.
- **Output:** 45 watts.

1955

AMPLIFIERS
TREMOLUX 1955–60

Fender's first amp to carry an onboard effect, the
Tremolux started life in the same cab as the Deluxe
but moved to a larger cab as used for the Pro.

- **Cabinet:** narrow-panel tweed.
- **Controls:** volume, volume, tone, speed, depth.
- **Speakers:** 12-inch Jensen P12Q.
- **Tubes:** 12AY7, 2x12AX7, 2x6V6GC, 5Y3GT
  rectifier (later 5U4G).
- **Output:** 18 watts.

1956

GUITARS
DUO-SONIC (first version) 1956–64

*Model name on headstock, neck pickup angled,
bridge pickup straight.*

- **Neck:** fretted maple (maple neck with rosewood
  fingerboard from 1959); 22.5-inch scale, 21 frets;
  truss-rod adjuster at body end; plastic tuner
  buttons; one string-guide.
- **Body:** slab; originally beige only but was later

offered in sunburst or colors.
- **Electronics:** two plain-top pickups (neck pickup
  angled); two controls (volume, tone), three-way
  selector and jack, all on pickguard.
- **Hardware:** eight-screw anodized metal pickguard
  (12-screw white or tortoiseshell laminated plastic
  from 1960); three-saddle bridge/tailpiece.

MUSICMASTER (first version) 1956–64

*Model name on headstock, one angled pickup at
neck.*

- **Neck:** fretted maple neck (maple neck with
  rosewood fingerboard from 1959); 22.5-inch
  scale, 21 frets; truss-rod adjuster at body end;
  plastic tuner buttons; one string-guide.
- **Body:** slab body; originally beige only, later
  sunburst or colors.
- **Electronics:** one plain-top pickup (angled at
  neck); two controls (volume, tone) and jack, all on
  pickguard.
- **Hardware:** eight-screw anodized pickguard (12-
  screw white or tortoiseshell laminated plastic from
  1960); three-saddle bridge/tailpiece.

AMPLIFIERS
HARVARD 1956–61

Shortlived student amp sized between Princeton and
Deluxe.

- **Cabinet:** narrow-panel tweed.
- **Controls:** volume, tone.
- **Speakers:** 1x8 Jensen (1x10 Jensen after 1958).
- **Tubes:** 6AT6, 12AX7, 2x6V6GTA, 5Y3GT rectifier
  (single 12AX7 and single 6V6GTA in final models).
- **Output:** 10 watts.

VIBROLUX 1956–60

Name implies otherwise, but Vibrolux also carried
tremolo, not true vibrato.

- **Cabinet:** narrow-panel tweed.
- **Controls:** volume, tone, speed, depth.
- **Speakers:** 10-inch Jensen P10R.
- **Tubes:** 2x12AX7, 2x6V6GC, 5Y3GT rectifier.
- **Output:** 18 watts.

58

A JAZZ GUITAR FOR THE SURF SCENE

In 1958, Fender introduced a new and quite different model that was intended to be its top-of-the-line electric guitar. The Jazzmaster was advertised as 'America's finest electric guitar;' it had a distinctive offset waist and dual-cutaway body, two entirely new pickups, a new wiring and switching circuit designed to offer two different preset sounds, and a new 'floating' vibrato system that was intended to have a smoother action and sound than that of the Stratocaster.

The Jazzmaster still had the Strat and Tele's 25.5-inch scale length and a similar neck, although with slightly different lines to the headstock. But it also carried another new element that seemed radical for Fender at the time: a rosewood fingerboard. From mid 1959 the Stratocaster, Telecaster, and Esquire would also receive rosewood fingerboards, and this component would partly typify the look of Fender guitars into the mid '60s.

Fenders were first fitted with what has become known as a 'slab board' fingerboard, which is to say a plank of rosewood milled flat on the underside and glued to a flat maple neck, radiused on the top side only. From mid 1962 a curved veneer of rosewood was fitted (sometimes referred to as the 'round-lam' fingerboard), and this became the standard thereafter.

The Jazzmaster failed to attract the players it was named for and in fact has rarely been seen for long in the hands of any reputable jazz artist. It did, however, make a pretty big splash with a lot of players on the surf and instrumental scenes that were big in the late 1950s and early '60s, and a decade and a half later became popular with a lot of punk and new wave players.

1958

GUITARS

JAZZMASTER 1958–80

Model name on headstock, two large rectangular pickups.

- **Neck:** maple with rosewood fingerboard (bound from 1965), dot markers (blocks from 1966); truss-rod adjuster at body end; one string-guide.
- **Body:** contoured offset-waist; sunburst or colors.
- **Electronics:** two large rectangular white (black from 1977) six-polepiece pickups; two controls (volume, tone), two rollers (volume, tone), three-way selector, slide-switch, jack, all on pickguard.
- **Hardware:** nine-screw anodized metal pickguard (13-screw white or tortoiseshell laminated plastic from 1959; black laminated plastic from 1976); six-saddle bridge, vibrato tailpiece.

Prototype examples with smaller headstock and/or fretted maple neck.
Some examples with gold-plated hardware.

1959

GUITARS

CUSTOM ESQUIRE 1959–69

Same as ESQUIRE (see 1950 listing) other than bound body.

CUSTOM TELECASTER 1959–72

Same as TELECASTER (see 1951 listing) other than bound body.

AMPLIFIERS

VIBRASONIC 1959–63

Fender's first Tolex-covered amplifier with forward-facing control panel.

- **Cabinet:** brown Tolex.
- **Controls:** normal: volume, treble, bass; vibrato: volume, treble, bass, speed, intensity; presence (tone and volume controls briefly reversed on introduction); brown control panel.
- **Speakers:** 1x15 JBL.

TOLEX, TOP AND FRONT

Shortlived it may have been, but the Vibrasonic amp was pivotal in Fender's evolution toward the modern era of amplification. Its front-mounted control panel and brown Tolex-covered cabinet arrived in 1959 when the rest of the line was clothed in narrow-panel tweed cabinets with top-mounted control panels, and its single 15-inch JBL speaker was the first of such quality ever used by Fender.

The Vibrasonic's two channels each had independent treble and bass controls rather than the shared EQ stage of other Fender amps, and the circuitry behind these controls was also something new: the 'tone stack', as it is often known, now came between the two gain stages of each channel's independent 12AX7 preamp tube, rather than being a 'cathode-follower' tone stack like that of the tweed amps.

The new model was louder than most other Fenders with two 6L6s, thanks to its big output transformer, the efficient JBL speaker, and a solid-state rectifier that helped develop bold, sag-free power (another first).

A new and considerably more complex effects circuit also helped the amp to live up to its name by producing a soft approximation of true vibrato rather than the tremolo of earlier Fender amps. This circuit required two full preamp tubes to achieve its sound (two and a half in a later revision) and was eventually dropped by Fender – probably in part because it was so complex – but it sounded glorious while it lasted.

The Vibrasonic didn't survive long but many of its innovations soon appeared as standard on other Fender models – and it clearly helped to pave the way for amps of the modern era. Many of its key circuit features appeared within other Fenders such as tweed models like the Deluxe, Pro, Bandmaster, Twin, and Bassman, while others evolved into the brown and blond Tolex amps of 1960 and after.

In 1963, Fender put reverb in its amps for the first time: the first to receive it was the shortlived brown Vibroverb (tremolo had arrived as the first onboard effect in the Tremolux model of 1955). This consolidated the features of the great amps of the 'blackface' era of the mid 1960s. With their improved headroom and clarity, higher output levels, contemporary features, and built-in effects, models such as the Princeton Reverb, Deluxe Reverb, Super Reverb, and Twin Reverb would earn all-time classic status.

- **Tubes:** 5x7025, 2x6L6GC, (solid-state rectifier).
- **Output:** 45 watts.

1960

AMPLIFIERS

BANDMASTER 1960–61

The Bandmaster, which had first appeared in the Fender line during 1952, retained its unusual 3x10 speaker configuration through its first year as a member of the company's new range of amps with front-mounted control panels.

- **Cabinet:** brown Tolex.
- **Controls:** normal ch: bass, treble, volume; vibrato ch: bass, treble, volume, speed, intensity; presence; brown control panel
- **Speakers:** 3x10 Jensen P10R.
- **Tubes:** 5x7025 (a.k.a. 12AX7), 2x6L6GC, (solid-state rectifier).
- **Output:** 30 watts.

CONCERT 1960–65

This 4x10 combo of the early Tolex years became redundant once the Super Reverb hit the scene.

- **Cabinet:** brown Tolex, then black Tolex from 1963.
- **Controls:** normal: volume, treble, bass; vibrato: volume, treble, bass, speed, intensity; presence (bright switches instead of presence from 1963); brown control panel, then blackface control panel from 1963.
- **Speakers:** 4x10 Jensen.
- **Tubes:** 5x7025, 2x6V6GC, (solid-state rectifier); one 7025 replaced by 2x12AX7s and 6L6GCs replaced by 5881s in 1962; from 1963/blackface: 2x7025, 12AX7, 12AT7, 2x6L6GC.
- **Output:** 40 watts.

PRO AMP 1960–65

This 1x15 guitar combo would evolve into the more popular 2x12 PRO REVERB (for which see under the 1965 listing).

- **Cabinet:** brown Tolex, then black Tolex from 1963.
- **Controls:** normal: volume, treble, bass; vibrato: volume, treble, bass, speed, intensity; presence (from 1963 presence is replaced by bright switches on both channels); brown control panel; blackface control panel from 1963.
- **Speakers:** 1x15 Jensen or Oxford.
- **Tubes:** 5x7025, 2x6L6GC, (solid-state rectifier); from 1961 4x7025, 2x12AX7, 2x5881; from 1963 2x7025, 12AX7, 12AT7, 2x6L6GC, GZ34 rectifier.
- **Output:** 35 watts.

SUPER 1960–63

A popular tweed model segues into the Tolex years.

- **Cabinet:** brown Tolex.
- **Controls:** normal: volume, bass, treble; vibrato: volume, bass, treble, speed, intensity; presence; brown control panel.
- **Speakers:** 2x10 Jensen or Oxford.
- **Tubes:** 5x7025, 2x6L6GC, 5U4G rectifier.
- **Output:** 50 watts.

TREMOLUX 1960–66

The first amp of the tweed years to receive the popular tremolo effect went through many changes as a smaller member of the piggy-back line of the Tolex years before being deleted in 1966.

- **Cabinet:** brown Tolex, blonde Tolex 1963–64, black Tolex 1965–66.
- **Controls:** bright: volume, treble, bass; normal: volume, treble, bass; speed, intensity (from 1964 tremolo speed & intensity on vibrato channel only, bright switches on both); brown control panel; blackface control panel from 1963.
- **Speakers:** 1x10 in separate cabinet; 2x10 from 1963.
- **Tubes:** 2x7025, 2x12AX7, 2x6V6GTA, GZ34 rectifier; 2x6BQ5 output tubes (a.k.a. EL84) used briefly in late 1960–61; 2x6L6GC output tubes from 1962.
- **Output:** 18 watts; 28 watts from 1962.

TWIN AMP 1960–63

The king of the tweed amps graduates to white Tolex.

- **Cabinet:** white Tolex.
- **Controls:** normal: volume, treble, bass; vibrato: volume, treble, bass, speed, intensity; presence; brown control panel.
- **Speakers:** 2x12 Jensen P12N.
- **Tubes:** 4x7025, 2x12AX7, 4x6L6GC, (solid-state rectifier).
- **Output:** 85 watts.

1961

AMPLIFIERS

BANDMASTER 1961–74

Goodbye to the Bandmaster combo, hello to one of the smaller members of the piggy-back line.

- **Cabinet:** blonde Tolex; then black Tolex.
- **Controls:** normal ch: volume, bass, treble; vibrato ch: volume, bass, treble, speed, intensity; presence (then bright switches from 1963–64); blackface control panel 1963–67; silverface control

panel from 1968–74.
- **Speakers:** 1x12 in separate cabinet, then 2x12 from 1963–64.
- **Tubes:** 4x7025 (a.k.a. 12AX7), 2x12AX7 (1x12AX7 and 1x12AT7 from mid 1960s), 2x5881 (a.k.a. 6L6GC), (solid-state rectifier).
- **Output:** 40 watts.

BASSMAN 1961–79
The legendary tweed Bassman evolved into a piggy-back amp that was a mainstay of its class for nearly

two decades and remained popular with guitarists too.
- **Cabinet:** brown Tolex, then blonde Tolex in 1963, then black Tolex from 1964.
- **Controls:** bass ch: volume, treble, bass; normal ch: volume, treble, bass; presence (from 1964 presence replaced by deep switch and bright switch respectively); brown control panel; blackface control panel from 1964; silverface from 1968.
- **Speakers:** 1x12 in separate cab, then from

A SURF GUITAR FOR THE SURF SCENE

If the Jazzmaster was an accidental hero of the surf-music crowd, the Jaguar, introduced in 1962, seemed to be aimed at these players. The Jaguar hit the scene with even more complex switching options than the Jazzmaster. It used the separate upper control plate that allowed the player to set up a preset rhythm sound for the neck pickup, as did the Jazzmaster, but also carried three somewhat enigmatic slider switches on a separate plate on the pickguard. They are in fact just an on-off switch for each pickup and a two-way tone switch.

The Jag also used the so-called 'Synchronized Tremolo' that first appeared on the Jazzmaster but added a muting pad designed specifically for the popular muted-picking sound used in a lot of surf instrumental recordings. (Any player worth their salt was always able to produce this sound by muting the strings with the edge of the palm, so a lot of people removed this clunky item from their Jaguars.)

Unlike the Jazzmaster, the Jaguar had a shorter 24-inch scale length. It also carried two new-design pickups, which were wound to be brighter than the Jazzmaster's. Each had unique steel 'claws' at the sides – actually U-shaped channels that the pickups sat in – and these helped to focus the magnetic field toward the coil and make the pickup a little fatter and more powerful sounding than such a bright pickup would have been without them.

The Jaguar too failed to live up to its billing as Fender's top-of-the-line electric guitar, and after a brief flurry of interest the Telecaster and Stratocaster continued to outsell it. But it did strike a chord with the surf and instrumental stylists at which it was originally aimed and, like the Jazzmaster, became popular with punk and new wave players in the late 1970s – perhaps because even pre-CBS examples remained far more affordable than Strats and Teles on the used market.

Two years after introducing the Jaguar, Fender revealed another, somewhat simpler 24-inch-scale model, the Mustang (also available for a time with a 22.5-inch scale). Its body edges were only slightly contoured and it had simple switching and a basic vibrato system, aiming the Mustang very much as a student or mid-level electric. As such it was a distinct success. It has even slipped into the hands of a number of professionals over the years, and good vintage examples have recently attained a certain collectable status, especially the sporty 'Competition Stripe' models, although prices hover far below those of the major pre- and early-CBS Fender models.

1962–63 2x12 in separate cab.
- **Tubes:** 4x7025 (later 3x12AX7, 12AT7), 2x6L6GC, GZ34 rectifier; solid-state rectifier from 1962–63.
- **Output:** 50 watts.

DELUXE 1961–66
Classic club amp evolves into the Tolex years.
- **Cabinet:** brown Tolex, then black Tolex from 1963–64.
- **Controls:** normal: volume, tone; bright: volume, tone; speed, intensity; brown control panel; then from 1963–64 blackface control panel with: normal: volume, bass, treble; vibrato: volume, bass, treble, speed, intensity.
- **Speakers:** 1x12.
- **Tubes:** 7025, 2x12AX7, 2x6V6GT, GZ34 rectifier; from 1963–64: 2x7025, 12AX7, 12AT7 in preamp.
- **Output:** 15 watts, then 20 watts from 1963–64.

PRINCETON 1961–79
One of Fender's earliest models evolves into an enduring mid-sized student amp. (See also 1982 listing for PRINCETON REVERB.)
- **Cabinet:** brown Tolex, then black Tolex from 1963.
- **Controls:** volume, tone, speed, intensity; brown control panel, then blackface control panel from 1963, then silverface control panel from 1968.
- **Speakers:** 1x10.
- **Tubes:** 7025, 12AX7, 2x6V6GTA, 5Y3GT rectifier.
- **Output:** 12 watts.

SHOWMAN 1961–69
A big, powerful piggy-back amplifier originally designed to help Dick Dale project his surf guitar to large dancehall audiences. Also known as DUAL SHOWMAN when paired with 2x15 speaker cabinet.
- **Cabinet:** blonde Tolex, then black Tolex from 1963.
- **Controls:** normal: volume, treble, bass; vibrato: volume, treble, bass, speed, intensity; presence (from 1963, presence is replaced by bright switches on each channel); brown control panel,

then blackface control panel from 1963, then silverface from 1968.
- **Speakers:** 1x12 JBL, then 1x15 JBL; 2x15 JBL with Dual Showman – all in external speaker cab.
- **Tubes:** 4x7025, 2x12AX7, 4x6L6GC, (solid-state rectifier).
- **Output:** 85 watts.

VIBROLUX 1961–65
Essentially a combo version of the TREMOLUX (see 1955 listing) except:
- **Speakers:** 1x12 Jensen, Oxford, Utah, or CTS.

1962
GUITARS
JAGUAR 1962–75
Model name on headstock, three metal control plates.
- **Neck:** maple with rosewood fingerboard (bound from 1965), dot markers (blocks from 1966); 24-inch scale, 22 frets; truss-rod adjuster at body end; one string-guide.
- **Body:** contoured offset-waist; sunburst or colors.
- **Electronics:** two rectangular white six-polepiece pickups, each with metal 'sawtooth' sides; two controls (volume, tone) and jack, all on lower metal plate adjoining pickguard; slide-switch and two roller controls (volume, tone), all on upper metal plate adjoining pickguard; three slide-switches on metal plate inset into pickguard.
- **Hardware:** ten-screw white or tortoiseshell laminated plastic pickguard; six-saddle bridge, spring-loaded string mute, vibrato tailpiece.
Some examples with gold-plated hardware.

1963
AMPLIFIERS
DELUXE REVERB 1963–82
The addition of reverb makes this one of the all-time favorites among smaller to medium-sized guitar combos.

Same as DELUXE (see previous listing) except:
- **Controls:** vibrato channel includes reverb control; volume control includes pull boost from around 1977; blackface control panel from around 1963–64 to 1968, silverface from 1968 to around 1979; new blackface control panel around 1980.
- **Tubes:** preamp has 3x7025, 2x12AT7, 12AX7.
- **Output:** 22 watts.

PRINCETON REVERB 1963–79
An enduring student amp that is also very popular with studio musicians.
Similar to PRINCETON from 1963 onward (see 1961 listing) except:
- **Controls:** added reverb control.
- **Speakers:** 1x10.
- **Tubes:** 7025, 2x12AX7, 12AT7, 2x6V6GTA, 5U4 rectifier.

SUPER REVERB 1963–82
The Super gains reverb and another two 10-inch speakers to become a legendary blues, jazz, and rock'n'roll amp.
- **Cabinet:** black Tolex.
- **Controls:** normal: volume, treble, middle, bass, bright switch; vibrato: volume, treble, middle, bass, reverb, speed, intensity, bright switch; master volume with pull distortion switch added 1976; blackface control panel; silverface from 1968; new blackface circa 1980–81.
- **Speakers:** 4x10 Oxford, Cambridge, Utah, or CTS speakers.
- **Tubes:** 3x7025, 2x12AT7, 12AX7, 2x6L6GC, 5AR4 rectifier.
- **Output:** 50 watts, then 70 watts with ultralinear output transformer late 70s.

TWIN REVERB 1963–82
Legendary big tube combo for players requiring loud, clean tones – suits anything from country to jazz to rock and pop.
- **Cabinet:** black Tolex.
- **Controls:** normal: volume, treble, middle, bass, bright switch; vibrato: volume, treble, middle, bass, reverb, speed, intensity, bright switch; master volume with pull distortion switch added 1973; blackface control panel; silverface from 1968, then new blackface circa 1980–81.
- **Speakers:** 2x12 Jensen, Oxford, Cambridge, Utah, or CTS.
- **Tubes:** 3x7025, 2x12AT7, 12AX7, 4x6L6GC, (solid-state rectifier).
- **Output:** 85 watts, then 100 watts from 1973, then 135 watts with ultralinear output transformer late 70s.

VIBROVERB 1963–65
This first Fender amp to receive onboard reverb remains a highly prized collector's item, especially in its brown Tolex configuration with 2x10 speakers.
- **Cabinet:** brown Tolex, then black Tolex during 1964.
- **Controls:** normal: volume, treble, bass; bright: volume, treble, bass, reverb; speed, intensity; brown control panel, then blackface control panel from mid 1964, bright channel becomes vibrato: volume, treble, bass, reverb, speed, intensity (with bright switch on each).
- **Speakers:** 2x10, then 1x15 from mid 1964.
- **Tubes:** 4x7025, 2x12AX7, 2x6L6GC, GZ34 rectifier.
- **Output:** 35 watts, 40 watts from mid 1964.

1964

GUITARS

DUO-SONIC (second version) 1964–69
Model name on enlarged headstock, both pickups angled, two slide switches.
- **Neck:** maple with rosewood fingerboard; 22.5-inch scale and 21 frets (or 24-inch scale and 22 frets; see next listing); enlarged headstock.
- **Body:** contoured offset-waist; red, white, or blue.
- **Electronics:** two white or black plain-top pickups (both angled). Two controls (volume, tone) and jack, all on metal plate adjoining pickguard; two

selector slide-switches on pickguard.
- **Hardware:** 12-screw white pearl or tortoiseshell laminated plastic re-styled pickguard; enlarged three-saddle bridge/tailpiece.

Early examples with slab body.

DUO-SONIC II 1964–69

Variant of the Duo-Sonic (second version; see previous listing) with 24-inch scale and 22 frets.

MUSICMASTER (second version) 1964–75

Model name on headstock, one angled pickup, controls on metal plate, enlarged headstock.
- **Neck:** maple with rosewood fingerboard (fretted maple option from 1970); 22.5-inch scale and 21 frets (or 24-inch scale and 22 frets; see next listing); enlarged headstock.
- **Body:** contoured offset-waist; red, white, or blue.
- **Electronics:** one white or black plain-top pickup

(angled at neck); two controls (volume, tone) and jack, all on metal plate adjoining pickguard.
- **Hardware:** 12-screw white pearl or tortoiseshell laminated plastic re-styled pickguard; enlarged three-saddle bridge/tailpiece.

Early examples with slab body. Version with 24-inch scale and 22 frets known as MUSICMASTER II (1964–69) then just MUSICMASTER (1969–75).

MUSICMASTER II 1964–69

Variant of the Musicmaster (second version; see previous listing) with 24-inch scale and 22 frets, known as MUSICMASTER II (1964–69) then simply MUSICMASTER (1969–75).

MUSTANG 1964–81

Model name on headstock, two angled pickups, two slide switches, vibrato tailpiece.
- **Neck:** maple with rosewood fingerboard (fretted

'64

THE CBS YEARS

At the very start of January 1965, Fender was sold to the enormous Columbia Broadcasting System Inc for a sum of $13 million, which was far and away the highest price paid for a musical instrument manufacturer to date.

It wasn't considered as such at the time, but the sale created an easy delineation for players and collectors, giving birth to the 'pre-CBS' tag that forever after has been the hallmark of some of the most desirable Fender guitars and amplifiers. It so happens, however, that some of the changes recognizable as 'post-CBS' had actually been launched in the previous year.

In summer 1964, the Stratocaster was given a version of the more modern-looking Fender logo that had appeared on the Jaguar way back in 1962. By the end of 1965, the headstock itself was also enlarged considerably to become the wide headstock that is so recognizable now as marking out the guitars of the late 1960s and '70s. The regular Telecasters, however, retained the thinner, old-style 'spaghetti logo' right into 1967.

Amplifiers too changed only gradually. Although the company name under the model name on the front control panel changed from Fender Electric Instrument Co (sometimes just 'Fender Elect Inst Co' where space was tight) to Fender Musical Instruments around the time of the CBS sale, the now-legendary blackface control panel remained until 1968, when a silver control panel finally replaced it.

The design and construction of both guitars and amps changed only gradually, too, a fact that has more recently been recognized by players and has helped early CBS-era guitars and amps to become quite collectable.

maple option from 1970); 22.5-inch scale and 21 frets (1964–69) or 24-inch scale and 22 frets; truss-rod adjuster at body end; plastic tuner buttons (metal from 1975); one string-guide (two from 1975).

- **Body:** contoured offset-waist; sunburst or colors.
- **Electronics:** two white or black plain-top pickups (both angled); two controls (volume, tone) and jack, all on metal plate adjoining pickguard; two selector slide-switches on pickguard.
- **Hardware:** 12-screw white pearl or tortoiseshell laminated plastic pickguard (black laminated plastic from 1975); six-saddle bridge with vibrato tailpiece.

Early examples with slab body.

AMPLIFIERS
CHAMP 1964–79
All-time classic student amp goes Tolex.
- **Cabinet:** black Tolex.
- **Controls:** volume, treble, bass; blackface control panel, then silverface from 1968.
- **Speakers:** 1x8.
- **Tubes:** 12AX7, 6V6GTA, 5Y3GT rectifier.
- **Output:** 5 watts.

VIBRO CHAMP 1964–79
Similar to CHAMP of same era (see earlier listing this year) except:
- **Controls:** volume, treble, bass, speed, intensity.
- **Tubes:** 2x12AX7, 6V6GTA, 5Y3GT rectifier.
- **Output:** 5 watts.

VIBROLUX REVERB 1964–79
This popular mid-sized club combo replaced the reverb-less Vibrolux.
- **Cabinet:** black Tolex.
- **Controls:** normal: volume, treble, bass, bright switch; vibrato: volume, treble, bass, speed, intensity, bright switch; blackface control panel.
- **Speakers:** 2x10.
- **Tubes:** 3x7025, 2x12AT7, 12AX7, 2x6L6GC, GZ34 rectifier.
- **Output:** 35 watts; 40 watts from 1970.

1965

GUITARS
ELECTRIC XII 12-string 1965–69
Model name on 12-string 'hockey-stick' headstock.
- **Neck:** maple with rosewood fingerboard (bound from 1965), dot markers (blocks from 1966); truss-rod adjuster at body end; one 'bracket' string-guide; six-tuners-per-side 'hockey-stick' headstock.
- **Body:** contoured offset-waist; sunburst or colors.
- **Electronics:** two black plain-top split pickups; two controls (volume, tone) and jack, all on metal plate adjoining pickguard; four-way rotary selector on pickguard.
- **Hardware:** 17-screw white pearl or tortoiseshell laminated plastic pickguard; 12-saddle bridge with through-body stringing.

STRATOCASTER (CBS Sixties) 1965–71
21 frets, enlarged headstock, one string-guide, four-screw neckplate, three controls.
- **Neck:** maple with rosewood fingerboard (maple option 1967–69, replaced by fretted maple from 1969); truss-rod adjuster at body end; one string-guide; enlarged headstock.
- **Body:** sunburst or colors.
- **Electronics:** three white six-polepiece pickups (bridge pickup angled); three controls (volume, two tone) and three-way selector, all on pickguard; jack in body face.
- **Hardware:** 11-screw white or tortoiseshell laminated plastic pickguard (only white from 1967); six-saddle bridge with through-body stringing or six-pivot bridge/vibrato unit.

Early examples with STRATOCASTER PRE-CBS small headstock (see 1954 listing). Some examples with bound rosewood fingerboard.

AMPLIFIERS
PRO REVERB 1965–82
Similar to post-1963 PRO AMP (see 1960 listing) except:

'66

SOLID STATE, SOLID GONE

Between 1968 and 1971, Fender attempted to revolutionize the amplifier world with the release of various Solid State models. The first of these merely shadowed an existing tube model: the Solid State Bassman, which was distinguished by a severely altered styling and the legend 'Solid State' printed in red letters on the amp's aluminum name plate. Also released at this time were the Super Reverb, Pro Reverb, Vibrolux Reverb, and Deluxe Reverb combos, all manufactured side by side with their tube-powered counterparts.

While solid-state technology was providing a new direction in everything from compact radios to hi-fi sets to televisions and more, the way in which these early Solid State Fenders amplified the electric guitar was perceived by the majority of musicians who tried them as cold, hard, and harsh when compared to the established tube designs. To compound the poor reception of these amplifiers' sonic abilities, a disproportionately high number of Solid State models proved poor performers in terms of reliability, too, a failing that is usually credited to workers on Fender's amplifier assembly lines being rushed into solid-state production without adequate training and preparation.

Fender introduced the massive, powerful transistorized Super Showman line in 1970. It consisted of a three-channel, preamp-only head partnered by either one or two XFL-1000 4x12 or XFL-2000 8x10 speaker cabs, both with internal 140-watt power amps (a potential of 280 watts total with two cabs connected).

In the same year, Fender reconfigured the first Solid State range into the far groovier (but equally misguided) theme of the Zodiac line, which included the Libra, Capricorn, Scorpio, and Taurus models.

After the demise of all of these amps in 1971 and '72, Fender would resist putting its name on a solid-state amp until the little budget-priced Harvard and Harvard Reverb of 1981.

In more recent years, however, considerable improvements in the sound of solid-state guitar amplification have helped lines like the Frontman and Dyna Touch models to become more successful, along with the company's digital/tube/solid-state hybrid amp, the Cyber-Twin.

- **Controls:** vibrato channel includes reverb control; master volume added 1976, pull distortion on master volume in late 70s, new blackface control panel 1980/81.
- **Speakers:** 2x12.
- **Tubes:** 3x7025, 12AX7, 2x12AT7, 2x6L6GC, 5U4GB rectifier.

1966

GUITARS

CORONADO I 1966–69
Model name on headstock, hollow twin-cutaway body, one pickup.
- **Neck:** maple with rosewood fingerboard; truss-rod adjuster at body end; plastic tuner buttons; single string-guide.
- **Body:** hollow twin-cutaway bound; long f-holes; sunburst or colors.
- **Electronics:** one metal-cover black-center six-polepiece pickup (at neck); two controls (volume, tone) on body; side-mounted jack.
- **Hardware:** White or gold laminated plastic pickguard; single-saddle wooden bridge, tailpiece; or six-saddle metal-top bridge, vibrato tailpiece.

CORONADO II 1966–69
Model name on headstock, hollow twin-cutaway body, two pickups.
Similar to CORONADO I (see previous listing) except:

- **Neck:** bound fingerboard, block markers.
- **Body:** bound long f-holes.
- **Electronics:** two pickups; four controls (two volume, two tone) and three-way selector, all on body.
- **Hardware:** six-saddle metal-top bridge, tailpiece with F inlay; or six-saddle all-metal bridge, vibrato tailpiece.

Prototype examples with unbound dot-marker neck and three-tuners-per-side headstock; truss-rod adjuster at headstock end; unbound body; black laminated plastic pickguard; six-section tailpiece.

CORONADO XII 12-string 1966–69
Model name on 12-string headstock, hollow twin-cutaway body, two pickups.
Similar to CORONADO II (see previous listing) except:
- **Neck:** one 'bracket' string-guide; six-tuners-per-side 'hockey stick' headstock.
- **Hardware:** six-saddle metal-top bridge; tailpiece with F inlay.

1967

GUITARS
BRONCO 1967–80
Model name on headstock, angled pickup at bridge.
- **Neck:** maple with rosewood fingerboard; 24-inch scale; truss-rod adjuster at body end; one string-guide; plastic tuner buttons (metal from 1975).
- **Body:** slab offset-waist; red only (black or white from 1975).
- **Electronics:** one black plain-top pickup (angled at bridge); two controls (volume, tone) and jack, all on pickguard.
- **Hardware:** 13-screw (15-screw from 1970) white laminated plastic pickguard (black laminated plastic from 1975); six-saddle bridge/vibrato unit.

CORONADO II ANTIGUA 1967–71
White/brown shaded hollow twin-cutaway body, two pickups.
Similar to CORONADO II (see 1966 listing) except:

- **Body:** white/brown shaded finish.
- **Hardware:** pearl tuner buttons; 'Antigua' on matching-color laminated plastic pickguard; six-saddle all-metal bridge, vibrato tailpiece only.

CORONADO XII ANTIGUA (12-string) 1967–71
12-string headstock, white/brown shaded hollow twin-cutaway body, two pickups.
Similar to CORONADO XII 12-string (see 1966 listing) except:
- **Body:** white/brown shaded finish.
- **Hardware:** pearl tuner buttons; 'Antigua' on matching-color laminated plastic pickguard.

CORONADO II WILDWOOD 1967–69
Colored wood hollow twin-cutaway body, two pickups.
Similar to CORONADO II (see 1966 listing) except:
- **Body:** six dye-injected color combinations.
- **Hardware:** pearl tuner buttons; 'Wildwood' on white laminated plastic pickguard; six-saddle all-metal bridge, vibrato tailpiece only.

CORONADO XII WILDWOOD (12-string) 1967–69
12-string headstock, colored wood hollow twin-cutaway body, two pickups.
Similar to CORONADO XII 12-string (see 1966 listing) except:
- **Body:** six dye-injected color combinations.
- **Hardware:** pearl tuner buttons; 'Wildwood' on white laminated plastic pickguard.

1968

GUITARS
BLUE FLOWER TELECASTER 1968–69
As TELECASTER of the period (see 1951 listing) but with blue floral-pattern body finish and clear plastic pickguard.

COMPETITION MUSTANG 1968–73
As MUSTANG of the period (see 1964 listing) but with stripes on body.

'68

COUNTRY STANDARD GETS CREATIVE

While the Stratocaster settled into a format that remained largely unchanged (other than in a handful of details, largely unseen) from 1965 to late 1971, the Telecaster became the subject of a lot of modification and experimentation in the late '60s.

Deluxe appointments had already visited twang-town in 1959 in the form of the Custom Telecaster (and Esquire), which had a bound body, sunburst finish – and later other colors too – and a triple-ply pickguard. (A sunburst finish was considered 'custom' on the normally blond Telecaster, while a blond finish was 'custom' on a normally sunburst Stratocaster – and collectors still pay a premium when they find them in this condition.)

In 1968, Fender offered a model with far more significant modifications: the Thinline Telecaster. Stocks of ash and alder timber had been growing heavier and heavier, and Fender found a means to lighten the load by partially routing the body of a Telecaster. This offered the cosmetic bonus of presenting a 'thinline' semi-acoustic appearance, with stylish f-hole.

Rather than putting a cap on a semi-hollow body, Fender sliced the back from slabs of solid ash or mahogany, routed out chambers on the bass and treble sides of the lower bout, cut an f-hole on the bass side (the pickguard would cover the other side), and glued the fillet of wood back on to the back of the guitar. The technique has provided an enduring alternative look for the Telecaster virtually ever since.

In the same year, Fender made a bid to appeal to the hippie scene with the Paisley Red and Blue Flower Telecasters. These were standard Teles (although fitted with maple-cap necks rather than rosewood) decorated with stick-on pink paisley or blue floral wallpaper front and back, sprayed around the edges in a pinkish-red or bright blue finish, and topped off with a plexiglass pickguard.

The ploy was far too obvious to appeal to many genuine flower children, but the Paisley model in particular was taken up by a handful of country players (notably James Burton, back in the day, and more recently Brad Paisley, naturally).

The tail-end of 1968 also witnessed Fender's presentation of a specially-made solid rosewood Telecaster to George Harrison of The Beatles. A now ultra-rare Rosewood Telecaster model was available on and off as a regular production model between 1969 and 1972.

LTD 1968–74

Hollow single-cutaway body, metal tailpiece, one floating pickup.

- **Neck:** maple with bound ebony fingerboard, 'diamond-in-block' markers; 20 frets; truss-rod adjuster at body end; three-tuners-per-side headstock.
- **Body:** hollow single-cutaway bound; carved top; sunburst or natural.
- **Electronics:** one metal-cover six-polepiece humbucker (mounted on neck-end); two controls (volume, tone) and jack, all on pickguard.
- **Hardware:** gold-plated; tortoiseshell laminated plastic pickguard; single-saddle wooden bridge, tailpiece with F inlay.

MONTEGO I 1968–74

Hollow single-cutaway body, one pickup, metal tailpiece.

- **Neck:** maple with bound ebony fingerboard, 'diamond-in-block' markers; 20 frets; truss-rod adjuster at body end; three-tuners-per-side headstock.
- **Body:** hollow single-cutaway bound; bound f-holes;

finished in sunburst or natural.
- **Electronics:** one metal-cover six-polepiece humbucker (at neck); two controls (volume, tone) on body; side-mounted jack.
- **Hardware:** Black laminated plastic pickguard; single-saddle wooden bridge, tailpiece with F inlay.

MONTEGO II 1968–74
Hollow single-cutaway body, two pickups, metal tailpiece.
Similar to MONTEGO I (see previous listing) except:
- **Electronics:** two humbuckers; four controls (two volume, two tone) and three-way selector, all on body.

PAISLEY RED TELECASTER 1968–69
As TELECASTER of the period (see 1951 listing) but with red paisley-pattern body finish and clear plastic pickguard.

THINLINE TELECASTER (first version) 1968–71
F-hole body, two single-coils, 12-screw white pearl pickguard.
- **Neck:** maple with maple fingerboard (fretted maple or maple with rosewood fingerboard from 1969); truss-rod adjuster at body end; one string-guide.
- **Body:** semi-solid slab single-cutaway with f-hole; sunburst or colors.
- **Electronics:** one plain metal-cover pickup with visible height-adjustment screws (at neck) and one black six-polepiece pickup (angled in bridgeplate); two controls (volume, tone) and three-way selector, all on pickguard; side-mounted jack.
- **Hardware:** 12-screw pearl laminated plastic pickguard; three-saddle raised-sides bridge with through-body stringing.

AMPLIFIERS
BRONCO 1968–74
Small Champ-like amp aimed at students and beginners.

- **Cabinet:** black Tolex.
- **Controls:** volume, bass, treble, speed, intensity; silverface control panel.
- **Speakers:** 1x8.
- **Tubes:** 2x12AX7, 6V6GTA, 5Y3GT rectifier.
- **Output:** 5 watts.

SOLID STATE BASSMAN 1968–70
A member of Fender's ill-fated first solid-state series.
- **Cabinet:** black Tolex.
- **Controls:** volume, treble, bass, style; aluminum control panel.
- **Speakers:** 3x12.
- **Output:** 100 watts.

SOLID STATE DELUXE REVERB 1968–70
A member of Fender's ill-fated first solid-state series.
- **Cabinet:** black Tolex.
- **Controls:** normal: volume, treble, bass, bright switch; vibrato: volume, treble, bass, reverb, speed, intensity, bright switch; aluminum control panel.
- **Speakers:** 1x12.
- **Output:** 25 watts.

SOLID STATE PRO REVERB 1968–70
A member of Fender's ill-fated first solid-state series.
- **Cabinet:** black Tolex.
- **Controls:** normal: volume, treble, bass, bright switch; vibrato: style, volume, treble, bass, speed, intensity, reverb, bright switch; aluminum control panel.
- **Speakers:** 2x12.
- **Output:** 50 watts.

SOLID STATE SUPER REVERB 1968–70
A member of Fender's ill-fated first solid-state series.
- **Cabinet:** black Tolex.
- **Controls:** normal: volume, treble, bass, bright switch; vibrato: volume, treble, bass, reverb, speed, intensity, bright switch; aluminum control panel.
- **Speakers:** 4x10.
- **Output:** 50 watts.

1968

SOLID STATE VIBROLUX REVERB 1968–70

A member of Fender's ill-fated first solid-state series.

- **Cabinet:** black Tolex.
- **Controls:** normal: volume, treble, bass, bright switch; vibrato: volume, speed, intensity, reverb, bright switch; aluminum control panel.
- **Speakers:** 2x10.
- **Output:** 35 watts.

1969

GUITARS

CUSTOM 1969–70

Model name on 'hockey stick' headstock.

- **Neck:** maple with bound rosewood fingerboard, block markers; truss-rod adjuster at body end; one 'bracket' string-guide; three-tuners-per-side 'hockey stick' headstock.
- **Body:** contoured offset-waist with pointed base; sunburst only.
- **Electronics:** two black plain-top split pickups; two controls (volume, tone) and jack, all on metal plate adjoining pickguard; four-way rotary selector on pickguard.
- **Hardware:** 17-screw tortoiseshell laminated plastic pickguard; six-saddle bridge with vibrato tailpiece.

Made using modified Electric XII parts, some with purpose-built necks. Some examples with MAVERICK model name, not Custom, on headstock.

MAVERICK 1969–70

See earlier CUSTOM listing this year.

ROSEWOOD TELECASTER 1969–72

As TELECASTER of the period (see 1951 listing) but with fretted rosewood neck, solid (later semi-solid) rosewood body, and black laminated plastic pickguard.

SWINGER 1969

Arrow-head-shape headstock, one angled pickup.

- **Neck:** maple with rosewood fingerboard; 22.5-inch scale, 21 frets; truss-rod adjuster at body end; one string-guide; 'arrow-head'

shape headstock.

- **Body:** contoured offset-waist with 'scoop' in base; various colors.
- **Electronics:** one black plain-top pickup (angled at neck); two controls (volume, tone) and jack, all on metal plate adjoining pickguard.
- **Hardware:** 12-screw white pearl or tortoiseshell laminated plastic pickguard; three-saddle bridge/tailpiece.

Made from modified Musicmaster and Mustang parts. Many examples have no Swinger logo on headstock. Also unofficially known as ARROW or MUSICLANDER.

AMPLIFIERS

DUAL SHOWMAN REVERB 1969–79

Similar to post-1968 SHOWMAN (see 1961 listing) except:

- **Controls:** vibrato: volume, treble, bass, middle, speed, intensity, reverb, bright switch.
- **Speakers:** 2x15 JBL in external speaker cab.
- **Tubes:** 3x7025, 2x12AX7, 12AX7, 4x6L6GC, (solid-state rectifier).
- **Output:** 100 watts.

1970

AMPLIFIERS

BANDMASTER REVERB 1970–81

Reverb and a tube rectifier for the midsized piggy-back amp.

- **Cabinet:** black Tolex.
- **Controls:** normal ch: volume, bass, treble, bright switch; vibrato ch: volume, bass, treble, speed, intensity, reverb, bright switch; silverface control panel.
- **Speakers:** 2x12 in separate cabinet.
- **Tubes:** 3x7025, 2x12AT7, 12AX7, 2x6L6GC, 5U4G rectifier.
- **Output:** 45 watts.

CAPRICORN 1970–72

From Fender's shortlived Zodiac range, the second series of solid-state amplifiers.

- **Cabinet:** black Tolex.
- **Controls:** normal: volume, treble, bass, bright switch; vibrato: volume, treble, middle, bass, reverb, speed, intensity, bright switch; black and aluminum control panel.
- **Speakers:** 3x12.
- **Output:** 105 watts.

LIBRA 1970–72

Another variant from the Zodiac solid-state line.

- **Cabinet:** black Tolex.
- **Controls:** normal: volume, treble, bass, bright switch; vibrato: volume, treble, middle, bass, reverb, speed, intensity, bright switch; black and aluminum control panel.
- **Speakers:** 4x12 JBL.
- **Output:** 105 watts.

QUAD REVERB 1970–79

A later Twin Reverb with 4x12 speakers. Big. Heavy.

- **Cabinet:** black Tolex.
- **Controls:** normal: volume, treble, middle, bass, bright switch; Vibrato: volume, treble, middle, bass, reverb, speed, intensity, bright switch; master volume (pull distortion on master volume from 1976); silverface control panel.
- **Speakers:** 4x12.
- **Tubes:** 3x7025, 2x12AT7, 12AX7, 4x6L6GC, (solid-state rectifier).
- **Output:** 100 watts.

SCORPIO 1970–72

Mid-sized model from the Zodiac solid-state line.

- **Cabinet:** black Tolex.
- **Controls:** normal: volume, treble, bass, bright

AND THEN THERE WERE THREE

In mid 1971, the Stratocaster became the subject of further changes when the new 'Tilt Neck' design was adopted. This also incorporated a three-screw neck attachment and 'bullet' style truss-rod adjustment nut at the headstock end of the body.

The 'three-bolt' neck is often derided as indicative of the gradual downward spiral in the quality of Fender instruments under CBS in the 1970s but, ironically, the Tilt Neck system was actually devised by Leo Fender. In principle, it's a clever idea. The heel end of the neck contains an adjustment bolt that enables fine-tuning of the neck pitch without removing and shimming the neck, and the headstock-end truss-rod adjustment nut is far easier to access than the nut previously implanted in the heel-end of Fender necks.

But it is generally accepted that the demands of mass production and other factors caused a general decline in the quality of the Stratocaster and other models – in the latter part of the early 1970s and more particularly in the mid '70s. The loss of one attachment screw and the truss-rod adjuster's journey to the other end of the neck have come to symbolize this decline.

Other changes made to the Strat's components in the early '70s served to take the instrument further from its pre-CBS format. The two-part tailpiece with separate screwed-on inertia block was replaced by a one-piece die-case unit in late 1971. Around the same time, the stamped steel saddles were replaced by die-cast saddles, and in 1974 the staggered polepieces on the pickups were replaced by polepieces of equal height.

On top of all this, the use of 'thick-skin' polyester finishes in place of the thinner nitro-cellulose finishes of the pre- and early-CBS years made the guitars feel, and even sound, quite different.

The regular Telecaster model did not receive the Tilt Neck system with three-screw attachment or the bullet-head truss-rod nut.

switch; vibrato: volume, treble, middle, bass, reverb, speed, intensity, bright switch; black and aluminum control panel.
- **Speakers:** 2x12 JBL.
- **Output:** 56 watts.

SUPER SHOWMAN 1970–72
A total departure in solid-state amplification, designed by former Gibson employee Seth Lover: a three-channel preamp coupled with powered speaker cabinets.
- **Cabinet:** black Tolex.
- **Controls:** normal: volume, treble, bass, bright switch; sound expander: volume, treble, bass, fuzz, Dimension IV; vibrato/reverb: speed, intensity, reverb, master volume; black and aluminum control panel.
- **Speakers:** 4x12 or 8x10 in single or multiple external cabinets.
- **Output:** 140 watts.

SUPER SIX REVERB 1970–79
Similar to the TWIN REVERB (see the entry in the 1963 listing) except:
- **Speakers:** 6x10.

TAURUS 1970–72
Another member of the Zodiac solid-state line.
- **Cabinet:** black Tolex.
- **Controls:** normal: volume, treble, bass, bright switch; vibrato: volume, treble, middle, bass, reverb, speed, intensity, bright switch; black and aluminum control panel.
- **Speakers:** 4x10 JBL.
- **Output:** 42 watts.

TRANSISTOR BASSMAN 1970–72
The sole survivor from the first solid-state series of 1968–70, identical to SOLID STATE BASSMAN (see 1968 listing) other than name and minor cosmetic changes.

1971

GUITARS
STRATOCASTER (CBS Seventies) 1971–81
21 frets, enlarged headstock, two string-guides, three-screw neckplate, three controls.
- **Neck:** fretted maple , or maple with rosewood fingerboard; 'bullet' truss-rod adjuster at headstock end; two string-guides; enlarged

---

A HUMBUCKER FOR THE TWANG CROWD
The 1970s saw further changes to the seminal Telecaster, mainly thanks to the arrival of a humbucking pickup at Fender. Seth Lover, the engineer who had developed the famous PAF humbucking pickup for Gibson, was hired by Fender in 1967, and he developed a somewhat different humbucking unit in 1970 that was known as the Fender Wide Range Humbucking Pickup.

This pickup was about the same size as the PAF but its six adjustable polepieces were staggered – three on the bass side of one coil, three on the treble side of the other – and it used cunife (copper-nickel-ferrite) polepieces rather than the alnico bar magnet mounted under Gibson's humbucker.

This powerful yet bright-sounding pickup first appeared on the revised Thinline model of 1971 and then in the neck position of the Telecaster Custom in 1972 (which retained a single-coil pickup in the bridge position). It also appeared in both positions on the brand new Telecaster Deluxe introduced in '72.

The humbucker-loaded Telecasters never quite outstripped the popularity of the standard model, but they did appeal to a lot of players who were seeking the power of a Gibson guitar in the guise of a Fender.

headstock; three-screw neckplate.

- **Body:** sunburst or colors.
- **Electronics:** three white (1971–75 and 1979–81) or black (1975–81) six-polepiece pickups (bridge pickup angled); three controls (volume, two tone) and three-way selector (five-way from 1977), all on pickguard; jack in body face.
- **Hardware:** 11-screw white (1971–75 and 1981) or black (1975–81) laminated pickguard; six-saddle bridge with through-body stringing or six-pivot bridge/vibrato unit.

Some late examples with truss-rod adjuster at body end and four-screw neckplate.

THINLINE TELECASTER (second version) 1971–79

F-hole body, two humbuckers.

Similar to THINLINE TELECASTER FIRST VERSION (see 1968 listing) except:

- **Neck:** fretted maple only; 'bullet' truss-rod adjuster at headstock; three-screw neckplate.
- **Electronics:** two metal-cover split-polepiece humbuckers.
- **Hardware:** 12-screw black, white or white pearl laminated plastic re-styled pickguard; six-saddle small bridge with through-body stringing.

1972

GUITARS

TELECASTER CUSTOM 1972–81

One humbucker and one single-coil, four controls.

- **Neck:** fretted maple , or maple with rosewood fingerboard; 'bullet' truss-rod adjuster at headstock end; two string-guides; three-screw neckplate.
- **Body:** slab single-cutaway; sunburst or colors.
- **Electronics:** one metal-cover split-polepiece humbucker (at neck) and one black six-polepiece pickup (angled in bridgeplate); four controls (two volume, two tone) and three-way selector, all on pickguard; side-mounted jack.
- **Hardware:** 16-screw black laminated plastic

pickguard; six-saddle raised-sides bridge with through-body stringing.

Earliest examples with 15-screw pickguard and/or three-saddle raised-sides bridge.

For Custom Telecaster (with bound body) see 1959 listing.

TELECASTER DELUXE 1972–81

Two covered humbuckers, normal Tele body.

- **Neck:** fretted maple; 'bullet' truss-rod adjuster at headstock end; two string-guides; large Stratocaster-style headstock; three-screw neckplate.
- **Body:** contoured single-cutaway; sunburst or colors.
- **Electronics:** two metal-cover split-polepiece humbuckers; four controls (two volume, two tone) and three-way selector, all on pickguard; side-mounted jack.
- **Hardware:** 16-screw black laminated plastic pickguard; six-saddle small bridge with through-body stringing.

Some examples with Stratocaster-type six-pivot bridge/vibrato unit.

AMPLIFIERS

BASSMAN 10 1972–82

Echoes of the 1950s Bassman in a new 4x10 combo.

- **Cabinet:** black Tolex.
- **Controls:** bass ch: volume, treble, bass, deep switch; normal ch: volume, treble, middle, bass; master volume; silverface control panel (revised blackface from 1981).
- **Speakers:** 4x10 in separate cab; from 1962–63, 2x12 in separate cab.
- **Tubes:** 2x7025, 12AT7, 2x6L6GC, (solid-state rectifier).
- **Output:** 50 watts (70 watts from 1981).

BASSMAN 50 1972–76

A variation of the piggy-back format for the mid 1970s.

- **Cabinet:** black Tolex.

75

MORE HEADROOM AND MASTER VOLUMES

Through the course of the 1970s, Fender engineers continually sought to make their amplifiers louder and more efficient – and thereby, in the estimation of many players, gradually robbed them of some of their hallowed tone in the process.

A small percentage of harmonic distortion, even in an amp perceived as 'clean,' helps to make an electric guitar sound fuller, richer, and more multi-dimensional. Take guitar amps further and further toward the realm of hi-fi amps and, ultimately, they don't make the guitar sound particularly good any more, for most genres of music at least.

The R&D teams at Fender went back and forth throughout the late 1960s and '70s between trying to improve the efficiency and headroom of their amplifiers and, after complaints from distributors that their customers "didn't like them as much as the older amps," trying to find ways of putting some of the 'oomph' back into them.

One result of this endeavor was the adoption of the master volume control, which proved a trend throughout the amp industry from the early '70s. A master volume is useful in helping players get a somewhat 'cranked up' overdriven sound at lower volumes, although the overdrive it helps to generate stems from preamp tube distortion rather than the combination of preamp and output tube distortion that many players love in vintage amps of the 1950s and '60s.

The master volume arrived first on big amps like the Twin Reverb and Showman in 1972 and made its way to most of the rest of the line through the course of the decade (although the Champ, Princeton, and Deluxe Reverb never received the upgrade).

Later in the 1970s, many amps were also given a 'pull boost' or 'pull distortion' function, accessed with a pull-switch on the volume or master volume control, in a bid to further slake players' thirst for distortion. At around the same time, the conversion of 50-watt amps to a 70-watt output and 100-watt amps to a 135-watt output – both thanks to the use of ultra-efficient ultralinear output transformers – helped to squelch any remnants of tone that remained in these much-altered silverface designs – according to the ears of the vast majority of players, at least.

- **Controls:** bass ch: volume, treble, bass, deep switch; normal ch: volume, treble, bass, bright switch; silverface control panel.
- **Speakers:** 2x15 in separate cab; from 1962–63, 2x12 in separate cab.
- **Tubes:** 4x7025 (later 3x12AX7, 12AT7), 2x6L6GC, GZ34 rectifier; solid-state rectifier from 1962–63.
- **Output:** 50 watts.

VIBRASONIC REVERB 1972–79
A name from the late 50s is revived as a 100-watter with reverb.
Similar to TWIN REVERB of same era (see 1963 listing) except:

- **Speakers:** 1x15 JBL.

1975

GUITARS

MUSICMASTER (third version) 1975–80
Model name on headstock, one angled pickup at neck, controls on black pickguard.
Similar to MUSICMASTER SECOND VERSION (see 1964 listing) except:

- **Neck:** 24-inch scale, 22 frets only.
- **Body:** black or white.
- **Electronics:** one black plain-top pickup (angled at neck); two controls (volume, tone) on pickguard.

- **Hardware:** 15-screw black laminated plastic pickguard.

RHINESTONE STRATOCASTER 1975

Based on STRATOCASTER CBS SEVENTIES (see 1971 listing) but with replacement bonded metal and fibreglass body by British sculptor Jon Douglas, specially ordered by Fender's UK agent in 1975. Front has heavy-relief floral leaf scroll design, inset with rhinestones on some examples. Very small quantity produced. Unauthorized 1990s versions are identifiable by a plaque on back of body.

1976

GUITARS

STARCASTER 1976–80

Model name on 'hooked' headstock with black edging, semi-acoustic offset-waist body.

- **Neck:** fretted maple; 22 frets; 'bullet' truss-rod adjuster at headstock end; one 'bracket' string-guide; three-screw neckplate; black edging on headstock.
- **Body:** Semi-acoustic offset-waist bound; f-holes; sunburst or colors.
- **Electronics:** two metal-cover split-polepiece humbuckers; five controls (two volume, two tone, master volume) and three-way selector, all on body; side-mounted jack.
- **Hardware:** Black laminated plastic pickguard; six-saddle bridge with through-body stringing.

AMPLIFIERS

SUPER TWIN 1976–81

Ultra high-powered amp using six output tubes and ultralinear output transformer.

- **Cabinet:** black Tolex, plus unusual black grille cloth.
- **Controls:** volume, treble, middle, bass, presence, distortion, output level, five-way EQ; black control panel.
- **Speakers:** 2x12.
- **Tubes:** 2x7025, 2AT7, 12AU7, 12AX7, 6x6L6GC,

(solid-state rectifier.

- **Output:** 180 watts.

300PS 1976–79

Guitar version of the mammoth stage rig for bass, with unusual 6V6-driven transformer phase inverter.

- **Cabinet:** black Tolex.
- **Controls:** volume, treble, middle, bass, presence, 5-band graphic EQ, distortion, output; black control panel.
- **Speakers:** amp top paired with 4x12 speaker cab.
- **Tubes:** 2x7025, 12AT7, 6V6GTA, 4x6550, (solid-state rectifier).
- **Output:** 300 watts.

1977

GUITARS

ANTIGUA MUSTANG 1977–79

As MUSTANG of the period (see 1964 listing) but with white/brown shaded body finish and matching-color laminated plastic pickguard.

ANTIGUA STRATOCASTER 1977–79

As STRATOCASTER CBS SEVENTIES (see 1971 listing) but with white/brown shaded body finish and matching-color laminated plastic pickguard.

ANTIGUA TELECASTER 1977–79

As TELECASTER of the period (see 1951 listing) but with white/brown shaded body finish and matching-color laminated plastic pickguard.

ANTIGUA TELECASTER CUSTOM 1977–79

As TELECASTER CUSTOM (see 1972 listing) but with white/brown shaded body finish and matching-color laminated plastic pickguard.

ANTIGUA TELECASTER DELUXE 1977–79

As Telecaster Deluxe (see 1973 listing) but with white/brown shaded body finish and matching-color laminated plastic pickguard.

1979

GUITARS

LEAD I 1979–82

Model name on headstock, one humbucker pickup, two switches.

- **Neck:** fretted maple , or maple with rosewood fingerboard; truss-rod adjuster at body end; two string-guides.
- **Body:** sunburst or colors.
- **Electronics:** one black or white 12-polepiece humbucker (at bridge); two controls (volume, tone), two two-way selectors, and jack, all on pickguard.
- **Hardware:** 11-screw black or white laminated plastic pickguard; six-saddle bridge with through-body stringing.

LEAD II 1979–82

Model name on headstock, two single-coils, two switches.

Similar to LEAD I (see previous listing) except:

- **Electronics:** two black or white six-polepiece pickups (both angled); one two-way selector, one three-way selector.

25th ANNIVERSARY STRATOCASTER 1979–80

'Anniversary' logo on body.

Similar to STRATOCASTER CBS SEVENTIES (see 1971 listing) except:

- **Neck:** fretted maple only; truss-rod adjuster at body end; commemorative four-screw neckplate.
- **Body:** silver (earliest examples white) with black 'Anniversary' logo.
- **Hardware:** Six-pivot bridge/vibrato unit only.

AMPLIFIERS

HARVARD 1979–82

Fender jumps back into solid state after a break of nearly ten years.

- **Cabinet:** black Tolex.
- **Controls:** volume, bass, treble, master volume; blackface control panel.

- **Speakers:** 1x10.
- **Output:** 20 watts.

30 1979–82

The smallest model in the last line of tube amps to be released by Fender under CBS.

- **Cabinet:** black Tolex.
- **Controls:** normal: volume, treble, bass, reverb: fain, treble, middle, bass, reverb, volume; black control panel.
- **Speakers:** 1x12 or 2x10.
- **Tubes:** 3x7025, 2x12AT7, 2x6L6GC, (solid-state rectifier).
- **Output:** 30 watts.

75 1979–83

Mid-sized tube amp for the modern musician, also available as an amp top.

- **Cabinet:** black Tolex.
- **Controls:** ch 1: gain, treble, middle, bass; ch 2: lead drive, reverb, lead level, master volume; black control panel.
- **Speakers:** 1x12 or 1x12.
- **Tubes:** 3x7025, 2x12AT7, 2x6L6GC, (solid-state rectifier).
- **Output:** 75 watts.

1980

GUITARS

HENDRIX STRATOCASTER 1980

Six-pivot vibrato, large inverted headstock.

- **Neck:** fretted maple; truss-rod adjuster at body end; two string-guides; large reverse headstock; four-screw neckplate.
- **Body:** with additional front contouring; white only.
- **Electronics:** three white six-polepiece pickups (bridge pickup angled); three controls (volume, two tone) and five-way selector, all on pickguard; jack in body face.
- **Hardware:** 11-screw white laminated plastic pickguard; six-pivot bridge/vibrato unit.

Only 25 produced.

STRAT 1980–83

Six-pivot vibrato, 'Strat' logo on headstock.

- **Neck:** fretted maple , or maple with rosewood fingerboard; truss-rod adjuster at body end; two string-guides; 'Strat' logo on re-styled headstock with face matching body color.
- **Body:** red, blue, or white.
- **Electronics:** three white six-polepiece pickups (bridge pickup angled); three controls (volume, tone, two-way rotary switch) and five-way selector, all situated on the guitar's pickguard; jack in body face.
- **Hardware:** gold-plated brass (early examples have chrome machine heads and polished brass hardware); 11-screw white laminated plastic pickguard; redesigned six-pivot bridge-and-vibrato unit.

AMPLIFIERS

140 1980–81

Shortlived big belter from the final CBS tube range.

- **Cabinet:** black Tolex.
- **Controls:** volume, treble, middle, bass, reverb, 5-band graphic EQ, lead drive, lead level, master volume; black control panel.
- **Speakers:** amp top only.
- **Tubes:** 4x7025, 2x12AT7, 4x6L6GC, (solid-state rectifier).
- **Output:** 135 watts.

1981

GUITARS

BLACK & GOLD TELECASTER 1981–83

Normal Tele pickup layout, 21 frets, black body, gold hardware.

Similar to 1981-period TELECASTER (see 1951 listing) except:

- **Neck:** black-face headstock.
- **Body:** black only.
- **Hardware:** gold-plated brass; black laminated plastic pickguard; six-saddle heavy-duty small bridge with through-body stringing.

BULLET (first version) 1981–83

Model name on headstock, single-cutaway body, bridge on metal pickguard.

- **Neck:** fretted maple, or maple with rosewood fingerboard; truss-rod adjuster at body end; one string-guide; Telecaster-style headstock.
- **Body:** slab single-cutaway; red or white.
- **Electronics:** two black or white plain-top pickups (neck pickup angled); two controls (volume, tone), three-way selector and jack, all situated on pickguard.
- **Hardware:** six-screw (plus four at bridge) white or black-painted metal pickguard; six-saddle bridge, raised 'lip' of pickguard forms tailpiece.

Earliest examples use some Korean-made components.

BULLET DELUXE 1981–83

Model name on headstock, single-cutaway body, separate bridge.

Similar to BULLET FIRST VERSION (see previous listing) except:

- **Hardware:** eight-screw white or black laminated plastic pickguard; separate six-saddle bridge with through-body stringing.

GOLD/GOLD STRATOCASTER 1981–83

Six-pivot vibrato, gold body and hardware.

Similar to STRAT (see 1980 listing) except:

- **Neck:** fretted maple only; 'Stratocaster' logo on headstock.
- **Body:** gold only; three controls (volume, two tone) and five-way selector.
- **Hardware:** gold-plated; normal-type six-pivot bridge/vibrato unit.

Some examples with pearl fingerboard position markers.

INTERNATIONAL COLOR STRATOCASTER 1981

As TELECASTER of the period (see 1951 listing) but with special color finishes, white laminated plastic pickguard, and black-plated pickguard screws.

EASTERN PROMISE

With well-made copies from Asian factories taking a bite out of sales in the U.S.A. and around the world in the late 1970s and early '80s, Fender made moves to beat the competition at its own game.

The Fender Japan Co. Ltd. was established in the spring of 1982, and its guitars, manufactured in Japan at the Fuji Gen-Gakki factory arrived on the market soon after (initially with parts shipped over from Fender in the U.S.A.). These first took the form of a line of Vintage Reissue-styled Stratocasters and Telecasters, which looked extremely similar to their U.S. counterparts, other than the small 'made in Japan' legend under the Fender logo.

To avoid confusion and to distinguish the Japan-made guitars further from instruments hailing from the California factory, Fender established the Squier brand, and Japanese guitars arriving in Europe and the U.S.A. by 1983 carried the Squier logo on their headstocks.

In the years to follow, Fender Japan would continue to produce a wide range of Squier models alongside Fender-branded models that were distributed widely in Japan itself, but also for various periods in the U.S.A. and other parts of the world.

INTERNATIONAL COLOR TELECASTER 1981

As Stratocaster CBS Seventies (see 1971 listing) but with special color finishes, white laminated plastic pickguard, and black-plated pickguard screws.

LEAD III 1981–2

Model name on headstock, two humbuckers, two switches.
Similar to Lead I (see 1979 listing) except:
- **Electronics:** two black or white 12-polepiece humbuckers; two three-way selectors.

STRATOCASTER STANDARD (first version) 1981–83

21 frets, small headstock, two string-guides, four-screw neckplate, three controls.
- **Neck:** fretted maple, or maple with rosewood fingerboard; truss-rod adjuster at body end; two string-guides; small headstock.
- **Body:** sunburst or colors.
- **Electronics:** three white six-polepiece pickups (bridge pickup angled); three controls (volume, two tone) and five-way selector, all on pickguard; jack in body face.
- **Hardware:** 11-screw white or black laminated plastic pickguard; six-saddle bridge with through-body stringing or six-pivot bridge/vibrato unit.

WALNUT STRAT 1981–83

As Strat (see 1980 listing) but with fretted walnut neck (some with walnut neck and ebony fingerboard), walnut body, black laminated plastic pickguard, and gold-plated hardware.

1982

GUITARS

SQUIER SERIES '52 TELECASTER (MIJ) 1982–83

Replica of 1952-period U.S. original (see Telecaster 1951 listing) with small Squier Series logo on headstock 1982–83. Known as 50s Telecaster 1990 onward. Sold under the Squier brandname (1983–85) and new Fender version introduced in 1990, although Japanese market manufacture continuous since 1982. Also Foto Flame fake figured wood finish option (1994).

SQUIER SERIES '57 STRATOCASTER (MIJ) 1982–83

Replica of 1957-period U.S. original (see

STRATOCASTER PRE-CBS 1954 listing) with small Squier Series logo on headstock 1982–83. Also version with six-saddle bridge and through-body stringing. Known as 50s STRATOCASTER from 1985 onward. Sold under the Squier brandname (1983–85) and new Fender version introduced in 1985, although Japanese market manufacture continuous since 1982. Also Foto Flame fake figured wood finish option (1992–94).

SQUIER SERIES '62 STRATOCASTER (MIJ) 1982–83

Replica of 1962-period U.S. original (see STRATOCASTER PRE-CBS 1954 listing) with small Squier Series logo on headstock 1982–83. Also version with six-saddle bridge and through-body stringing. Known as 60s STRATOCASTER from 1985 onward. Sold under the Squier brandname (1983–85) and new Fender version introduced in 1985, although Japanese market manufacture continuous since 1982. Also Foto Flame fake figured wood finish option (1992–94).

AMPLIFIERS

CHAMP II 1982–85

Student amp on steroids.
- **Cabinet:** black Tolex.
- **Controls:** volume, treble, bass, master volume; blackface control panel.
- **Speakers:** 1x10.
- **Tubes:** 2x12AX7, 2x6V6GTA, (solid-state rectifier).
- **Output:** 15 watts.

CONCERT 112, 210, 410 1982–85

One of the hot-rodded 'II' series amps designed by Paul Rivera, with channel switching and pull-boost functions.
- **Cabinet:** black Tolex.
- **Controls:** ch 1: volume, treble, bass; ch 2: volume, gain, master, treble, middle, bass; reverb, presence; blackface control panel.
- **Speakers:** 1x12, 2x10, 4x10.
- **Tubes:** 5x7025, 2x12AT7, 2x6L6GC, (solid-state rectifier).
- **Output:** 50 watts.

DELUXE REVERB II 1982–85

One of the hot-rodded 'II' series amps designed by Paul Rivera, with channel switching and pull-boost functions.
- **Cabinet:** black Tolex.
- **Controls:** ch 1: volume, treble, bass; ch 2: volume, gain, master, treble, middle, bass; reverb, presence; blackface control panel.
- **Speakers:** 1x12.
- **Tubes:** 5x7025, 12AT7, 2x6V6GTA, (solid-state rectifier).
- **Output:** 20 watts.

HARVARD REVERB II 1982–85

A basic transistorized student amp with reverb.
- **Cabinet:** black Tolex.
- **Controls:** volume, gain, master, treble, middle, bass, reverb; blackface control panel.
- **Speakers:** 1x10.
- **Output:** 20 watts.

PRINCETON REVERB II 1982–85

This lower-mid-sized amp was part of the popular but shortlived hotrodded line that was designed by Paul Rivera.
- **Cabinet:** black Tolex.
- **Controls:** volume, treble, middle, bass, reverb, lead level, master volume, presence; blackface control panel.
- **Speakers:** 1x12.
- **Tubes:** 3x7025, 12AT7, 2x6V6GTA, (solid-state rectifier).
- **Output:** 20 watts.

SUPER CHAMP 1982–85

A steroid injection for the tiny tube amp.
- **Cabinet:** black Tolex.
- **Controls:** volume, treble, bass, reverb, lead level, master volume.
- **Speakers:** 1x10 (Electrovoice speaker optional).
- **Tubes:** 2x7025, 2x6V6GTA, (solid-state rectifier).
- **Output:** 18 watts.

TWIN REVERB II 1982–85

Paul Rivera's souped-up version of the big 100-watt mainstay.
- **Cabinet:** black Tolex.
- **Controls:** ch 1: volume, treble, bass; ch 2: volume, gain, master, treble, middle, bass; reverb, presence; blackface control panel.
- **Speakers:** 2x12.
- **Tubes:** 4x7025, 2x12AT7, 4x6L6GC, (solid-state rectifier).
- **Output:** 105 watts

YALE REVERB 1982–85

A bump up the Ivy League ladder: essentially a Harvard Reverb II with a 12-inch speaker and more power.
- **Cabinet:** black Tolex.
- **Controls:** volume, gain, master, treble, middle, bass, reverb.
- **Speakers:** 1x12.
- **Output:** 50 watts.

1983

GUITARS

BULLET (second version) 1983

Model name on headstock, offset-cutaway body, two single-coils, bridge on metal pickguard.
- **Neck:** fretted maple; truss-rod adjuster at body end; one string-guide; Telecaster-style headstock.
- **Body:** slab offset-cutaway; red or white.
- **Electronics:** two white plain-top pickups (neck pickup angled); two controls (volume, tone), three-way selector and jack, all on pickguard.
- **Hardware:** six-screw (plus four at bridge) white-painted metal pickguard; six-saddle bridge, raised 'lip' of pickguard forms tailpiece.

BULLET H1 1983

'Bullet' name on headstock, offset-cutaway body, one humbucker, bridge on metal pickguard.
Similar to BULLET SECOND VERSION (see previous listing) except:

- **Electronics:** one white plain-top humbucker (at bridge); pushbutton coil-switch replaces three-way selector.

BULLET H2 1983

'Bullet' name on headstock, offset-cutaway body, two humbuckers, separate bridge.
Similar to BULLET SECOND VERSION (see earlier listing this year) except:
- **Body:** sunburst or colors.
- **Electronics:** two white plain-top humbuckers; three-way selector, plus two pushbutton coil-switches.
- **Hardware:** nine-screw white laminated plastic pickguard; six-saddle separate bridge with through-body stringing.

BULLET S2 1983

'Bullet' name on headstock, offset-cutaway body, two single-coils, separate bridge.
Similar to BULLET SECOND VERSION (see earlier listing this year) except:
- **Body:** sunburst or colors.
- **Hardware:** nine-screw white laminated plastic pickguard; six-saddle separate bridge with through-body stringing.

BULLET S3 1983

'Bullet' name on headstock, offset-cutaway body, three single-coils, separate bridge.
Similar to BULLET SECOND VERSION (see earlier listing this year) except:
- **Body:** sunburst or colors.
- **Electronics:** three black or white plain-top pickups (bridge pickup angled); five-way selector.
- **Hardware:** nine-screw white laminated plastic pickguard; six-saddle separate bridge with through-body stringing.

ELITE STRATOCASTER 1983–84

Single-pivot vibrato, three pushbutton switches.
- **Neck:** fretted maple , or maple with rosewood fingerboard; truss-rod adjuster at headstock end;

two string-guides.
- **Body:** sunburst or colors.
- **Electronics:** three white plain-top pickups (bridge pickup angled); three controls (volume, two tone) and three pushbutton selectors, all on pickguard; side-mounted jack; active circuit.
- **Hardware:** 11-screw white laminated plastic pickguard; redesigned six-saddle bridge/tailpiece or single-pivot bridge/vibrato unit.

ELITE TELECASTER 1983–84
Two white plain-top humbuckers.
- **Neck:** fretted maple , or maple with rosewood fingerboard; truss-rod adjuster at headstock end; two string-guides.
- **Body:** slab single-cutaway bound; sunburst or colors.
- **Electronics:** two white plain-top humbuckers; four controls (two volume, two tone) and three-way selector, all on body; side-mounted jack; active circuit.
- **Hardware:** white laminated plastic optional mini pickguard; re-designed six-saddle bridge/tailpiece.

GOLD ELITE STRATOCASTER 1983–84
As ELITE STRATOCASTER listing this year but with pearl tuner buttons and gold-plated hardware.

GOLD ELITE TELECASTER 1983–84
As ELITE TELECASTER listing this year but with pearl tuner buttons and gold-plated hardware.

STRATOCASTER STANDARD (second version) 1983–84
21 frets, small headstock, two string-guides, four-screw neckplate, two controls.
- **Neck:** fretted maple only; truss-rod adjuster at headstock end; two string-guides; small headstock.
- **Body:** sunburst or colors; also in red, yellow, or blue streaked finish, unofficially known as BOWLING BALL or MARBLE STRATOCASTER (1984).

- **Electronics:** three white six-polepiece pickups (bridge pickup angled); two controls (volume, tone) and jack, all on pickguard.
- **Hardware:** 12-screw white plastic pickguard; re-designed six-saddle bridge/tailpiece or single-pivot bridge/vibrato unit.

TELECASTER STANDARD 1983–84
21 frets, slab single-cutaway body, two single-coils, six-saddle bridge/tailpiece.
- **Neck:** fretted maple; truss-rod adjuster at headstock end; two string-guides.
- **Body:** slab single-cutaway; sunburst or colors; also in red, yellow, or blue streaked finish, unofficially known as BOWLING BALL or MARBLE TELECASTER (1984).
- **Electronics:** one plain metal-cover pickup at neck and one black six-polepiece pickup (angled in bridgeplate); two controls (volume, tone) and three-way selector, all on metal plate adjoining pickguard; side-mounted jack.
- **Hardware:** five-screw (originally eight-screw) white plastic pickguard; six-saddle flat bridge/tailpiece (no through-body stringing).

WALNUT ELITE STRATOCASTER 1983–84
As ELITE STRATOCASTER listing this year but with walnut neck and ebony fingerboard, walnut body, pearl tuner buttons, and gold-plated hardware.

WALNUT ELITE TELECASTER 1983–84
As ELITE TELECASTER listing this year but with walnut neck and ebony fingerboard, walnut body, pearl tuner buttons, and gold-plated hardware.

'52 TELECASTER 1983–84, 86–98
Replica of 1952-period original (see 1951 listing).

'57 STRATOCASTER 1983–85, 86–98
Replica of 1957-period original (see 1954 listing).

'62 STRATOCASTER 1983–85, 86–98
Replica of 1962-period original (see 1954 listing).

'83

VINTAGE REISSUES AND THE DECLINE OF CBS

Although the 1970s are usually thought of as the CBS years, Fender remained under the Columbia Broadcasting System's ownership until early 1985, when the company was sold to a group of investors headed by William Schultz, president of Fender Musical Instruments, and including Dan Smith and other Fender managers.

Smith in particular had recognized the decline in quality that had resulted from CBS's failure to invest in Fender from the late 1970s onward. He also perceived that the best way forward for the company might involve, in some measure, a lingering look into the rearview mirror.

While Fender was still a part of CBS, and virtually simultaneous to the move to develop a more affordable Japan-made line for the brand, Smith and the Fender R&D team began studying and measuring vintage models. Toward the end of 1982 they announced the Vintage Reissue Series. The '52 Telecaster, '57 Stratocaster, and '62 Stratocaster went into regular production in 1983 and were very well received.

Purists were swift to point out certain inconsistencies between the reissues and original vintage examples from the respective periods – unlikely neck profiles (back shapes), wrongly spaced 12th-fret position markers, a lack of 'clay' dots and 'green' celluloid pickguard on the '62 model – but overall these new instruments were closer to the guitars that Fender had produced 20 years ago and better than anything that had been available for, well, 20 years.

When Schultz, Smith, and the other managers and investors purchased Fender they didn't have the funds to also purchase the enormous Fullerton factory. So for approximately the first three-quarters of 1985 Fender guitars were made in Japan only, until the new factory in Corona, CA, came online in October 1985. When it did, the newly popular Vintage Reissues were the first guitars to go into production, at which time Fender took the opportunity to improve some of the finer points to make these guitars more vintage-correct.

A newly revitalized, independently owned Fender Musical Instruments Corp went on to introduce the American Standard Stratocaster in late 1986 and the Strat Plus in 1987. Since that time the company has gone from strength to strength with very few major hiccups, regaining both the quality and the reputation that it enjoyed in the first two decades of its existence.

AMPLIFIERS

LONDON REVERB 1983–85

This London Reverb model was one member of a line of fully-featured solid-state combos and head/cab sets.

- **Cabinet:** black Tolex.
- **Controls:** ch 1: volume, treble, bass; ch 2: volume, gain, master, treble, mid 1, mid 2, bass, reverb 1, reverb 2, five-band EQ; black control panel.
- **Speakers:** 1x12 or 2x10, or top (head) only.
- **Output:** 100 watts.

SIDEKICK REVERB 20 (MIJ) 1983–85

One of the first amplifiers manufactured by Fender Japan.

- **Cabinet:** black Tolex.
- **Controls:** volume, master, treble, middle, bass, reverb.
- **Speakers:** 1x10.
- **Output:** 20 watts.

SIDEKICK REVERB 30 (MIJ) 1983–85

Another solid-state amp from Fender Japan.

- **Cabinet:** black Tolex.

- **Controls:** volume, master, treble, middle, bass, presence, reverb.
- **Speakers:** 1x12.
- **Output:** 30 watts.

SIDEKICK 10 (MIJ) 1983–85
Small solid-state amp from Fender Japan.
- **Cabinet:** black Tolex.
- **Controls:** volume, master, treble, middle, bass.
- **Speakers:** 1x8.
- **Output:** 10 watts.

SHOWMAN 112 / 212 / 115 / 210 1983–85
Powerful flagship of the mid '80s solid-state range.
- **Cabinet:** black Tolex.
- **Controls:** ch 1: volume, treble, bass; ch 2: volume, gain, master, treble, mid 1, mid 2, bass, reverb 1, reverb 2; five-way graphic EQ; black control panel.
- **Speakers:** 1x12, 2x12, 1x15, 2x10, according to model.
- **Output:** 200 watts.

STAGE LEAD 1983–85
Shortlived high-powered solid-state amp with channel switching.
- **Cabinet:** black Tolex.
- **Controls:** ch 1: volume, treble, middle, bass; ch 2: volume, gain, master, treble, middle, bass, reverb; blackface control panel.
- **Speakers:** 1x12.
- **Output:** 100 watts.

STAGE LEAD 212 1983–85
Similar to STAGE LEAD (see previous listing) except:
- **Speakers:** 2x12.

STUDIO LEAD 1983–85
Shortlived mid-powered solid-state amp with channel switching.
- **Cabinet:** black Tolex.
- **Controls:** ch 1: volume, treble, middle, bass; ch 2: volume, gain, master, treble, middle, bass, reverb; blackface control panel.

- **Speakers:** 1x12.
- **Output:** 50 watts.

1984

GUITARS

BOWLING BALL STRATOCASTER 1984
Also known as Marble Stratocaster. See STRATOCASTER STANDARD SECOND VERSION 1983 listing.

BOWLING BALL TELECASTER 1984
Also known as Marble Telecaster. See TELECASTER STANDARD 1983 listing.

D'AQUISTO ELITE (MIJ) 1984, 1989–94
Hollow single-cutaway body, one pickup, wooden tailpiece.
Similar to D'AQUISTO STANDARD (see next listing) except:
- **Neck:** bound ebony fingerboard, block markers; ebony tuner buttons.
- **Electronics:** one black 12-polepiece humbucker pickup (one metal-cover six-polepiece humbucker 1989–94); two controls (volume, tone) on body.
- **Hardware:** gold-plated.

D'AQUISTO STANDARD (MIJ) 1984
Hollow single-cutaway body, two pickups, wooden tailpiece.
- **Neck:** maple glued-in, with bound rosewood fingerboard; 24.75-inch scale, 20 frets; truss-rod adjuster at headstock end; pearl tuner buttons; three-tuners-per-side headstock.
- **Body:** hollow archtop single-cutaway bound; f-holes; sunburst, natural or black.
- **Electronics:** two black 12-polepiece humbuckers; four controls (two volume, two tone) and three-way selector, all on body; side-mounted jack.
- **Hardware:** bound floating wooden pickguard; single-saddle wooden bridge, wooden tailpiece.

ESPRIT ELITE (MIJ) 1984
Three-tuners-per-side headstock, Elite on truss-rod

cover, twin-cutaway body, two humbuckers.
Similar to ESPRIT STANDARD (see next listing) except:
- **Neck:** snowflake position markers; pearl tuner buttons; Elite on truss-rod cover.
- **Body:** sunburst or colors.
- **Electronics:** four controls (two volume, two tone), three-way selector and coil-switch, all on body.
- **Hardware:** fine-tuner tailpiece.

ESPRIT STANDARD (MIJ) 1984

Three-tuners-per-side headstock, twin-cutaway body, two humbuckers.
- **Neck:** maple glued-in, with bound rosewood fingerboard; 24.75-inch scale, 22 frets; truss-rod adjuster at headstock end; three-tuners-per-side headstock; neck matches body color.
- **Body:** semi-solid twin-cutaway bound; sunburst or black.
- **Electronics:** two black 12-polepiece humbucker pickups; two controls (volume, tone) and three-way selector, all on body; side-mounted jack.
- **Hardware:** six-saddle bridge, tailpiece.

ESPRIT ULTRA (MIJ) 1984

Three-tuners-per-side headstock, Ultra on truss-rod cover, twin-cutaway body, two humbuckers.
Similar to ESPRIT STANDARD (see previous listing) except:
- **Neck:** bound ebony fingerboard, split-block position markers; ebony tuner buttons; Ultra on truss-rod cover.
- **Body:** sunburst or colors.
- **Electronics:** four controls (two volume, two tone), three-way selector and coil-switch, all situated on body.
- **Hardware:** gold-plated; fine-tuner tailpiece.

FLAME STANDARD (MIJ) 1984

Three-tuners-per-side headstock, offset-cutaway body, two humbuckers.
Similar to ESPRIT STANDARD (see earlier listing this year) except:
- **Body:** smaller, semi-solid offset-cutaway.

1985

GUITARS

CONTEMPORARY STRATOCASTER (MIJ) (first type) 1985–87

One humbucker, normal logo, black neck.
- **Neck:** maple with rosewood fingerboard; 22 frets; truss-rod adjuster at headstock end; string-clamp; black neck.
- **Body:** various colors.
- **Electronics:** one black coverless humbucker (at bridge); one control (volume) on body; side-mounted jack.
- **Hardware:** black-plated; no pickguard; two-pivot bridge/vibrato unit.

CONTEMPORARY STRATOCASTER (MIJ) (second type) 1985–87

Two humbuckers, black neck.
Similar to CONTEMPORARY STRATOCASTER FIRST TYPE (see previous listing) except:
- **Electronics:** two black coverless humbuckers; two controls (volume, tone) and three-way selector, all on pickguard.
- **Hardware:** 11-screw black plastic pickguard.

CONTEMPORARY STRATOCASTER (MIJ) (third type) 1985–87

Two single-coils and one humbucker, black neck,
Similar to CONTEMPORARY STRATOCASTER FIRST TYPE (see earlier listing this year) except:
- **Electronics:** two black six-polepiece pickups and one black coverless humbucker (at bridge); two controls (volume, tone), five-way selector and coil-switch, all on pickguard.
- **Hardware:** 11-screw black plastic pickguard.

CONTEMPORARY STRATOCASTER (MIJ) (fourth type) 1985–87

Lever-type locking nut, two single-coils and one black coverless humbucker.
Similar to CONTEMPORARY STRATOCASTER FIRST TYPE (see earlier listing this year) except:

'84

- **Neck:** two string-guides; lever-type locking nut; black-face headstock.
- **Electronics:** two black six-polepiece pickups and one black coverless humbucker (at bridge); two controls (volume, tone), five-way selector and coil-switch, all on pickguard.
- **Hardware:** chrome-plated; 11-screw black plastic pickguard.

CONTEMPORARY STRATOCASTER DELUXE (MIJ) (first type) 1985–87

Two humbuckers, normal color neck.
Similar to CONTEMPORARY STRATOCASTER FIRST TYPE (see earlier listing this year) except:
- **Neck:** two string-guides; lever-type locking nut; black-face headstock.
- **Electronics:** two black cover humbuckers; two controls (volume, tone), three-way selector and coil-switch, all on pickguard.
- **Hardware:** chrome-plated; 11-screw black plastic pickguard.

CONTEMPORARY STRATOCASTER DELUXE (MIJ) (second type) 1985–87

Two single-coils and one covered humbucker.
Similar to CONTEMPORARY STRATOCASTER FIRST TYPE (see earlier listing this year) except:
- **Neck:** two string-guides; lever-type locking nut; black-face headstock.
- **Electronics:** two black six-polepiece pickups and one black cover humbucker (at bridge); two controls (volume, tone), five-way selector and coil-switch, all on pickguard.
- **Hardware:** chrome-plated; 11-screw black plastic pickguard.

CONTEMPORARY TELECASTER (MIJ) (first type) 1985–87

Black neck, two humbuckers.
- **Neck:** maple neck with rosewood fingerboard; 22 frets; truss-rod adjuster at headstock end; string clamp; black neck.
- **Body:** slab single-cutaway body; various colors.

- **Electronics:** two black coverless humbuckers; two controls (volume, tone), three-way selector and coil-switch, all on body; side-mounted jack.
- **Hardware:** black-plated; no pickguard; two-pivot bridge/vibrato unit.

CONTEMPORARY TELECASTER (MIJ) (second type) 1985–87

Black neck, two single-coils and one humbucker.
Similar to CONTEMPORARY TELECASTER FIRST TYPE (see previous listing) except:
- **Electronics:** two black six-polepiece pickups and one black coverless humbucker (at bridge); two controls (volume, tone) and three mini-switches, all on body.

CUSTOM TELECASTER '62 (MIJ) 1985–onward

Replica of 1962-period U.S. original with bound-body (see 1959 listing). Foto Flame fake figured wood finish option (1994–96).

KATANA (MIJ) 1985–86

Model name on headstock, wedge-shape body.
- **Neck:** maple glued-in with bound rosewood fingerboard, offset triangle markers; 24.75-inch scale, 22 frets; truss-rod adjuster at headstock end; string clamp; arrow-head-shape headstock; neck matches body color.
- **Body:** bevelled-edge wedge; various colors.
- **Electronics:** two black coverless humbuckers; two controls (volume, tone) and three-way selector, all on body; side-mounted jack.
- **Hardware:** two-pivot bridge/vibrato unit.

PERFORMER (MIJ) 1985–86

Model name on headstock, two angled white plain-top pickups.
- **Neck:** maple with rosewood fingerboard; 24 frets; truss-rod adjuster at headstock end; string clamp; 'arrow-head' shape headstock.
- **Body:** contoured offset-waist with 'hooked' horns; sunburst or colors.

- **Electronics:** two white plain-top humbuckers (both angled); two controls (volume, tone), three-way selector and coil-switch, all on pickguard; side-mounted jack.
- **Hardware:** ten-screw white laminated plastic pickguard; two-pivot bridge/vibrato unit.

STANDARD STRATOCASTER (first version) 1985–89

22 frets, two-pivot bridge/vibrato unit.
- **Neck:** fretted maple, or maple with rosewood fingerboard; 22 frets; truss-rod adjuster at headstock end; string clamp (locking nut from 1988).
- **Body:** sunburst or colors.
- **Electronics:** three white six-polepiece pickups (bridge pickup angled); three controls (volume, two tone) and five-way selector, all on pickguard; jack in body face.
- **Hardware:** 11-screw white laminated plastic pickguard; two-pivot bridge/vibrato unit (locking type from 1988).

STRATOCASTER '72 (MIJ) 1985–onward

Replica of 1972-period U.S. original (see 1971 listing).

50s STRATOCASTER (MIJ) 1985–onward

See SQUIER SERIES '57 STRATOCASTER 1982 listing.

60s STRATOCASTER (MIJ) 1985–onward

See SQUIER SERIES '62 STRATOCASTER 1982 listing.

1986

GUITARS

AMERICAN STANDARD STRATOCASTER 1986–2000

22 frets, small headstock, two string-guides, four-screw neckplate, three controls.
- **Neck:** fretted maple neck, or maple neck with rosewood fingerboard; 22 frets; truss-rod adjuster at headstock end; two string-guides.

- **Body:** sunburst or colors.
- **Electronics:** three white six-polepiece pickups (bridge pickup angled); three controls (volume, two tone) and five-way selector, all on pickguard; jack in body face.
- **Hardware:** 11-screw white laminated plastic pickguard; two-pivot bridge/vibrato unit.

Also with 40th Anniversary medallion on headstock and commemorative neckplate (1994).
Also with anodized aluminum hollow-body option (1994–95).
Succeeded by AMERICAN STRATOCASTER (see entry in the 2000 listing).

BLUE FLOWER TELECASTER (MIJ) 1986–onward

Replica of 1969-period U.S. original with blue floral pattern-finish body (see 1968 listing).

CUSTOM ESQUIRE (MIJ) 1986–onward

Replica of 1962-period U.S. original with bound body (see 1959 listing).

ESQUIRE (MIJ) 1986–onward

Replica of 1954-period U.S. original (see 1950 listing).

JAGUAR (MIJ) 1986–onward

Replica of early 1960s-period U.S. original (see 1962 listing). Gold-plated hardware option (1994). Foto Flame fake figured wood finish option (1994–96). Also ANTIGUA JAGUAR, with white/brown shaded body finish and matching pickguard (2004).

JAZZMASTER (MIJ) 1986–onward

Replica of early 1960s-period U.S. original (see 1958 listing). Gold-plated hardware option (1994). Foto Flame fake figured wood finish option (1994–96).

MUSTANG (MIJ) 1986–onward

Replica of 1969-period U.S. original with 24-inch scale (see 1964 listing). Also COMPETITION MUSTANG, with stripes on body (2002–03).

CUSTOM SHOP GUITARS, REISSUED AMPLIFIERS

After their Corona factory was up and running from 1986, Fender set about establishing a Custom Shop next door in 1987 under the supervision of master luthiers John Page and Michael Stevens. This facility concentrated at first on one-offs, extremely limited runs, and major artist models but soon began to manufacture lines of 'standard' Custom Shop models. Such production would expand considerably through the course of the '90s, with the introduction of numerous Custom Shop Signature Models based on the guitars of famous artists and the popular distressed-look Relic models.

The Custom Shop currently produces general catalogue models, which are noted in the main U.S. listing here and indicated as 'Custom Shop production.' The Shop also makes limited-edition instruments, which over the years have variously been called Builder Select, Custom Team Built, Dealer Select, Limited Edition, Limited Release, Master Builder, Master Built, Master Design Limited Edition, Stock Team Built, Tribute Series, and probably more besides.

These limited editions are clearly still big business, with the majority ordered by distributors or stores worldwide. Quantities of each item can range from tens to hundreds, and the number of models so far is considerable – making it impossible to identify and itemize all of them here, especially as Fender cannot supply complete records. Regardless of order size, all official Custom Shop instruments carry an identifying logo on the back of the headstock. Originally oval, the logo was later amended to the current 'V' shape.

After the shortlived but innovative and relatively successful hotrodded 'II' series tube amps of 1982–85, designed for Fender by Paul Rivera, the newly independent Fender Musical Instruments Corp survived through the lean years of 1985–86 on leftovers from the end of the CBS years and a few solid-state imports from Japan.

In 1986–87 the first new U.S.-made tube amps emerged in the form of the Champ 12, The Twin, and the Dual Showman. In 1990, Fender finally gave its amplifiers the treatment that had helped to turn around the guitars in the early '80s by reissuing vintage-styled versions of the highly collectible '59 Bassman and '63 Vibroverb. A Custom Amp Shop joined the club during 1993, releasing the hand-wired Vibro King and Tonemaster, which were followed by the Dual Professional and Prosonic, the latter blending vintage looks with modern features.

Meanwhile, a new 'standard' line of Fender tube amps was issued in 1993 in the form of the Tweed Series, which captured a look from the late '50s – and a degree of the tone – but with more modern functionality. The Pro Junior, Blues Junior, Blues Deluxe, and Blues De Ville have since become modern working-man's classics. Further additions to the Vintage Reissue line such as the Deluxe Reverb, Twin Reverb, and Super Reverb have brought more vintage tones back into the hands of the everyday guitarist.

Not merely content to roll forward by looking backward, Fender has also developed a number of amplifiers (alongside many more guitars) that cater to the needs of a wide range of musicians, from the digital Cyber series begun in 2001 to deluxe-featured, high-gain tube amps such as the Super-Sonic and Twin-Amp of 2006.

PAISLEY TELECASTER 1986–onward

Replica of 1969-period U.S. original with paisley-pattern body finish (see 1968 listing).

ROSEWOOD TELECASTER (MIJ) 1986–onward

Replica of 1969-period U.S. original with rosewood neck and body (see 1969 listing).

TELECASTER CUSTOM '72 (MIJ) 1986–onward

Replica of 1972-period U.S. original with humbucker and single-coil (see 1972 listing).

THINLINE TELECASTER '69 (MIJ) 1986–onward

Replica of 1969-period U.S. original with two single-coils (see 1968 listing).

THINLINE TELECASTER '72 (MIJ) 1986–onward

Replica of 1972-period U.S. original with two humbuckers (see 1971 listing).

AMPLIFIERS

CHAMP 12 1986–92

More power from a 6L6GC output tube.

- **Cabinet:** black Tolex (optional custom coverings in red, white, gray and snakeskin).
- **Controls:** treble, bass, volume, overdrive gain, overdrive volume, reverb; blackface control panel.
- **Speakers:** 1x12.
- **Tubes:** 2x12AX7, 6L6GC, (solid-state rectifier).
- **Output:** 12 watts.

SIDEKICK 35 REVERB (MIJ) 1986–90

Similar to SIDEKICK REVERB 30 (see 1983 listing) except:

- **Controls:** volume, gain, master, treble, middle, bass, presence, reverb.
- **Output:** 35 watts.

SIDEKICK 65 REVERB (MIJ) 1986–88

Big boy solid-state amp of the Japan-made Sidekick line.

- **Cabinet:** black Tolex.
- **Controls:** ch A: volume, treble, bass; ch B: volume, gain, master, treble, middle, bass, presence, reverb.
- **Speakers:** 1x12.
- **Output:** 65 watts.

1987

GUITARS

STRAT PLUS 1987–98

Two-pivot vibrato, no string-guides, three same-type Lace Sensor pickups.

- **Neck:** fretted maple, or maple with rosewood fingerboard; 22 frets; truss-rod adjuster at headstock end; locking tuners; roller nut.
- **Body:** sunburst or colors.
- **Electronics:** three same-type white plain-top Lace Sensor pickups (bridge pickup angled); three controls (volume, two tone) and five-way selector, all on pickguard; jack in body face.
- **Hardware:** 11-screw white or white pearl laminated plastic pickguard; two-pivot bridge/vibrato unit.

Also with anodized aluminum hollow body option (1994–95).

AMPLIFIERS

DUAL SHOWMAN 1987–94

An update of the 1960s and 70s DUAL SHOWMAN REVERB (see 1961 and 1969 listings); similar except:

- **Controls:** ch 1: volume, treble, middle, bass; ch 2: gain, treble, middle, bass, presence, volume; blackface control panel.
- **Speakers:** choice of cabinets.
- **Tubes:** 4x12AX7, 12AT7, 4x6L6GC, (solid-state rectifier).
- **Output:** 100 watts.

THE TWIN 1987–94

First amplifier out of the gate from the newly-owned Fender company of 1985.

- **Cabinet:** black Tolex.

- **Controls:** ch 1: volume, treble, middle, bass; ch 2: gain, treble, middle, bass, presence, volume, reverb (plus assorted pull switches for boost and overdrive).
- **Speakers:** 2x12 Eminence.
- **Tubes:** 5x12AX7, 2x12AT7, 4x6L6GC, (solid-state rectifier).
- **Output:** 100 watts.

1988

GUITARS

AMERICAN STANDARD TELECASTER 1988–2000

22 frets, slab single-cutaway body, two single-coils, six-saddle bridge.

- **Neck:** fretted maple, or maple with rosewood fingerboard; 22 frets; truss-rod adjuster at headstock end; one string-guide.
- **Body:** slab single-cutaway; finished in sunburst or colours.
- **Electronics:** one plain metal-cover pickup with visible height-adjustment screws (at neck) and one black six-polepiece pickup (angled in bridgeplate); two controls (volume, tone) and three-way selector, all on metal plate adjoining pickguard; side-mounted jack.
- **Hardware:** eight-screw white laminated plastic pickguard; six-saddle flat bridge with through-body stringing (earliest examples with raised-sides type).

Also with anodized aluminum hollow body option (1994–95).
Succeeded by AMERICAN TELECASTER (see 2000 listing).

BLUE FLOWER STRATOCASTER (first version) (MIJ) 1988–93

Blue floral-pattern body finish, large headstock.
Similar to STRATOCASTER '72 (see 1985 listing) except:
- **Neck:** fretted maple only.
- **Body:** blue floral-pattern only.
- **Hardware:** 11-screw blue floral-pattern pickguard.

ERIC CLAPTON STRATOCASTER (first version) 1988–2001

Signature on headstock, three white plain-top pickups, active circuit.

- **Neck:** fretted maple; 22 frets; truss-rod adjuster at headstock end; one string-guide; Eric Clapton signature on headstock.
- **Body:** various colors.
- **Electronics:** three white plain-top Lace Sensor pickups (bridge pickup angled); three controls (volume, two tone) and five-way selector, all on pickguard; jack in body face; active circuit.
- **Hardware:** eight-screw white plastic pickguard; six-pivot bridge/vibrato unit.

Earliest examples with 21 frets and/or mini-switch.

HM POWER STRAT (MIJ) (first type) 1988–89

One humbucker, black-face headstock with large flamboyant 'Strat' logo.

- **Neck:** fretted maple, or maple with rosewood fingerboard; 25-inch scale, 24 frets; truss-rod adjuster at headstock end; locking nut; flamboyant 'Strat' logo on black-face headstock.
- **Body:** smaller; various colours.
- **Electronics:** one black coverless humbucker (at bridge); two controls (volume, tone) and coil-switch, all on body; side-mounted jack.
- **Hardware:** black-plated; no pickguard; two-pivot locking bridge/vibrato unit.

Some examples with International Series logo on headstock.

PAISLEY STRATOCASTER (MIJ) 1988–onward

Pink paisley-pattern body finish.
Similar to STRATOCASTER '72 (see 1985 listing) except:
- **Neck:** fretted maple only.
- **Body:** pink paisley-pattern only.
- **Hardware:** 11-screw pink paisley-pattern pickguard.

STANDARD STRATOCASTER (second version) 1988–91

21 frets, two string-guides.

Similar to 50s STRATOCASTER and 60s STRATOCASTER (see 1985 listings) except:
• **Neck:** two string-guides.
Also version with six-saddle bridge and through-body stringing.
Previously sold under Squier brandname (1986–88). Later, production moved to Mexico (see 1991 listing).

STANDARD TELECASTER (MIJ) 1988–91

Two string-guides, five-screw pickguard, six-saddle bridge/tailpiece with no through-body stringing.
• **Neck:** fretted maple; truss-rod adjuster at body end; two string-guides.
• **Body:** slab single-cutaway; black or blond.
• **Electronics:** one plain metal cover pickup (at neck) and one black six-polepiece pickup (angled in bridgeplate); two controls (volume, tone) and three-way selector, all on metal plate adjoining pickguard; side-mounted jack.
• **Hardware:** five-screw white plastic pickguard; six-saddle flat bridge/tailpiece with no through-body stringing.
Previously marketed under the Squier brandname (1985–88). Later, production moved to Mexico (see 1991 listing).

STRAT XII 12-string (MIJ) 1988–onward

12-string headstock, offset-cutaway body.
• **Neck:** maple with rosewood fingerboard; 24.75-inch scale, 22 frets; truss-rod adjuster at body end; one 'bracket' string-guide; six-tuners-per-side headstock.
• **Body:** sunburst or colors.
• **Electronics:** three white six-polepiece pickups (bridge pickup angled); three controls (volume, two tone) and five-way selector, all on pickguard; jack in body face.
• **Hardware:** 11-screw white laminated plastic pickguard; 12-saddle bridge with through-body stringing.

STRATOCASTER '68 (MIJ) 1988–onward

Replica of 1968-period U.S. original (see

STRATOCASTER CBS SIXTIES 1965 listing).

YNGWIE MALMSTEEN STRATOCASTER (first version) 1988–98

Signature on small headstock, two-pivot vibrato.
• **Neck** fretted maple, or maple with rosewood fingerboard, both with scalloping between frets; truss-rod adjuster at body end; one string-guide; brass nut; Yngwie Malmsteen signature on headstock.
• **Body** red, white, or blue.
• **Electronics** three white six-polepiece pickups (bridge pickup angled); three controls (volume, two tone) and five-way selector, all on pickguard; jack socket in body face.
• **Hardware** 11-screw white laminated plastic pickguard; two-pivot bridge/vibrato unit.

AMPLIFIERS

LONDON 185 1988–92

One of a line of fully featured solid-state combos and head/cab sets.
• **Cabinet:** black Tolex.
• **Controls:** ch 1: volume, treble, bass; ch 2: gain, boost, treble, middle, bass, contour, presence, reverb, volume; black control panel.
• **Speakers:** various.
• **Output:** 160 watts.

STUDIO 85 1988

Solid state; renamed simply 85 immediately after introduction.
• **Cabinet:** black Tolex.
• **Controls:** volume, treble, middle, bass, reverb, gain, limiter, presence, volume.
• **Speakers:** 1x12 Eminence.
• **Output:** 65 watts.

SUPER 112 1988–93

Tube amp, also available as piggy-back top and rack-mounted versions.
• **Cabinet:** black Tolex.
• **Controls:** ch A: volume, treble, middle, bass; ch

OVER THE BORDER

Like so many American manufacturers, Fender sought more affordable production in the late 1980s and early '90s. A short hop over the boarder to a plant in Ensenada, Baja California, Mexico, provided considerable savings on labor costs while still allowing easy control of quality and production from Fender's main U.S. factory in Corona, CA, less than 180 miles north. (The location also allowed for the comforting, if easily misunderstood, 'Made in Ensenada, Baja California' label of origin on the backs of many Mexican-made Fender products.)

Fender amps began rolling out of Mexico in 1989, and the factory produced its first guitars in 1991. Production ramped up from around 175 instruments a day in 1992 to some 600 a day by 1995 (following the rebuilding of the factory after a fire in 1994). By 1998, the Ensenada plant had a workforce approximately 40 per cent larger than that of the Corona plant and was producing nearly twice the number of instruments.

This capacity was put to good use. Mexican production took over the Standard line of Fender guitar models that had come from Japan since the early 1980s, while Japanese Fenders were relegated almost exclusively to domestic sales within Japan.

The most prominent Mexican models would take shape in 1999 as the Classic 50s, 60s, and 70s Stratocaster and Classic 50s Telecaster (and a Classic 60s Telecaster with rosewood fingerboard arrived in 2001). Alongside these came numerous revised and modified models – such as the Tex-Mex Strat, Traditional Fat Strat, Deluxe Nashville Tele, and Deluxe Powerhouse Strat – and a pair of popular new retro models, the Toronado and Cyclone.

Meanwhile, in 1998 Fender U.S.A. opened a new state-of-the-art factory in Corona. Since the start of production at Corona in 1985, after the curtain fell on CBS's ownership, Fender's production facility had grown to encompass ten buildings spread around Corona, with a total of 115,000 square feet of space. The new 177,000-square-foot factory cost $20 million to build. It centralized production and offered room for expansion. In addition, the new factory included a finishing department with zero toxic emission, a boon to both environmental conservation and statutory compliance, given California's stringent environmental laws.

1989

B: volume, gain; presence, reverb; black control panel.
- **Speakers:** 1x12 Eminence (Celestion optional).
- **Tubes:** 2x12AX7, 12AT7, 2x6L6GC, (solid-state rectifier).
- **Output:** 50 watts.

SUPER 210 1988–93
Same as Super 112 except:
- **Speakers:** 2x10 Eminence.

85 1988–92
Same as STUDIO 85 (see earlier listing this year).

1989

GUITARS

AMERICAN STANDARD DELUXE STRATOCASTER 1989–90
Two string-guides, three Lace Sensor pickups.
Similar to AMERICAN STANDARD STRATOCASTER (see 1986 listing) except:
- **Electronics:** three white plain top Lace Sensor pickups (bridge pickup angled).

HM STRAT (first type) 1989–90
Two-pivot locking vibrato system, two single-coils

and one humbucker, black-face headstock.

- **Neck:** fretted maple, or maple with rosewood fingerboard; 25-inch scale, 24 frets; truss-rod adjuster at headstock end; locking nut; large flamboyant 'Strat' logo on black-face headstock.
- **Body:** smaller; various colors.
- **Electronics:** two black six-polepiece pickups and one black coverless humbucker (at bridge); three controls (volume, two tone), five-way selector and coil-switch, all situated on body; side-mounted jack.
- **Hardware:** black-plated; no pickguard; two-pivot locking bridge/vibrato unit.

HM STRAT (second type) 1989–90

Two-pivot locking vibrato system, one angled Lace Sensor pickup and one humbucker.
Similar to HM STRAT FIRST TYPE (see previous listing) except:

- **Electronics:** one angled black plain-top Lace Sensor and one black coverless humbucker (at bridge); two controls (volume, tone), three-way selector and coil-switch, all on body.
- **Hardware:** black laminated plastic pickguard.

HM STRAT (third type) 1989–90

Two-pivot locking vibrato system, two humbuckers.
Similar to HM STRAT FIRST TYPE (see earlier listing this year) except:

- **Electronics:** two black two coverless humbuckers; two controls (volume, tone), three-way selector and coil-switch, all on body.

ROBBEN FORD (MIJ) 1989–94

Name on truss-rod cover.
Similar to ESPRIT ULTRA (see 1984 listing) except:
- **Neck:** 'Robben Ford' on truss-rod cover.
- **Body:** sunburst, natural, or black.
- **Electronics:** two black coverless humbucker pickups.

SHORT-SCALE STRATOCASTER (MIJ) 1989–95

Two controls, 22 frets.

- **Neck:** fretted maple, or maple with rosewood fingerboard; 24-inch scale, 22 frets; truss-rod adjuster at headstock end; one string-guide.
- **Body:** sunburst or colors.
- **Electronics:** three white six-polepiece pickups (bridge pickup angled); two controls (volume, tone) and five-way selector, all on pickguard; jack in body face.
- **Hardware:** eight-screw white laminated plastic pickguard; two-pivot bridge/vibrato unit.

STRAT PLUS DELUXE 1989–98

Two-pivot vibrato, no string-guides, three differing Lace Sensor pickups.
Similar to STRAT PLUS (see 1987 listing) except:

- **Electronics:** three differing white plain-top Lace Sensor pickups (bridge pickup angled).
- **Hardware:** 11-screw white, white pearl, or tortoiseshell laminated plastic pickguard; two-pivot bridge/vibrato unit.

Also with anodized aluminum hollow body option (1994–95).

U.S. CONTEMPORARY STRATOCASTER 1989–91

Two-pivot locking vibrato system, two single-coils and one humbucker, straight-sided humbucker cut-out in pickguard.

- **Neck:** maple with rosewood fingerboard; 22 frets; truss-rod adjuster at headstock end; locking nut.
- **Body:** sunburst or colors.
- **Electronics:** two white six-polepiece pickups and one white coverless humbucker (at bridge); three controls (volume, two tone) and five-way selector, all on pickguard; jack in body face.
- **Hardware:** 11-screw white laminated plastic pickguard; two-pivot locking bridge/vibrato unit.

AMPLIFIERS

PRINCETON CHORUS 1989–2001

Mid-sized solid-state stereo amp with chorus.
- **Cabinet:** black Tolex.
- **Controls:** volume, treble, middle, bass, reverb,

gain, limiter, presence, volume, chorus rate &
depth; black control panel.
- **Speakers:** 2x10 Eminence.
- **Output:** 2x25 watts.

PRO 185 1989–92

*Large, powerful solid-state amp with channel
switching and modern features.*
- **Cabinet:** black Tolex.
- **Controls:** ch A: volume, treble, middle, bass; ch
  B: gain, gain boost, treble, middle, bass, mid
  boost, contour, tilt, presence, reverb; black control
  panel.
- **Speakers:** 2x12 Eminence.
- **Output:** 160 watts.

STAGE 185 1989–92

Similar to Pro 185 (see previous listing) except:
- **Speakers:** 1x12 Eminence.

SUPER 60 1989–93

*Later tube amp with channel switching and modern
features.*
- **Cabinet:** black Tolex.
- **Controls:** ch A: clean, bright switch; ch B:
  overdrive volume, gain; both: treble, middle, bass,
  reverb, presence; black control panel.
- **Speakers:** 1x12 Eminence (Celestion optional).
- **Tubes:** 2x12AX7, 12AT7, 2x6L6GC, (solid-state
  rectifier).
- **Output:** 50 watts.

1990

`GUITARS`

ALBERT COLLINS TELECASTER
1990–current

Signature on headstock.
- **Neck:** maple with maple fingerboard; truss-rod
  adjuster at body end; one string-guide; Albert
  Collins signature on headstock.
- **Body:** slab single-cutaway bound; natural only.
- **Electronics:** one metal-cover six-polepiece

humbucker (at neck) and one black six-polepiece
pickup (angled in bridgeplate); two controls
(volume, tone) and three-way selector, all on metal
plate adjoining pickguard; side-mounted jack.
- **Hardware:** eight-screw white laminated plastic
  pickguard; six-saddle raised-sides bridge with
  through-body stringing.
Custom Shop production.

DANNY GATTON TELECASTER 1990–current

Signature on headstock.
- **Neck:** fretted maple; 22 frets; truss-rod adjuster at
  body end; one string-guide; Danny Gatton
  signature on headstock.
- **Body:** slab single-cutaway; blond or gold.
- **Electronics:** two black twin-blade humbuckers
  (bridge pickup angled); two controls (volume, tone)
  and three-way selector, all on metal plate adjoining
  pickguard; side-mounted jack.
- **Hardware:** five-screw cream plastic pickguard;
  modified three-saddle raised-sides bridge with
  through-body stringing.
Custom Shop production.

HM STRAT ULTRA 1990–92

*Two-pivot locking vibrato system, four Lace Sensor
pickups.*
Similar to HM STRAT FIRST TYPE (see 1989 listing)
except:
- **Neck:** ebony fingerboard with split-triangle
  markers.
- **Electronics:** four black plain-top Lace Sensor
  pickups (two at bridge).

HRR STRATOCASTER (MIJ) 1990–94

*22 frets, three controls on pickguard with rectangular
hole for humbucker, locking bridge/vibrato system.*
- **Neck:** fretted maple, or maple with rosewood
  fingerboard; 22 frets; truss-rod adjuster at
  headstock end; single-bar string-guide; locking
  nut.
- **Body:** sunburst or colors.
- **Electronics:** two white six-polepiece pickups and

one coverless humbucker (at bridge); three controls (volume, two tone) and five-way selector, all situated on the guitar's pickguard; jack in body face.
- **Hardware:** 11-screw white plastic or laminated plastic pickguard; two-pivot locking bridge/vibrato unit.

Also known as FLOYD ROSE HRR STRATOCASTER *(1992–94). Foto Flame fake figured wood finish option (1992–94).*

JAMES BURTON TELECASTER (first version) 1990–2005

Signature on headstock.
- **Neck:** fretted maple; truss-rod adjuster at body end; one string-guide; pearl tuner buttons; James Burton signature on headstock.
- **Body:** slab single-cutaway; black with gold or red paisley-pattern, red or white.
- **Electronics:** three black plain-top Lace Sensor pickups (bridge pickup angled); two controls (volume, tone) and five-way selector, all on metal plate; side-mounted jack.
- **Hardware:** black-plated or gold-plated; no pickguard; six-saddle small bridge with through-body stringing.

STRAT ULTRA 1990–98

Two-pivot vibrato, no string-guides, four Lace Sensor pickups (two at bridge), bolt-on neck.
- **Neck:** maple with ebony fingerboard; 22 frets; truss-rod adjuster at headstock end; locking tuners; roller nut.
- **Body:** sunburst or colors.
- **Electronics:** four white plain-top Lace Sensor pickups (two at bridge); three controls (volume, two tone), five-way selector and coil-switch, all on pickguard; jack in body face.
- **Hardware:** 11-screw white or white pearl laminated plastic pickguard; two-pivot bridge/vibrato unit.

Also with anodized aluminum hollow body option (1994–95).

TELE PLUS (first version) 1990–95

Three Lace Sensor pickups (two at bridge).
- **Neck:** fretted maple, or maple with rosewood fingerboard; 22 frets; truss-rod adjuster at headstock end; one string-guide.
- **Body:** slab single-cutaway; sunburst or colors.
- **Electronics:** three black plain-top Lace Sensor pickups (two in single separate surround at bridge); two controls (volume, tone), three-way selector and coil-switch, all on metal plate adjoining pickguard; side-mounted jack.
- **Hardware:** eight-screw white laminated plastic pickguard; six-saddle small bridge with through-body stringing.

50s TELECASTER (MIJ) 1990–onward

Replica of 1952-period U.S. original (see 1951 listing). Previously known in UK as SQUIER SERIES '52 TELECASTER, with small Squier Series logo on headstock (1982–83). Sold under the Squier brandname (1983–85) and new Fender version introduced in 1990, although Japanese market manufacture continuous since 1982. Foto Flame fake figured wood finish option (1994).

AMPLIFIERS

H.O.T. 1990–95

Smaller member of an affordable solid-state line.
- **Cabinet:** gray carpet covering, then black from 1992.
- **Controls:** contour, volume, tone; blackface control panel.
- **Speakers:** 1x10.
- **Output:** 25 watts.

J.A.M. 1990–95

Smaller member of an affordable solid-state line.
- **Cabinet:** gray carpet covering, then black from 1992.
- **Controls:** contour, volume, reverb, rate & depth (for chorus effect); blackface control panel.
- **Speakers:** 1x12.
- **Output:** 25 watts.

M-80 1990–95

Mid-level solid-state platform available in a range of formats: basic combo; Chorus combo; basic head; Chorus head; and Pro head.

- **Cabinet:** gray carpet covering, then black carpet from 1992.
- **Controls:** clean: volume, treble, middle, bass; overdrive: volume, gain, contour, presence, volume (plus depth and rate for Chorus models); black control panel.
- **Speakers:** 1x12 or 2x12, or other separate cabs.
- **Output:** 90 watts.

R.A.D. 1990–95

Baby member of an affordable solid-state line.

- **Cabinet:** gray carpet covering, then black from 1992.
- **Controls:** contour, volume, switches for tone control; blackface control panel.
- **Speakers:** 1x8.
- **Output:** 20 watts.

'59 BASSMAN VINTAGE REISSUE 1990–2004

Similar to original tweed BASSMAN (see 1954 listing) except:

- **Tubes:** 3x12AX7, 2x6L6GC, (plug-in solid-state rectifier, can be replaced by GZ34/5AR4 or 5U4G); printed circuit board rather than original hand-wired eyelet board.

'63 VIBROVERB VINTAGE REISSUE 1990–96

Replica of the original brown Tolex model with 2x10 speakers (see 1963 listing); printed circuit board rather than original hand-wired eyelet board.

1991

GUITARS

HM STRAT (first type) (MIJ) 1991–92

Black-face headstock with 'stencil'-style 'Strat' logo.

- **Neck:** fretted maple, or maple with rosewood fingerboard; 25.1-inch scale, 24 frets; truss-rod adjuster at headstock end; single-bar string-guide;

locking nut; 'stencil'-style Strat logo on black-face headstock.
- **Body:** smaller; various colors.
- **Electronics:** two black six-polepiece pickups and one black coverless humbucker (at bridge); two controls (volume, tone) and five-way selector, all on body; side-mounted jack.
- **Hardware:** black-plated; no pickguard; two-pivot locking bridge/vibrato unit.

HM STRAT (second type) (MIJ) 1991–92

Drooped black-face headstock with long 'streamlined' Fender logo.

- **Neck:** fretted maple, or maple with rosewood fingerboard; 25.1-inch scale, 22 frets; truss-rod adjuster at headstock end; single-bar string-guide; locking nut; long 'streamlined' Fender logo on drooped black-face headstock.
- **Body:** smaller; various colors.
- **Electronics:** two black coverless humbuckers and one black six-polepiece pickup (in center); two controls (volume, tone) and five-way selector, all situated on the guitar's pickguard; side-mounted jack.
- **Hardware:** black-plated; eight-screw black laminated plastic pickguard; two-pivot locking bridge/vibrato unit.

HMT ACOUSTIC-ELECTRIC (first version) (MIJ) 1991–94

Stratocaster-style headstock, wooden-base bridge.

- **Neck:** maple with rosewood fingerboard; 25.1-inch scale, 22 frets; truss-rod adjuster at headstock end; one string-guide; large Stratocaster-style headstock with black-face.
- **Body:** enlarged semi-solid slab single-cutaway bound; f-hole; sunburst or colors.
- **Electronics:** one black plain-top Lace Sensor (angled at neck) and piezo pickup (in bridge); three controls (volume, tone, pan,) all on body; side-mounted jack; active circuit.
- **Hardware:** no pickguard; single-saddle wooden-base bridge.

HMT TELECASTER (first version) (MIJ) 1991–92

Stratocaster-style headstock, F-hole body, two humbuckers.

- **Neck:** maple with rosewood fingerboard; 25.1-inch scale, 22 frets; truss-rod adjuster at headstock end; Stratocaster-style black-face headstock.
- **Body:** larger semi-solid slab single-cutaway bound; f-hole; sunburst or colors.
- **Electronics:** two black coverless humbuckers; two controls (volume, tone), three-way selector and coil-switch, all on body; side-mounted jack.
- **Hardware:** no pickguard; six-saddle small bridge with through-body stringing.

HMT TELECASTER (second version) (MIJ) 1991–92

Drooped headstock with long 'streamlined' Fender logo, f-hole body, angled Lace Sensor and humbucker.

Similar to HMT TELECASTER FIRST VERSION (see previous listing) except:

- **Neck:** split-triangle markers; locking nut; long 'streamlined' Fender logo on drooped black-face headstock.
- **Electronics:** one black plain-top Lace Sensor pickup (angled at neck) and one black coverless humbucker (at bridge).
- **Hardware:** two-pivot locking bridge/vibrato unit.

JEFF BECK STRATOCASTER (first version) 1991–2001

Signature on headstock, four white plain-top pickups.

- **Neck:** maple with rosewood fingerboard; 22 frets; truss-rod adjuster at headstock end; locking tuners; roller nut; Jeff Beck signature on headstock.
- **Body:** white, green or purple. Four white plain-top Lace Sensor pickups (two at bridge); three controls (volume, two tone), five-way selector and pushbutton coil-switch, all on pickguard; jack in body face.

- **Hardware:** 11-screw white laminated plastic pickguard; two-pivot bridge/vibrato unit.

PRODIGY 1991–93

Prodigy on headstock, two single-coils and one humbucker, six-pivot bridge/vibrato unit.

- **Neck:** fretted maple, or maple with rosewood fingerboard; 22 frets; truss-rod adjuster at headstock end; one string-guide.
- **Body:** contoured offset-waist; various colors.
- **Electronics:** two black six-polepiece pickups and one black coverless humbucker (at bridge); two controls (volume, tone), five-way selector and jack, all on pickguard.
- **Hardware:** eight-screw black laminated plastic pickguard; six-pivot bridge/vibrato unit.

PRODIGY II 1991–92

Prodigy on headstock, two single-coils and one humbucker, locking vibrato system.

Similar to PRODIGY (see previous listing) except:

- **Neck:** no string-guide; locking nut.
- **Hardware:** chrome-plated or black-plated; two-pivot locking bridge/vibrato unit.

SET NECK TELECASTER 1991–95

Two coverless humbuckers, glued-in neck.

- **Neck:** mahogany glued-in with rosewood fingerboard (pao ferro from 1993); 22 frets; truss-rod adjuster at headstock end; two string-guides; neck and headstock face match body color.
- **Body:** semi-solid slab single-cutaway bound; various colors.
- **Electronics:** two black coverless humbuckers; two controls (volume, tone), three-way selector and coil-tap, all on body; side-mounted jack.
- **Hardware:** no pickguard; six-saddle small bridge with through-body stringing.

Custom Shop production.

SET NECK TELECASTER FLOYD ROSE 1991–92

Two coverless humbuckers and one single-coil,

glued-in neck, locking vibrato system.
Similar to SET NECK TELECASTER (see previous listing)
except:
- **Neck:** ebony fingerboard; locking nut.
- **Electronics:** two black coverless humbuckers and
  one black six-polepiece pickup (in center); two
  controls (volume, tone), five-way selector and coil-
  tap, all on body; side-mounted jack.
- **Hardware:** two-pivot locking bridge/vibrato unit.
Custom Shop production.

SET NECK TELECASTER PLUS 1991–92

Two coverless humbuckers, glued-in neck, vibrato.
Similar to SET NECK TELECASTER (see earlier listing this
year) except:
- **Neck:** ebony fingerboard; locking tuners; roller
  nut.
- **Hardware:** two-pivot bridge/vibrato unit.
Custom Shop production.

STANDARD STRATOCASTER (MIM)
1991–current

*Modern-style 'thick' Fender headstock logo in silver,
three single-coils, six-pivot vibrato.*
- **Neck:** fretted maple, or maple with rosewood
  fingerboard; truss-rod adjuster at headstock end;
  one string-guide.
- **Body:** sunburst or colors.
- **Electronics:** three white six-polepiece pickups
  (bridge pickup angled); three controls (volume, two
  tone) and five-way selector, all on pickguard; jack
  in body face.
- **Hardware:** 11-screw white laminated plastic
  pickguard; six-pivot bridge/vibrato unit.

STANDARD TELECASTER (MIM) 1991–current

*Modern-style 'thick' Fender headstock logo in silver,
two single-coils.*
- **Neck:** fretted maple; truss-rod adjuster at
  headstock end; one string-guide.
- **Body:** slab single-cutaway; sunburst or colors.
- **Electronics:** one plain metal-cover pickup with
  visible height-adjustment screws (at neck) and one

black six-polepiece pickup (angled in bridgeplate);
two controls (volume, tone) and three-way
selector, all on metal plate adjoining pickguard;
side-mounted jack.
- **Hardware:** eight-screw white laminated plastic
  pickguard; six-saddle flat bridge/tailpiece (no
  through-body stringing).

TELE PLUS DELUXE 1991–92

Three Lace Sensor pickups (two at bridge), vibrato.
Similar to TELE PLUS FIRST VERSION (see 1990 listing)
except:
- **Neck:** no string-guide; locking tuners; roller nut.
- **Hardware:** two-pivot bridge/vibrato unit.

YNGWIE MALMSTEEN STANDARD
STRATOCASTER 1991–94

Signature on headstock.
- **Neck:** scalloped fretted maple; 'bullet' truss-rod
  adjuster at headstock end; two string-guides;
  three-screw neckplate.
- **Body:** black, blue, or white.
- **Electronics:** three black six-polepiece pickups
  (pickup at bridge is angled); three controls
  (volume, two tones) and five-way selector, all on
  pickguard; jack in body face.
- **Hardware:** 11-screw white laminated plastic
  pickguard; six-pivot bridge/vibrato unit.

AMPLIFIERS
POWER CHORUS 1991–93

Powerful solid-state stereo amp with chorus, later
known as the ULTRA CHORUS.
- **Cabinet:** black Tolex.
- **Controls:** ch 1: volume, treble, middle, bass; ch 2:
  gain, boost, treble, middle, bass, contour,
  presence, volume, reverb, chorus rate & depth;
  black control panel.
- **Speakers:** 2x12 Eminence.
- **Output:** 2x65 watts.

SK CHORUS 20 (MIJ) 1991–92

Further developments from the Sidekick template

with this small, stereo chorus amp, part of a range of similar combos.
- **Cabinet:** black Tolex.
- **Controls:** overdrive, gain, volume, treble, middle, bass, presence, chorus rate, chorus depth.
- **Speakers:** 2x8.
- **Output:** 2x10 watts.

1992

GUITARS

AMERICAN CLASSIC STRATOCASTER 1992–99
Two-pivot vibrato, one string-guide.
Similar to AMERICAN STANDARD STRATOCASTER (see 1986 listing) except:
- **Neck:** one string-guide.
- **Hardware:** 11-screw white pearl or tortoiseshell laminated plastic pickguard.
Gold-plated hardware option. Custom Shop production.

BAJO SEXTO TELECASTER baritone 1992–98
Model name on headstock, long-scale neck.
- **Neck:** fretted maple; 30.2-inch scale; 24 frets; truss-rod adjuster at body end; one string-guide; Bajo Sexto on headstock.
- **Body:** slab single-cutaway; sunburst or blond.
- **Electronics:** one plain metal-cover pickup (at neck) and one black six-polepiece pickup (angled in bridgeplate); two controls (volume, tone) and three-way selector, all on metal plate adjoining pickguard; side-mounted jack.
- **Hardware:** five-screw black plastic pickguard; three-saddle raised-sides bridge with through-body stringing.
Custom Shop production.

FLOYD ROSE CLASSIC STRATOCASTER 1992–98
Two-pivot locking vibrato system, two single-coils and one humbucker, curved-ends humbucker cut-out in pickguard.

- **Neck:** fretted maple, or maple with rosewood fingerboard; 22 frets; truss-rod adjuster at headstock end; single-bar string-guide; locking nut.
- **Body:** sunburst or colors.
- **Electronics:** two white six-polepiece pickups and one white coverless humbucker (at bridge); three controls (volume, two tone) and five-way selector, all on pickguard; jack in body face.
- **Hardware:** 11-screw white laminated plastic pickguard; two-pivot locking bridge/vibrato unit.
Replaced by FLOYD ROSE CLASSIC STRAT HSS (see 1998 listing).

FLOYD ROSE HRR STRATOCASTER (MIJ) 1992–94
Another name for the HRR Stratocaster (see 1990 listing).

JD TELECASTER (MIJ) 1992–99
'JD' on headstock, black six-polepiece pickup at neck.
- **Neck:** fretted maple; truss-rod adjuster at body end; one string-guide; Jerry Donahue initials on headstock.
- **Body:** slab single-cutaway bound; sunburst or colors.
- **Electronics:** two black six-polepiece pickups (bridgeplate pickup angled); two controls (volume, tone) and five-way selector, all on metal plate adjoining pickguard; side-mounted jack.
- **Hardware:** eight-screw black laminated plastic pickguard; three-saddle raised-sides bridge with through-body stringing.
Based on signature model of U.S. Custom Shop (see next listing).

JERRY DONAHUE TELECASTER 1992–2001
Signature on headstock.
- **Neck:** fretted maple; truss-rod adjuster at body end; one string-guide; Jerry Donahue signature on headstock.
- **Body:** slab single-cutaway; sunburst, blue or red.
- **Electronics:** two black six-polepiece pickups (bridgeplate pickup angled); two controls (volume,

tone) and five-way selector, all on metal plate adjoining pickguard; side-mounted jack.
- **Hardware:** gold-plated; five-screw black laminated plastic pickguard; three-saddle raised-sides bridge with through-body stringing.

Custom Shop production.

ROBERT CRAY STRATOCASTER 1992–current
Signature on headstock.
- **Neck:** maple with rosewood fingerboard; truss-rod adjuster at body end; one string-guide; Robert Cray signature on headstock.
- **Body:** sunburst, silver, or violet.
- **Electronics:** three white six-polepiece pickups (bridge pickup angled); three controls (volume, two tone) and five-way selector, all on pickguard; jack in body face.
- **Hardware:** 11-screw white laminated plastic pickguard; six-saddle bridge with through-body stringing.

Also with gold-plated hardware (1998–current). Custom Shop production.

SET NECK FLOYD ROSE STRATOCASTER 1992–95
Two-pivot locking vibrato system, two single-coils and one humbucker, reverse headstock, glued-in neck.
- **Neck:** maple glued-in with ebony fingerboard; 22 frets; truss-rod adjuster at headstock end; locking nut; black-face reverse headstock.
- **Body:** smaller; sunburst or colors.
- **Electronics:** two black six-polepiece pickups and one black coverless humbucker (at bridge); two controls (volume, tone) and five-way selector, all on body; side-mounted jack.
- **Hardware:** black-plated or gold-plated; no pickguard; two-pivot locking bridge/vibrato unit.

Custom Shop production.

SET NECK STRATOCASTER (first version) 1992–95
Two-pivot vibrato, no string-guides, four Lace Sensor pickups (two at bridge), glued-in neck.
- **Neck:** maple glued-in with ebony fingerboard; 22 frets; truss-rod adjuster at headstock end; locking tuners; roller nut.
- **Body:** with figured top; sunburst or colors.
- **Electronics:** four white plain-top Lace Sensor pickups (two at bridge); three controls (volume, two tone), five-way selector and coil-switch, all on pickguard; jack in body face.
- **Hardware:** 11-screw white laminated plastic pickguard; two-pivot bridge/vibrato unit.

Custom Shop production. Also Custom Shop limited edition.

SET NECK TELECASTER COUNTRY ARTIST 1992–95
One humbucker and one single-coil, glued-in neck. Similar to SET NECK TELECASTER (see 1991 listing) except:
- **Electronics:** one black coverless humbucker (at neck) and one black six-polepiece pickup (angled in bridgeplate).
- **Hardware:** five-screw tortoiseshell laminated plastic small pickguard.
- **Hardware:** gold-plated; six-saddle flat bridge with through-body stringing.

Custom Shop production.

SPARKLE TELECASTER 1992–95
Colored sparkle finish on body.
- **Neck:** fretted maple, or maple with rosewood fingerboard; truss-rod adjuster at body end; one string-guide.
- **Body:** slab single-cutaway; sparkle colors.
- **Electronics:** one plain metal-cover pickup (at neck) and one black six-polepiece pickup (angled in bridgeplate); two controls (volume, tone) and three-way selector, all on metal plate adjoining pickguard; side-mounted jack.
- **Hardware:** eight-screw white laminated plastic pickguard; three-saddle raised-sides bridge with through-body stringing.

Custom Shop production.

SQUIER SERIES FLOYD ROSE STANDARD STRATOCASTER (MIJ) 1992–96

Another name for the FLOYD ROSE STANDARD STRATOCASTER (see 1994 listing).

SQUIER SERIES STANDARD STRATOCASTER (MIK) 1992–94

Modern-style 'thick' Fender headstock logo in black, three single-coils.

- **Neck:** fretted maple, or maple with rosewood fingerboard; truss-rod adjuster at headstock end; one string-guide.
- **Body:** black, red, or white.
- **Electronics:** three white six-polepiece pickups (bridge pickup angled); three controls (volume, two tone) and five-way selector, all on pickguard; jack in body face.
- **Hardware:** 11-screw white laminated plastic pickguard; six-pivot bridge/vibrato unit.

Later made in Mexico, with small Squier Series logo on headstock (see 1994 listing), then name changed to TRADITIONAL STRATOCASTER (see 1996 listing).

SQUIER SERIES STANDARD TELECASTER (MIK) 1992–94

Modern-style 'thick' Fender headstock logo in black, two single-coils.

Similar to vintage-style Telecaster except:

- **Neck:** fretted maple; truss-rod adjuster at headstock end; one string-guide.
- **Body:** slab single-cutaway; black, red or white.
- **Electronics:** one plain metal-cover pickup with visible height-adjustment screws (at neck) and one black six-polepiece pickup (angled in bridgeplate); two controls (volume, tone) and three-way selector, all on metal plate adjoining pickguard; side-mounted jack.
- **Hardware:** eight-screw white laminated plastic pickguard; six-saddle flat bridge/tailpiece (no through-body stringing).

Later made in Mexico, with small Squier Series logo on headstock (see 1994 listing), then name changed to TRADITIONAL STRATOCASTER (see 1996 listing).

STEVIE RAY VAUGHAN STRATOCASTER 1992–current

Signature on headstock.

- **Neck:** maple with pao ferro fingerboard; truss-rod adjuster at body end; one string-guide; Stevie Ray Vaughan signature on headstock.
- **Body:** sunburst only.
- **Electronics:** three white six-polepiece pickups (bridge pickup angled); three controls (volume, two tone) and five-way selector, all on pickguard; jack in body face.
- **Hardware:** gold-plated; eight-screw black laminated plastic pickguard with 'SRV' engraving; left-handed six-pivot bridge/vibrato unit.

'54 STRATOCASTER 1992–98

Replica of 1954-period original (see 1954 listing). Gold-plated hardware option. Custom Shop production.

'60 STRATOCASTER (first version) 1992–98

Replica of 1960-period original (see 1954 listing). Gold-plated hardware option. Custom Shop production.

AMPLIFIERS

CHAMP 25 1992–94

A hybrid amp with solid-state preamp and tube output stage.

- **Cabinet:** black Tolex.
- **Controls:** normal: volume, treble, middle, bass; drive: gain, overdrive, treble, bass, volume; reverb; black control panel.
- **Speakers:** 1x12.
- **Tubes:** (solid-state preamp); 2x5881 (6L6GC) output tubes, (solid-state rectifier).
- **Output:** 25 watts.

CONCERT 1992–1996

Many classic Fender features in a modern tube combo with channel switching.

- **Cabinet:** black Tolex.
- **Controls:** ch 1: volume, treble, middle, bass; ch 2:

gain 1, gain 2, treble, bass, middle, volume; mix, reverb; blackface control panel.
- **Speakers:** 1x12.
- **Tubes:** 4x12AX7, 2x12AT7, 2x6V6GC, (solid-state rectifier).
- **Output:** 50 watts.

STAGE 112SE 1992–99
Evolution of the solid-state STAGE 185 (see 1989 listing).
- **Cabinet:** black Tolex.
- **Controls:** normal: volume, treble, middle, bass; drive: gain, contour, treble, bass, volume, reverb; black control panel.
- **Speakers:** 1x12.
- **Output:** 160 watts.

SUPER AMP 1992–96
Hotrodded channel-switcher with traditional blackface looks.
- **Cabinet:** black Tolex.
- **Controls:** ch 1: volume, treble, middle, bass; ch 2: gain 1, gain 2, treble, bass, middle, volume; mix and reverb; blackface control panel.
- **Speakers:** 4x10 Eminence Legend alnico-magnet speakers.
- **Tubes:** 4x12AX7, 2x12AT7, 2x6L6GC, (solid-state rectifier).
- **Output:** 50 watts.

'65 TWIN REVERB VINTAGE REISSUE 1992–current
Replica of the TWIN REVERB circa 1964–65 (see 1963 listing); printed circuit board rather than original hand-wired eyelet board.

1993

GUITARS

CLARENCE WHITE TELECASTER 1993–2001
Signature on headstock.
- **Neck:** fretted maple; truss-rod adjuster at body end; Scruggs Peg banjo-style de-tuners for 1st

and 6th strings; Clarence White signature on headstock.
- **Body:** slab single-cutaway; sunburst only.
- **Electronics:** one white six-polepiece pickup (at neck) and one black six-polepiece pickup (angled in bridgeplate); two controls (volume, tone) and three-way selector, all on metal plate adjoining pickguard; side-mounted jack.
- **Hardware:** eight-screw tortoiseshell laminated plastic pickguard; three-saddle raised-sides bridge with through-body stringing; factory-fitted B-Bender built-in bending device for 2nd string.
Custom Shop production.

DUO-SONIC (MIM) 1993–97
Model name on headstock, 20-fret neck, two angled pickups.
- **Neck:** fretted maple; 22.7-inch scale, 20 frets; truss-rod adjuster at body end; one string-guide.
- **Body:** slab offset-cutaway; black, red, or white.
- **Electronics:** two white six-polepiece pickups (both angled); two controls (volume, tone), three-way selector and jack, all on pickguard.
- **Hardware:** 12-screw white plastic pickguard; three-saddle bridge/tailpiece.
Based on U.S. original (see DUO-SONIC FIRST VERSION 1956 listing).

ELAN I (MIM) 1993
Three-tuners-per-side headstock, EL on truss-rod cover, offset-cutaway body, two humbuckers.
- **Neck:** mahogany glued-in, with bound ebony fingerboard; 25.1-inch scale, 22 frets; truss-rod adjuster at headstock end; pearl tuner buttons; three-tuners-per-side headstock; neck matches body color; EL on truss-rod cover.
- **Body:** offset-cutaway carved-top bound; sunburst or colors.
- **Electronics:** two black coverless humbuckers; two controls (volume, tone) and five-way selector, all on body; side-mounted jack.
- **Hardware:** six-saddle bridge with through-body stringing.

Previously with 'Heartfield' or 'Heartfield by Fender' on headstock as part of Elan series.

RICHIE SAMBORA STRATOCASTER (first version) 1993–99

Signature on headstock.

- **Neck:** fretted maple, star position markers; 22 frets; truss-rod adjuster at headstock end; single-bar string-guide; locking nut; Richie Sambora signature on headstock.
- **Body:** sunburst or white.
- **Electronics:** two white six-polepiece pickups and one white coverless humbucker (at bridge); three controls (volume, two tone), five-way selector and push-switch, all on pickguard; jack in body face; active circuit.
- **Hardware:** 11-screw white laminated plastic pickguard; two-pivot locking bridge/vibrato unit.

RR-58 (MIJ) 1993

RR on truss-rod cover, two humbuckers, fixed bridge.

- **Neck:** mahogany glued-in, with rosewood fingerboard; 24.75-inch scale, 22 frets; truss-rod adjuster at headstock end; neck matches body color; RR on truss-rod cover.
- **Body:** blond, green, or red
- **Electronics:** two black plain-top humbuckers; two controls (volume, tone) and five-way selector, all on body; side-mounted jack.
- **Hardware:** four-screw black laminated plastic pickguard; six-saddle bridge with through-body stringing.

Previously with 'Heartfield' or 'Heartfield by Fender' on headstock as part of RR series.

SPECIAL EDITION 1993 STRATOCASTER 1993

Commemorative neckplate.

Similar to AMERICAN STANDARD STRATOCASTER (see 1986 listing) except:

- **Hardware:** gold-plated; 11-screw white pearl laminated plastic pickguard; commemorative neckplate.

AMPLIFIERS

BLUES DE VILLE 1993–current

Tweed stylings (Tolex optional) for a modern amp with many classic Fender features.

- **Cabinet:** tweed; blonde Tolex optional from 1995, or black Tolex.
- **Controls:** volume, volume, bass, middle, treble, presence, reverb.
- **Speakers:** 4x10 (2x12 available from 1994).
- **Tubes:** 3x12AX7, 2x6L6GC, (solid-state rectifier).
- **Output:** 50 watts.

BLUES DELUXE 1993–current

A modern amp with many classic Fender features.

- **Cabinet:** tweed; blonde Tolex optional from 1995, or black Tolex.
- **Controls:** volume, volume, bass, middle, treble, presence, reverb.
- **Speakers:** 1x12.
- **Tubes:** 3x12AX7, 2x6L6GC, (solid-state rectifier).
- **Output:** 40 watts.

BRONCO 1993–current

Solid-state guts in a little tweed box.

- **Cabinet:** narrow-panel tweed.
- **Controls:** volume, bass, treble.
- **Speakers:** 1x8.
- **Output:** 15 watts.

BULLET 1993–current

Small solid-state amp for students and beginners.

- **Cabinet:** black Tolex.
- **Controls:** volume, gain, volume, treble, middle, bass.
- **Speakers:** 1x8.
- **Output:** 15 watts.

CHAMPION 110 1993–1999

Mid-sized solid-state combo.

- **Cabinet:** black Tolex.
- **Controls:** volume, overdrive gain, overdrive volume, bass, middle, treble, reverb; blackface control panel.

- **Speakers:** 1x10.
- **Output:** 25 watts.

PERFORMER 1000 1993–96

Fender's second stab at a hybrid design, with a tube in the preamp and all-solid-state output stage. Available as combo or piggy-back set.

- **Cabinet:** black Tolex.
- **Controls:** ch 1: volume, treble, middle, bass; ch 2: gain, treble, middle, bass, volume; reverb and effects mix; black control panel.
- **Speakers:** 1x12, or as head with separate 1x12 or 4x12 cab.
- **Tubes:** 12AX7 in preamp, otherwise solid state.
- **Output:** 100.

PRINCETON 112 1993–95

A member of the solid-state Standard line introduced in 1993.

- **Cabinet:** black Tolex.
- **Controls:** normal: volume, treble, bass; drive: gain, contour, treble, bass, volume, reverb; black control panel.
- **Speakers:** 1x12.
- **Output:** 40 watts.

TONE-MASTER 1993–2003

Hand-wired tube-amp head from the Custom Shop.

- **Cabinet:** blonde Tolex.
- **Controls:** ch 1: volume, treble, middle, bass; ch 2: volume, treble, middle, bass, reverb.
- **Speakers:** 2x12 or 4x12 Celestions in separate cab.
- **Tubes:** 3x12AX7, 4x6L6GC, (solid-state rectifier).
- **Output:** 100 watts.

ULTRA CHORUS 1993–95

Solid-state amp similar to Power Chorus (see 1991 listing) except:

- **Controls:** normal: volume, treble, middle, bass, reverb; drive: gain, contour, volume, treble, middle, bass, reverb, chorus rate & depth; black control panel.

VIBRO-KING 1993–current

Another hand-wired Custom Shop offering, adding onboard three-knob tube reverb to classic early-'60s looks. Later this model was known as the Vibro-King Custom.

- **Cabinet:** blonde Tolex, then black Tolex.
- **Controls:** dwell, mix, tone (these all for the reverb), fat switch, volume, treble, bass, middle, speed, intensity; blackface control panel.
- **Speakers:** 3x10.
- **Tubes:** 5x12AX7, EL84 reverb driver (6V6 used in later years), 2x6L6GC, (solid-state rectifier).
- **Output:** 50 watts.

'65 DELUXE REVERB 1993–current

A replica of the blackface DELUXE REVERB (see 1963 listing), similar except:

- **Tubes:** preamp has 4x12AX7, 2x12AT7; printed circuit board rather than original hand-wired eyelet board.

1994

GUITARS

ALUMINUM-BODY STRATOCASTER 1994–95

Anodized aluminum hollow-body option offered on AMERICAN STANDARD STRATOCASTER, STRAT PLUS, STRAT PLUS DELUXE, and STRAT ULTRA (see the relevant entries in the listings for 1986, for 1987, for 1989, and for 1990).

ALUMINUM-BODY TELECASTER 1994–95

Anodized aluminum hollow-body option for AMERICAN STANDARD TELECASTER (see 1988 listing).

D'AQUISTO ELITE 1994–95, 2000–01

Hollow single-cutaway body, one floating pickup, wooden tailpiece.
Similar to D'AQUISTO DELUXE (see 1995 listing) except:

- **Neck:** split-block markers; ebony tuner buttons.
- **Body:** sunburst or natural.
- **Electronics:** floating humbucker.

Custom Shop production

DICK DALE STRATOCASTER 1994–current
Signature on headstock.
- **Neck:** maple with rosewood fingerboard; truss-rod adjuster at body end; two string guides; Dick Dale signature on reverse headstock.
- **Body:** gold only.
- **Electronics:** three white six-polepiece pickups (bridge pickup reverse-angled); one control (volume), three-way selector and two-way switch, all on pickguard; jack in body face.
- **Hardware:** 11-screw white laminated plastic pickguard, metal covers over three 'spare' holes; six-pivot bridge/vibrato unit.
Custom Shop production.

FLOYD ROSE STANDARD STRATOCASTER (MIJ) 1994–96
Two single-coils and one coverless humbucker, normal color neck, locking vibrato system.
- **Neck:** maple with rosewood fingerboard; truss-rod adjuster at headstock end; single-bar string-guide; locking nut.
- **Body:** with Foto Flame fake figured wood finish; sunburst, blue, or red.
- **Electronics:** two white six-polepiece pickups and one white coverless humbucker (at bridge); two controls (volume, tone) and five-way selector, all on pickguard; jack in body face.
- **Hardware:** 11-screw white laminated plastic pickguard; two-pivot locking bridge/vibrato unit.
Also known as SQUIER SERIES FLOYD ROSE STANDARD STRATOCASTER, with small Squier Series logo on headstock (see 1992 listing).

FLOYD ROSE STANDARD STRATOCASTER (MIM) 1994–98
Two-pivot locking vibrato system, two white single-coils and one white humbucker, white pickguard, small headstock, two controls.
Similar to STANDARD STRATOCASTER (see 1991 listing) except:
- **Neck:** single-bar string-guide; locking nut.
- **Body:** black or white.

- **Electronics:** two white six-polepiece pickups and one white coverless humbucker (at bridge); two controls (volume, tone) and five-way selector, all on pickguard.
- **Hardware:** two-pivot locking bridge/vibrato unit.
Also known as SQUIER SERIES FLOYD ROSE STANDARD STRATOCASTER, with small Squier Series logo on headstock (see later listing this year).

RICHIE SAMBORA STANDARD STRATOCASTER (MIM) 1994–2002
Signature on headstock.
Similar to STANDARD STRATOCASTER (see 1991 listing) except:
- **Neck:** maple with rosewood fingerboard only; single-bar string-guide; locking nut; Richie Sambora signature on headstock.
- **Body:** various colors.
- **Electronics:** two white six-polepiece pickups and one white coverless humbucker (at bridge); two-pivot locking bridge/vibrato unit.

ROBBEN FORD ELITE 1994–2001
Signature on headstock, unbound fingerboard, twin-cutaway body.
- **Neck:** mahogany glued-in, with unbound ebony fingerboard (pao ferro from 1997); 24.625-inch scale, 22 frets; truss-rod adjuster at headstock end; three-tuners-per-side headstock.
- **Body:** twin-cutaway bound; sunburst, black, or red.
- **Electronics:** two metal-cover six-polepiece humbuckers; four controls (two volume, two tone), three-way selector and coil-switch, all on body; side-mounted jack.
- **Hardware:** six-saddle bridge, fine-tuner tailpiece.
Custom Shop production.

ROBBEN FORD ULTRA FM 1994–2001
Signature on headstock, bound fingerboard, twin-cutaway body.
Similar to ROBBEN FORD ELITE (see previous listing) except:

- **Neck:** bound ebony fingerboard with split-block position markers.

Custom Shop production.

ROBBEN FORD ULTRA SP 1994–2001

Signature on headstock, bound fingerboard, twin-cutaway body, gold-plated hardware.

Similar to ROBBEN FORD ELITE (see earlier listing this year) except:

- **Neck:** bound ebony fingerboard with split-block position markers; ebony tuner buttons.
- **Body:** semi-solid.
- **Hardware:** gold-plated.

Custom Shop production.

SPECIAL EDITION 1994 STRATOCASTER 1994

Commemorative neckplate.

Similar to AMERICAN STANDARD STRATOCASTER (see 1986 listing) except:

- **Body:** black or blond.
- **Hardware:** 11-screw grey pearl or tortoiseshell laminated plastic pickguard; commemorative neckplate.

SPECIAL EDITION 1994 TELECASTER 1994

Commemorative neckplate.

Similar to AMERICAN STANDARD TELECASTER (see 1988 listing) except:

- **Body:** black or blond.
- **Hardware:** eight-screw grey pearl or tortoiseshell laminated plastic pickguard; commemorative neckplate

SQUIER SERIES FLOYD ROSE STANDARD STRATOCASTER (MIM) 1994–96

Another name for FLOYD ROSE STANDARD STRATOCASTER (see earlier listing this year).

SQUIER SERIES STANDARD STRATOCASTER (MIM) 1994–96

Another name for TRADITIONAL STRATOCASTER (see 1996 listing).

SQUIER SERIES STANDARD TELECASTER (MIM) 1994–96

Another name for TRADITIONAL TELECASTER (see 1996 listing).

STRAT SPECIAL (MIM) 1994–96

Black pickups and pickguard.

Similar to STANDARD STRATOCASTER (see 1991 listing) except:

- **Electronics:** two black six-polepiece pickups and one black coverless humbucker (at bridge); two controls (volume, tone), five-way selector and coil-switch, all on pickguard.
- **Hardware:** black-plated; 11-screw black laminated plastic pickguard.

TELE SPECIAL (MIM) 1994–96

Humbucker at neck, black pickguard.

Similar to STANDARD TELECASTER (see 1991 listing) except:

- **Electronics:** one metal-cover six-polepiece humbucker (at neck) and one black six-polepiece pickup (angled in bridgeplate); two controls (volume, tone) and five-way selector.
- **Hardware:** eight-screw black laminated plastic pickguard; six-saddle raised-sides bridge with through-body stringing.

40th ANNIVERSARY 1954 STRATOCASTER 1994

Replica of 1954-period original (see STRATOCASTER PRE-CBS 1954 listing) but with commemorative neckplate. Numbered factory production run of 1,954.

AMPLIFIERS

DUAL PROFESSIONAL 1994–current

A powerful combo from the Custom Shop combining vintage looks and features with some contemporary functions such as channel switching.

- **Cabinet:** blonde Tolex.
- **Controls:** dwell, mix, tone (for reverb); volume ch A, volume ch B, treble, bass, mid, speed,

intensity, ch A/B switch, ch A fat switch, ch B fat switch; blackface control panel.
- **Speakers:** 2x12 Celestion Vintage 30 speakers.
- **Tubes:** 5x12AX7, 12AT7, 4x6L6GC, (solid-state rectifier).
- **Output:** 100 watts.

PRO JUNIOR 1994–current

A member of the Tweed Series and essentially Fender's modern-day equivalent of the Champ but with different output tubes and more power.
- **Cabinet:** narrow panel tweed, later available in black Tolex.
- **Controls:** volume, tone.
- **Speakers:** 1x10 Eminence.
- **Tubes:** 2x12AX7, 2xEL84, (solid-state rectifier).
- **Output:** 15 watts.

1995

GUITARS

AMERICAN CLASSIC TELECASTER (first version) 1995–99

Three single-coils (two white, one black), inverted control plate, five-way selector.
Similar to AMERICAN STANDARD TELECASTER (see 1988 listing) except:
- **Electronics:** two white six-polepiece pickups and one black six-polepiece pickup (angled in bridgeplate); two controls (volume, tone) and five-way selector, all on inverted control plate adjoining pickguard.
- **Hardware:** gold-plated option; eight-screw white pearl or tortoiseshell laminated plastic pickguard.
Custom Shop production.

AMERICAN STANDARD B-BENDER TELECASTER 1995–97

Standard Tele pickup layout, 22 frets, B-Bender string-bending device installed.
Similar to AMERICAN STANDARD TELECASTER (see 1988 listing) except:
- **Neck:** fretted maple only.

- **Hardware:** factory-fitted B-Bender (built-in bending device for 2nd string).

AMERICAN STANDARD ROLAND GR-READY STRATOCASTER 1995–98

Two-pivot vibrato, two string-guides, extra slim white pickup at bridge.
Similar to AMERICAN STANDARD STRATOCASTER (see 1986 listing) except:
- **Electronics:** additional slim white plain-top Roland synthesizer pickup (at bridge); three controls (volume, tone, synth volume), five-way selector, two pushbuttons and mini-switch, all on pickguard; jack in body face; side-mounted multi-pin synth output.

BONNIE RAITT STRATOCASTER 1995–2001

Signature on headstock.
- **Neck:** narrow, maple, with rosewood fingerboard; 22 frets; truss-rod adjuster at headstock end; one string-guide; Bonnie Raitt signature on large headstock.
- **Body:** sunburst or blueburst.
- **Electronics:** three white six-polepiece pickups (bridge pickup angled); three controls (volume, two tone) and five-way selector, all on pickguard; jack in body face.
- **Hardware:** 11-screw white pearl laminated plastic pickguard; six-pivot bridge/vibrato unit.
Also Custom Shop limited edition.

BUDDY GUY STRATOCASTER 1995–current

Signature on headstock.
- **Neck:** fretted maple; 22 frets; truss-rod adjuster at headstock end; one string-guide; Buddy Guy signature on headstock.
- **Body:** sunburst or blond.
- **Electronics:** three white plain-top Lace Sensor pickups (bridge pickup angled); three controls (volume, tone, boost), five-way selector and mini-switch, all on pickguard; jack in body face; active circuit.
- **Hardware:** eight-screw (11-screw from 2000)

white pearl or tortoiseshell laminated plastic pickguard; six-pivot bridge/vibrato unit.

CARVED TOP STRAT 1995–98

Two-pivot vibrato, no string-guides, two single-coils and one humbucker, figured carved-top body.

- **Neck:** fretted maple, or maple with rosewood fingerboard; 22 frets; truss-rod adjuster at headstock end; locking tuners; roller nut.
- **Body:** with figured carved top; sunburst or colors.
- **Electronics:** two cream six-polepiece pickups and one black/cream coverless humbucker (at bridge); two controls (volume, tone) and five-way selector, all on body; side-mounted jack.
- **Hardware:** no pickguard; two-pivot bridge/vibrato unit.

Known as CARVED TOP STRAT HSS (1998).
Custom Shop production.

CONTEMPORARY STRAT 1995–98

Two-pivot vibrato, no string-guides, two single-coils and one humbucker, smaller body with slimmer horns.

- **Neck:** fretted maple, or maple with rosewood fingerboard; 22 frets; truss-rod adjuster at headstock end; locking tuners; roller nut.
- **Body:** smaller, with slimmer horns; sunburst or colors.
- **Electronics:** two white six-polepiece pickups and one white coverless humbucker (at bridge).
- **Hardware:** 11-screw white pearl laminated plastic pickguard; two-pivot bridge/vibrato unit.

Custom Shop production.

CONTEMPORARY STRAT FMT 1995–98

Similar to CONTEMPORARY STRAT (see previous listing) but with figured-top body and two-pivot locking bridge/vibrato unit. Custom Shop production.

D'AQUISTO DELUXE 1995–2001

Hollow single-cutaway body, one pickup, wooden tailpiece.

- **Neck:** maple glued-in, with bound ebony

fingerboard, block markers; 25.125-inch scale, 22 frets; truss-rod adjuster at headstock end; three-tuners-per-side headstock.
- **Body:** hollow archtop single-cutaway bound; f-holes; sunburst, natural, or red.
- **Electronics:** one metal-cover six-polepiece humbucker (at neck); two controls (volume, tone) on body; side-mounted jack.
- **Hardware:** gold-plated; bound wooden pickguard; single-saddle wooden bridge, wooden tailpiece.

Custom Shop production

HMT ACOUSTIC-ELECTRIC (second version) (MIJ) 1995–97

Telecaster headstock, wooden-base bridge.
Similar to HMT ACOUSTIC-ELECTRIC FIRST VERSION (see 1991 listing) except:
- **Neck:** Telecaster headstock.
- **Body:** sunburst or black.
- **Electronics:** one black plain-top pickup (angled at neck) and piezo pickup (in bridge).

JAMES BURTON STANDARD TELECASTER (MIM) 1995–current

Signature on headstock.
Similar to STANDARD TELECASTER (see 1991 listing) except:
- **Neck:** James Burton signature on headstock.
- **Hardware:** eight-screw white plastic pickguard; six-saddle raised-sides bridge with through-body stringing.

SET NECK STRATOCASTER (second version) 1995–98

Two-pivot vibrato, no string-guides, two single-coils and one humbucker, glued-in neck.
Similar to SET NECK STRATOCASTER FIRST VERSION (see 1992 listing) except:
- **Neck:** rosewood fingerboard.
- **Body:** sunburst or natural.
- **Electronics:** two white six-polepiece pickups and one white coverless humbucker (at bridge).

Custom Shop production.

TELE JNR 1995–2000

Two large black rectangular pickups.

- **Neck:** mahogany glued-in, with pao ferro fingerboard; 22 frets; truss-rod adjuster at headstock end; one string-guide; neck and headstock face match body color.
- **Body:** semi-solid slab single-cutaway; sunburst or colors.
- **Electronics:** two large black six-polepiece pickups; two controls (volume, tone) and three-way selector, all on inverted metal plate adjoining pickguard; side-mounted jack.
- **Hardware:** small tortoiseshell plastic, or white pearl, tortoiseshell or black laminated plastic pickguard; six-saddle small bridge with through-body stringing.

Custom Shop production.

TELE PLUS (second version) 1995–98

Three Lace Sensor pickups (one angled in bridgeplate).

- **Neck:** fretted maple, or maple with rosewood fingerboard; 22 frets; truss-rod adjuster at headstock end; one string-guide.
- **Body:** slab single-cutaway bound; sunburst or colors.
- **Electronics:** three plain-top Lace Sensor pickups (bridgeplate pickup angled); two controls (volume, tone) and three-way selector, all on metal plate adjoining pickguard; side-mounted jack.
- **Hardware:** eight-screw white pearl or tortoiseshell laminated plastic pickguard; six-saddle flat bridge with through-body stringing.

TELECASTER XII 12-string 1995–98

Model name on 12-string headstock.

- **Neck:** fretted maple, or maple with rosewood fingerboard; truss-rod adjuster at headstock end; one 'bracket' string-guide; six-tuners-per-side headstock.
- **Body:** slab single-cutaway; sunburst or colors.
- **Electronics:** one plain metal-cover pickup (at neck) and one black six-polepiece pickup (angled in bridgeplate); two controls (volume, tone) and three-way selector, all on metal plate adjoining pickguard; side-mounted jack.
- **Hardware:** five-screw black or white plastic, or white pearl laminated plastic pickguard; 12-saddle bridge with through-body stringing.

Custom Shop production.

WAYLON JENNINGS TRIBUTE TELECASTER 1995–2003

Signature on headstock.

- **Neck:** fretted maple; truss-rod adjuster at body end; one string-guide; pearl tuner buttons; Scruggs Peg banjo-style de-tuner for 6th string; 'W' inlay at 12th fret and Waylon Jennings signature on headstock.
- **Body:** slab single-cutaway bound; black only with white leather inlay.
- **Electronics:** one plain metal-cover pickup with visible height-adjustment screws (at neck) and one black six-polepiece pickup (angled in bridgeplate); two controls (volume, tone) and three-way selector, all on metal plate adjoining pickguard; side-mounted jack.
- **Hardware:** eight-screw white laminated plastic pickguard; six-saddle flat bridge with through-body stringing.

Custom Shop production.

'54 STRATOCASTER FMT 1995–98

Replica of 1954-period original (see STRATOCASTER PRE-CBS 1954 listing) but with figured body top. Gold-plated hardware option. Custom Shop production.

'60 STRATOCASTER FMT 1995–98

Replica of 1960-period original (see STRATOCASTER PRE-CBS 1954 listing) but with figured body top. Gold-plated hardware option. Custom Shop production.

90s TELECASTER CUSTOM (MIJ) 1995–98

Black or white bound body with matching headstock face, pearl pickguard, gold-plated hardware.

CUSTOM AGED

Fender's strength continued to grow alongside the breadth of its catalog in the 1990s, but a studied look back over the shoulder continued to offer a reliable means of success in model development. Namely, more players than ever seemed to want guitars that not only were made like they were in the old days but also looked like they were made 40 or 50 years ago.

After building a handful of aged or 'distressed' instruments for name artists, often as replicas of much-played favorite guitars that had become too valuable to take on tour, the Fender Custom Shop formally introduced its Relic series in 1995. These guitars included intentional dings, scuffs, and scratches and 'arm rubs' in the finish, along with artificially aged and tarnished hardware.

The line proved extremely popular, and in fact the Mary Kaye Stratocaster (a blonde-finish version of the 1956 Stratocaster with gold-plated hardware) proved the Custom Shop's best seller of the late 1990s. Between the official launch of the Relics in 1995 and May of 1999, the ageing of bodies, necks, and parts that would be assembled at the Custom Shop was outsourced to Vince Cunetto, who established a shop and workforce in Bolivar, Missouri, for this purpose.

Cunetto's own aged custom-made Fender replicas had impressed his friend Jay Black, a Custom Shop Master Builder, who in turn showed the work to Custom Shop Manager John Page. Page was equally impressed and hired the craftsman to provide the look that would define the Relic series. An occasional request for a 'slightly less aged' guitar led Cunetto to develop the less-distressed models, dubbed Closet Classics in 1998 for their 'gently played but cared for' look.

Later in '98 Fender formally expanded the distressed line into the Time Machine series, which included the relatively well-aged Relics, the gently aged Closet Classics, and the entirely un-distressed N.O.S. guitars. The N.O.S models were intended to look as if an original vintage model had been zapped into the future by a time machine. (N.O.S. means 'new old stock,' a term commonly used for amplifier tubes manufactured many years ago but which have remained unused on the shelf and therefore in 'new' condition.)

In 1999, Fender moved the ageing of all Time Machine models in-house, although the majority of Closet Classic guitars were already being produced in the Custom Shop itself during 1998, as of course were the non-aged N.O.S. guitars. In the intervening years, the Relics of 1995-'99, known in collector's parlance as 'Cunetto-era' instruments, have become collector's items, just a notch down on the desirability ladder from refinished original vintage guitars, themselves a notch below entirely original examples. It's worth nothing that Cunetto never 'made' guitars for Fender but simply finished and aged bodies, necks, and parts that were sent to him by Fender.

- **Neck:** maple with rosewood fingerboard; truss-rod adjuster at body end; one string-guide; black- or white-face headstock.
- **Body:** slab single-cutaway bound; black or white.
- **Electronics:** one plain metal cover pickup (at neck) and one black six-polepiece pickup (angled in bridgeplate); two controls (volume, tone) and three-way selector, all on metal plate adjoining pickguard; side-mounted jack.
- **Hardware:** gold-plated; eight-screw grey or white pearl laminated plastic pickguard; six-saddle flat bridge with through-body stringing.

90s TELECASTER DELUXE (MIJ) 1995–98

Contoured body, three six-polepiece pickups, reversed control plate.

- **Neck:** maple with rosewood fingerboard; truss-rod adjuster at body end; one string-guide.
- **Body:** single-cutaway; sunburst or colors.
- **Electronics:** two white six-polepiece pickups (neck and center) and one black six-polepiece pickup (angled in bridgeplate); two controls (volume, tone) and five-way selector, all on reversed metal plate adjoining pickguard; side-mounted jack.
- **Hardware:** eight-screw white pearl laminated plastic pickguard; six-saddle flat bridge with through-body stringing.

Foto Flame fake figured wood finish option (1995–96).

AMPLIFIERS

BLUES JUNIOR 1995–current
Similar to Pro Junior (see 1994 listing) except:
- **Cabinet:** narrow panel tweed, later available in black Tolex.
- **Controls:** volume, bass, middle, treble, master volume, reverb, fat switch.
- **Speakers:** 1x12 Eminence.
- **Tubes:** 3x12AX7, 2xEL84, (solid-state rectifier).
- **Output:** 15 watts.

'CUSTOM' VIBROLUX REVERB 1995–current
This model appears as a reissue of an early '60s Fender amp but is not a direct replica of any vintage design.
- **Cabinet:** blonde Tolex.
- **Controls:** normal: volume, treble, bass; bright: volume, treble, bass; reverb, speed, intensity; brown control panel.
- **Speakers:** 2x10 Eminence Legend Alnico, then Jensen P10R Reissue from 2001–02.
- **Tubes:** 5x7025, 12AT7, 2x6L6GC, (solid-state rectifier).
- **Output:** 40 watts.

PROSONIC 1995–2001
First venture into solid state for the new post-'95 Fender regime.

- **Cabinet:** black Tolex.
- **Controls:** volume, treble, middle, bass, reverb, gain, limiter, presence, volume; black control panel.
- **Speakers:** 1x12 or 2x12.
- **Output:** 65 watts.

1996

GUITARS

HANK MARVIN STRATOCASTER (MIJ) 1996–97
Signature on headstock.
Similar to Japan-made 50s Stratocaster (see 1985 listing) except:
- **Neck:** Hank Marvin signature on headstock.
- **Body:** red only.

JAG-STANG (MIJ) 1996–onward
Model name on headstock, angled single-coil and humbucker.
- **Neck:** maple with rosewood fingerboard; 24-inch scale, 22 frets;
truss-rod adjuster at body end; one string-guide.
- **Body:** contoured offset-waist; blue or red.
- **Electronics:** one white six-polepiece pickup (at neck) and one white coverless humbucker (at bridge), both angled; two controls (volume, tone) and jack, all on metal plate adjoining pickguard; two selector slide-switches on pickguard.
- **Hardware:** Ten-screw white pearl laminated plastic pickguard; six-saddle bridge with vibrato unit.

LONE STAR STRAT 1996–2000
Two-pivot vibrato, two string-guides, two single-coils and one humbucker.
Similar to American Standard Stratocaster (see 1986 listing) except:
- **Electronics:** two white six-polepiece pickups and one Seymour Duncan-logo white coverless humbucker (at bridge).

- **Hardware:** 11-screw white pearl or tortoiseshell laminated plastic pickguard.

NOKIE EDWARDS TELECASTER (MIJ) 1996
Signature on headstock, two twin-blade humbuckers.
- **Neck:** maple with ebony fingerboard; 22 frets; truss-rod adjuster at body end; brass nut; optional Scruggs Peg banjo-style de-tuner for 6th string; Nokie Edwards signature on headstock.
- **Body:** Single-cutaway with figured front; natural only.
- **Electronics:** two black twin-blade humbucker pickups; two controls (volume, tone) and three-way selector, all on body, side-mounted jack.
- **Hardware:** gold-plated; no pickguard; six-saddle small bridge with through-body stringing.
Optional Nokie Edwards logo for body.

RELIC 50s NOCASTER 1996–98
Distressed-finish replica of 1950s-period original with no model name on headstock (see BROADCASTER 1950 listing). Custom Shop production.

RELIC 50s STRATOCASTER 1996–98
Distressed-finish replica of 1950s-period original (see STRATOCASTER PRE-CBS 1954 listing). Gold-plated hardware option. Custom Shop production.

RELIC 60s STRATOCASTER 1996–98
Distressed-finish replica of early 1960s-period original (see STRATOCASTER PRE-CBS 1954 listing). Gold-plated hardware option. Custom Shop production.

RICHIE SAMBORA PAISLEY STRATOCASTER (MIJ) 1996
Signature on headstock, black paisley-pattern body finish.
- **Neck:** fretted maple, star markers; 22 frets; truss-rod adjuster at headstock end; pearl tuner buttons; single-bar string-guide; locking nut; Richie Sambora signature on headstock.
- **Body:** black paisley-pattern only.

- **Electronics:** two black six-polepiece pickups and one black coverless humbucker (at bridge); three controls (volume, two tone) and five-way selector, all on pickguard; jack in body face.
- **Hardware:** 11-screw black paisley laminated plastic pickguard; two-pivot locking bridge/vibrato unit.

TEX-MEX STRAT (MIM) 1996–97
Vintage-style 'thin' Fender headstock logo in gold, three single-coils.
Similar to STANDARD STRATOCASTER (see 1991 listing) except:
- **Neck:** Headstock with vintage-style Fender headstock logo in gold.
Fitted with different specification but visually similar pickups.

THE VENTURES JAZZMASTER (MIJ) 1996
The Ventures logo on headstock, two large white pickups.
- **Neck:** maple with bound rosewood fingerboard, block markers; 22 frets; truss-rod adjuster at body end; two string guides; The Ventures logo on black-face headstock.
- **Body:** contoured offset-waist; black only.
- **Electronics:** two large white rectangular six-polepiece pickups; two controls (volume, tone), three-way selector and jack, all on pickguard.
- **Hardware:** gold-plated; 11-screw white pearl laminated plastic pickguard; six-saddle bridge, vibrato tailpiece.
Optional Ventures logo for body.

THE VENTURES STRATOCASTER (MIJ) 1996
The Ventures logo on headstock, three Lace Sensor pickups.
- **Neck:** maple with bound rosewood fingerboard, block markers; 22 frets; truss-rod adjuster at body end; one string-guide; The Ventures logo on black-face headstock.
- **Body:** black only.
- **Electronics:** three white plain-top Lace Sensor

pickups (pickup at bridge is angled); three controls (volume, tone, boost) and five-way selector, all on pickguard; jack in body face; active circuit.

- **Hardware:** gold-plated; 11-screw white pearl laminated plastic pickguard; six-pivot bridge/vibrato unit.

Optional Ventures logo for body.

TRADITIONAL FAT STRAT (MIM) 1996–98

Modern-style 'thick' Fender headstock logo in black, two single-coils and one humbucker.

Similar to TRADITIONAL STRATOCASTER (see next listing) except:

- **Electronics:** two white six-polepiece pickups and one white coverless humbucker (at bridge).

TRADITIONAL STRATOCASTER (MIM) 1996–98

Modern-style 'thick' Fender headstock logo in black, three single-coils.

- **Neck:** fretted maple, or maple neck with rosewood fingerboard; truss-rod adjuster at headstock end; one string-guide.
- **Body:** black, red, or white.
- **Electronics:** three white six-polepiece pickups (bridge pickup angled); three controls (volume, two tone) and five-way selector, all on pickguard; jack in body face.
- **Hardware:** 11-screw white laminated plastic pickguard; six-pivot bridge/vibrato unit.

Previously known as SQUIER SERIES STANDARD STRATOCASTER, with small Squier Series logo on headstock (see 1994 listing).

TRADITIONAL TELECASTER (MIM) 1996–98

Modern-style 'thick' Fender headstock logo in black, two single-coils.

Similar to vintage-style Telecaster except:

- **Neck:** fretted maple; truss-rod adjuster at headstock end; one string-guide.
- **Body:** slab single-cutaway; black, red, or white.
- **Electronics:** one plain metal-cover pickup with visible height-adjustment screws (at neck) and one

black six-polepiece pickup (angled in bridgeplate); two controls (volume, tone) and three-way selector, all on metal plate adjoining pickguard; side-mounted jack.

- **Hardware:** eight-screw white laminated plastic pickguard; six-saddle flat bridge/tailpiece (no through-body stringing).

Previously known as SQUIER SERIES STANDARD TELECASTER, with small Squier Series logo on headstock (see 1994 listing).

50s TELECASTER 1996–98

Replica of 1950s-period original (see TELECASTER 1951 listing). Gold-plated hardware option. Custom Shop production.

50th ANNIVERSARY STRATOCASTER 1996

Commemorative neckplate.

Similar to AMERICAN STANDARD STRATOCASTER (see 1986 listing) except:

- **Neck:** maple with rosewood fingerboard only; commemorative neckplate.
- **Body:** sunburst only.
- **Hardware:** gold-plated.

Numbered factory production run of 2,500. Also Custom Shop limited editions.

50th ANNIVERSARY TELECASTER 1996

Commemorative neckplate.

Similar to AMERICAN STANDARD TELECASTER (see 1988 listing) except:

- **Neck:** fretted maple; commemorative neckplate.
- **Body:** sunburst only.
- **Hardware:** gold-plated.

Numbered factory production run of 1,250.

'58 STRATOCASTER 1996–98

Replica of 1958-period original (see STRATOCASTER PRE-CBS 1954 listing). Gold-plated hardware option. Custom Shop production.

60s TELECASTER CUSTOM 1996–98

Replica of 1960s-period original (see TELECASTER

1951 listing). Gold-plated hardware option. Custom Shop production.

'69 STRATOCASTER (first version) 1996–98
Replica of 1969-period original (see STRATOCASTER CBS SIXTIES entry in the 1965 listing). Custom Shop production.

1997

GUITARS

BIG APPLE STRAT 1997–2000
Two-pivot vibrato, two string-guides, two white humbuckers.
Similar to AMERICAN STANDARD STRATOCASTER (see 1986 listing) except:
- **Electronics:** two white coverless humbuckers.
- **Hardware:** 11-screw white pearl or tortoiseshell laminated plastic pickguard.

CALIFORNIA FAT STRAT 1997–98
Six-pivot vibrato, 'California Series' on headstock, two singles-coils and one humbucker.
- **Neck:** fretted maple, or maple neck with rosewood fingerboard; truss-rod adjuster at headstock end; one string-guide; California Series on headstock.
- **Body:** sunburst or colors.
- **Electronics:** two white six-polepiece pickups and one white coverless humbucker (at bridge); three controls (volume, two tone) and five-way selector, all on pickguard; jack in body face.
- **Hardware:** 11-screw white laminated plastic pickguard; six-pivot bridge/vibrato unit.

CALIFORNIA FAT TELE 1997–98
'California Series' on headstock, one humbucker and one single-coil.
- **Neck:** fretted maple; truss-rod adjuster at headstock end; one string-guide; 'California Series' on headstock.
- **Body:** slab single-cutaway; sunburst or colors.
- **Electronics:** one metal-cover six-polepiece humbucker (at neck) and one black six-polepiece pickup (angled in bridgeplate); two controls (volume, tone) and three-way selector, all on metal plate adjoining pickguard; side-mounted jack.
- **Hardware:** eight-screw white laminated plastic pickguard; six-saddle raised-sides bridge with through-body stringing.

CALIFORNIA STRAT 1997–current
Six-pivot vibrato, 'California Series' on headstock, three single-coils.
Similar to CALIFORNIA FAT STRAT (see earlier listing this year) except:
- **Electronics:** three white six-polepiece pickups (bridge pickup angled).

CALIFORNIA TELE 1997–current
'California Series' on headstock, two single-coils.
Similar to CALIFORNIA FAT TELE (see 1997 listing) except:
- **Neck:** fretted maple, or maple with rosewood fingerboard.
- **Electronics:** one white six-polepiece pickup (at neck) and one black six-polepiece pickup (angled in bridgeplate).

COLLECTORS EDITION STRATOCASTER 1997
Six-pivot vibrato, '1997' inlay at 12th fret position.
- **Neck:** maple with rosewood fingerboard; truss-rod adjuster at body end; one string-guide; oval-shape 1997 inlay at 12th fret.
- **Body:** sunburst only.
- **Electronics:** three white six-polepiece pickups (bridge pickup angled); three controls (volume, two tone) and five-way selector, all on pickguard; jack in body face.
- **Hardware:** gold-plated; 11-screw tortoiseshell laminated plastic pickguard; six-pivot bridge/vibrato unit.
Numbered factory production run of 1,997.

DELUXE NASHVILLE TELE (MIM) 1997–current
White six-polepiece pickup in center position.

Similar to STANDARD TELECASTER (see 1991 listing) except:
- **Neck:** fretted maple, or maple with rosewood fingerboard.
- **Body:** sunburst or colors.
- **Electronics:** one plain metal-cover pickup with visible height-adjustment screws (at neck), one white six-polepiece pickup (in center) and one black six-polepiece pickup (angled in bridgeplate); white six-polepiece pickup (in center); two controls (volume, tone) and five-way selector.
- **Hardware:** eight-screw tortoiseshell laminated plastic pickguard; six-saddle raised-sides bridge with through-body stringing.

DELUXE POWERHOUSE STRAT (MIM) 1997–current
White pearl pickguard, active circuit.
Similar to STANDARD STRATOCASTER (see 1991 listing) except:
- **Body:** various colors.
- **Electronics:** three controls (volume, tone, boost) and five-way selector, all on pickguard; active circuit.
- **Hardware:** 11-screw white pearloid plastic pickguard.

DELUXE SUPER STRAT (MIM) 1997–2004
Gold-plated hardware, push-switch.
Similar to STANDARD STRATOCASTER (see 1991 listing) except:
- **Electronics:** Three controls (volume, two tone), five-way selector and push-switch, all on pickguard.
- **Hardware:** gold-plated; 11-screw tortoiseshell laminated plastic pickguard.

HANK MARVIN STRATOCASTER (MIM) 1997
Signature on body.
Similar to TRADITIONAL STRATOCASTER (see 1996 listing) except:
- **Neck:** fretted maple only; Hank Marvin signature on body.

- **Body:** red only.
Limited edition of 300.

JERRY DONAHUE HELLECASTERS STRATOCASTER (MIJ) 1997–98
Signature on headstock, 'Hellecasters' inlay at 12th fret.
- **Neck:** fretted maple; truss-rod adjuster at headstock end; one string-guide; roller nut; 'Hellecasters' inlay at 12th fret; Jerry Donahue signature on headstock.
- **Body:** blue only.
- **Electronics:** three white six-polepiece pickups (bridge pickup angled); three controls (volume, tone, two-way rotary switch) and five-way selector, all on pickguard; jack in body face.
- **Hardware:** 11-screw blue sparkle laminated plastic pickguard; six-pivot bridge/vibrato unit.

JIMI HENDRIX STRATOCASTER 1997–2000
Mirror-image Fender Stratocaster logo on large inverted headstock.
- **Neck:** fretted maple; truss-rod adjuster at body end; one string-guide; mirror-image Fender Stratocaster logo on large reverse headstock.
- **Body:** left-handed; white only.
- **Electronics:** three white six-polepiece pickups (bridge pickup reverse-angled); three controls (volume, two tone) and five-way selector, all on pickguard; jack in body face.
- **Hardware:** left-handed 11-screw white laminated plastic pickguard; left-handed six-pivot bridge/vibrato unit.

JIMMIE VAUGHAN TEX-MEX STRATOCASTER (MIM) 1997–current
Signature on back of headstock.
Similar to STANDARD STRATOCASTER (see 1991 listing) except:
- **Neck:** fretted maple only; Jimmie Vaughan signature on back of headstock.
- **Electronics:** modified control operation.
- **Hardware:** 11-screw white plastic pickguard.

JOHN JORGENSON HELLECASTER (MIJ) 1997–98

Signature and model name on headstock, three split pickups.

- **Neck:** maple with rosewood fingerboard, gold sparkle dot markers; 22 frets; truss-rod adjuster at headstock end; locking tuners; 'Hellecasters' inlay at 12th fret; John Jorgenson signature on large Stratocaster reverse headstock.
- **Body:** black sparkle only.
- **Electronics:** three black plain-top split pickups (bridge pickup angled); three controls (volume, two tone) and five-way selector, all on pickguard; jack in body face.
- **Hardware:** gold-plated; 11-screw gold sparkle laminated plastic pickguard; two -pivot bridge/vibrato unit.

MERLE HAGGARD TELE 1997–current

Signature on headstock.

- **Neck:** fretted maple; 22 frets; truss-rod adjuster at body end; one string-guide; pearl tuner buttons; 'Tuff Dog Tele' inlay and Merle Haggard signature on headstock.
- **Body:** slab single-cutaway bound; sunburst only.
- **Electronics:** one plain metal-cover pickup (at neck) and one black six-polepiece pickup (angled in bridgeplate); two controls (volume, tone) and four-way selector, all on metal plate adjoining pickguard; side-mounted jack.
- **Hardware:** gold-plated; seven-screw cream plastic re-styled pickguard; six-saddle flat bridge with through-body stringing.

Custom Shop production.

Catalogue name varies: Merle Haggard Tribute Tuff Dog Tele (1997–2000); Merle Haggard Tribute Tele (2001–03); Merle Haggard Signature Telecaster (2004–current).

ROADHOUSE STRAT 1997–2000

Two-pivot vibrato, two string-guides, three single-coils, white pearl or tortoiseshell pickguard.
Similar to AMERICAN STANDARD STRATOCASTER (see 1986 listing) except:

- **Electronics:** visually similar pickups but different specification.
- **Hardware:** 11-screw white pearl or tortoiseshell laminated plastic pickguard.

TEX-MEX STRAT SPECIAL (MIM) 1997

Vintage-style 'thin' Fender headstock logo in gold, two single-coils and one humbucker.
Similar to STANDARD STRATOCASTER (see 1991 listing) except:

- **Electronics:** two white six-polepiece pickups and one white coverless humbucker (at bridge).

TEX-MEX TELE SPECIAL (MIM) 1997

Humbucker at neck, white pickguard.
Similar to STANDARD TELECASTER (see 1991 listing) except:

- **Electronics:** one metal-cover six-polepiece humbucker (at neck) and one black six-polepiece pickup (angled in bridgeplate); two controls (volume, tone) and five-way selector.
- **Hardware:** six-saddle raised-sides bridge with through-body stringing.

WILL RAY JAZZ-A-CASTER (MIJ) 1997–98

Signature and model name on headstock, two large white pickups.

- **Neck:** maple with rosewood fingerboard, triangle markers; 22 frets; truss-rod adjuster at headstock end; one string guide; locking tuners; 'Hellecasters' inlay at 12th fret; Will Ray signature on small Stratocaster-style headstock.
- **Body:** slab single-cutaway; gold foil leaf only.
- **Electronics:** two large white rectangular six-polepiece pickups (bridge pickup angled); two controls (volume, tone) and four-way selector, all on metal plate adjoining pickguard; side-mounted jack.
- **Hardware:** eight-screw white pearl laminated plastic pickguard; modified six-saddle bridge with through-body stringing; Hipshot bending device on 2nd string.

90s TELE THINLINE 1997–2001

F-hole body, 22 frets.

- **Neck:** fretted maple, or maple with rosewood fingerboard; 22 frets; truss-rod adjuster at headstock end; one string-guide.
- **Body:** semi-solid slab single-cutaway bound; sunburst or colors.
- **Electronics:** one plain metal-cover pickup with visible height-adjustment screws (at neck) and one black six-polepiece pickup (angled in bridgeplate); two controls (volume, tone) and three-way selector, all on pickguard; side-mounted jack.
- **Hardware:** 12-screw white pearl or tortoiseshell laminated plastic pickguard; six-saddle flat bridge with through-body stringing.

AMPLIFIERS

FRONTMAN 15G (MII) 1997–current

Entry-level solid-state combo, now graduated to the Frontman II Series.

- **Cabinet:** black Tolex.
- **Controls:** normal volume, gain, drive volume, treble, middle, bass, aux inputs/headphone outputs; black control panel.
- **Speakers:** 1x8.
- **Output:** 15 watts.

FRONTMAN 15R (MII) 1997–current

Identical to FRONTMAN 15G (see previous listing) except:

- **Controls:** includes reverb.

FRONTMAN 25R (MII) 1997–current

Simliar to FRONTMAN 15R (see previous listing) except:

- **Speakers:** 1x10 (in a larger cab).
- **Output:** 25 watts.

1998

GUITARS

AMERICAN DELUXE FAT STRAT 1998–2003

Two Noiseless logo white pickups and one white humbucker, staggered height locking tuners, two-pivot vibrato.

Similar to AMERICAN DELUXE STRATOCASTER FIRST VERSION (see later listing this year) except:

- **Neck:** no string-guide; roller nut.
- **Electronics:** two Noiseless logo white six-polepiece pickups and one white coverless humbucker (at bridge).

AMERICAN DELUXE FAT STRAT/LOCKING TREM 1998–2003

Two Noiseless logo white pickups and one white humbucker, staggered height locking tuners, two-pivot locking vibrato.

Similar to AMERICAN DELUXE STRATOCASTER FIRST VERSION (see next listing) except:

- **Neck:** no string-guide; roller nut.
- **Electronics:** two Noiseless logo white six-polepiece pickups and one white coverless humbucker (at bridge).
- **Hardware:** two-pivot locking bridge/vibrato unit.

AMERICAN DELUXE STRATOCASTER (first version) 1998–2003

Three Noiseless logo white pickups, staggered height locking tuners, two-pivot vibrato.

- **Neck:** fretted maple, or maple with rosewood fingerboard; 22 frets; truss-rod adjuster at headstock end; staggered height locking tuners; one string-guide.
- **Body:** sunburst or colors.
- **Electronics:** three Noiseless logo white six-polepiece pickups (bridge pickup angled); three controls (volume, two tone) and five-way selector, all on pickguard; jack in body face.
- **Hardware:** 11-screw white laminated plastic pickguard; two-pivot bridge/vibrato unit.

AMERICAN DELUXE TELECASTER (first version) 1998–99

Contoured bound body, 22 frets, additional center pickup.

Similar to AMERICAN STANDARD TELECASTER (see 1986 listing) except:

- **Body:** contoured single-cutaway, bound.

- **Electronics:** one plain metal-cover pickup with visible height-adjustment screws (at neck), one white six-polepiece pickup (in center) and one black six-polepiece pickup (angled in bridgeplate); two controls (volume, tone), five-way selector and mini-switch, all on metal plate adjoining pickguard.
- **Hardware:** eight-screw white or tortoiseshell laminated plastic pickguard.

AMERICAN STANDARD STRATOCASTER HARD-TAIL 1998–2000

22 frets, small headstock, two string-guides, four-screw neckplate, three controls, six-saddle bridge with through-body stringing.
Similar to AMERICAN STANDARD STRATOCASTER (see 1986 listing) except:
- **Hardware:** six-saddle bridge with through-body stringing.

AMERICAN VINTAGE '52 TELECASTER 1998–current

Replica of 1952 original (see TELECASTER 1951 listing).

AMERICAN VINTAGE '57 STRATOCASTER 1998–current

Replica of 1957-period original (see STRATOCASTER PRE-CBS 1954 listing).

AMERICAN VINTAGE '62 STRATOCASTER 1998–current

Replica of 1962-period original (see STRATOCASTER PRE-CBS 1954 listing).

BIG APPLE STRAT HARD-TAIL 1998–2000

Two string-guides, two white humbuckers, six-saddle bridge with through-body stringing.
Similar to BIG APPLE STRAT (see 1997 listing) except:
- **Hardware:** six-saddle small bridge with through-body stringing.

BUCK OWENS TELECASTER (MIJ) 1998

Signature on headstock, red, silver and blue sparkle striped body front.

- **Neck:** maple with rosewood fingerboard; truss-rod adjuster at body end; one string- guide; red, silver and blue sparkle striped headstock face; Buck Owens signature on headstock.
- **Body:** slab single-cutaway, bound; red, silver, and blue sparkle striped front.
- **Electronics:** one plain metal-cover pickup (at neck) and one black six-polepiece pickup (angled in bridgeplate); two controls (volume, tone) and three-way selector, all on metal plate adjoining pickguard; side-mounted jack.
- **Hardware:** gold-plated; eight-screw gold pickguard; three-saddle raised-sides bridge with through-body stringing.

CARVED TOP STRAT HH 1998

Carved top, two metal-cover humbuckers.
Similar to CARVED TOP STRAT (see 1995 listing) except:
- **Electronics:** two metal-cover humbuckers.

CARVED TOP STRAT HSS 1998

Another name for CARVED TOP STRAT (see 1995 listing).

CLASSIC PLAYER STRAT 1998–2005

Custom Shop headstock logo, two-pivot vibrato, no string-guides, three Noiseless logo white pickups.
- **Neck:** fretted maple, or maple with rosewood fingerboard; 22 frets; truss-rod adjuster at headstock end; staggered height locking tuners.
- **Body:** sunburst or colors.
- **Electronics:** three Noiseless logo white six-polepiece pickups (bridge pickup angled); three controls (volume, two tone) and five-way selector, all on pickguard; jack in body face.
- **Hardware:** eight-screw white laminated plastic or anodized metal pickguard; two-pivot bridge/vibrato unit.
Custom Shop production.

CLASSIC '69 TELECASTER THINLINE (MIM) 1998–current

Replica of 1969-period original (see THINLINE TELECASTER FIRST VERSION 1968 listing).

CYCLONE (MIM) 1998–2006

Name on headstock, one angled single-coil and one humbucker.

- **Neck:** maple with rosewood fingerboard; 24.75-inch scale, 22 frets; truss-rod adjuster at headstock end; one string-guide.
- **Body:** contoured offset-waist; sunburst or colors.
- **Electronics:** one white six-polepiece pickup (angled at neck) and one white/black coverless humbucker (at bridge); two controls (volume, tone) and jack, all on metal plate adjoining pickguard; three-way selector on pickguard.
- **Hardware:** nine-screw white pearl laminated plastic pickguard; six-pivot bridge/vibrato unit.

DELUXE DOUBLE FAT STRAT FLOYD ROSE (MIM) 1998–2004

Two-pivot locking vibrato system, two black humbuckers, black pickguard, large headstock.
Similar to DELUXE FAT STRAT (see 1999 listing) except:
- **Neck:** single-bar string-guide; locking nut.
- **Electronics:** two black coverless humbuckers.
- **Hardware:** two-pivot locking bridge/vibrato unit.
Known as DELUXE DOUBLE FAT STRAT HH WITH LOCKING TREMOLO (see 2002 listing).
Known as DELUXE STRAT HH WITH LOCKING TREMOLO (see 2004 listing).

DELUXE FAT STRAT HSS FLOYD ROSE (MIM) 1998–2005

Two-pivot locking vibrato system, two black single-coils and one black humbucker, black pickguard, large headstock.
Similar to DELUXE FAT STRAT (see 1999 listing) except:
- **Neck:** single-bar string-guide; locking nut.
- **Hardware:** two-pivot locking bridge/vibrato unit.
Known as DELUXE FAT STRAT HSS WITH LOCKING TREMOLO (see 2002 listing).
Known as DELUXE STRAT HSS WITH LOCKING TREMOLO (see 2004 listing).

FLOYD ROSE CLASSIC STRAT HH 1998–2002

Two-pivot locking vibrato system, two humbuckers, three-screw fixing for each humbucker.
Similar to FLOYD ROSE CLASSIC STRAT HSS (see next listing) except:
- **Electronics:** two white coverless humbucker pickups.
Known as STRAT SPECIAL WITH LOCKING TREMOLO HH (see 2002 listing).

FLOYD ROSE CLASSIC STRAT HSS 1998–2002

Two-pivot locking vibrato system, two single-coils and one humbucker, three-screw fixing for humbucker.
Similar to FLOYD ROSE CLASSIC STRATOCASTER (see 1992 listing) except:
- **Hardware:** three-screw fixing for humbucker pickup; no curved-ends humbucker cut-out in pickguard.
Known as STRAT SPECIAL WITH LOCKING TREMOLO HSS (see 2002 listing).

JOHN JORGENSON TELECASTER 1998–2001

Signature on headstock.
- **Neck:** maple with rosewood or ebony fingerboard; 22 frets; truss-rod adjuster at headstock end; no string-guide; locking tuners; John Jorgenson signature on headstock.
- **Body:** slab single-cutaway, bound; black or sparkle colors.
- **Electronics:** two plain metal-cover pickups (at neck) and two black six-polepiece pickups (angled in bridgeplate); two controls (volume, tone) and five-way selector, all on metal plate adjoining pickguard; side-mounted jack.
- **Hardware:** eight-screw clear plastic pickguard; three-saddle raised-sides bridge with through-body stringing.
Custom Shop production.

MATTHIAS JABS STRATOCASTER (MIJ) 1998

Ringed planet position markers.
- **Neck:** maple with rosewood fingerboard, 'ringed planet' position markers; 22 frets; truss-rod

adjuster at headstock end; locking tuners; scroll inlay at 12th fret.
- **Body:** red only.
- **Electronics:** two white six-polepiece pickups and one white coverless humbucker (at bridge); three controls (two volume, tone) and five-way selector, all on pickguard; jack in body face.
- **Hardware:** 11-screw white plastic pickguard; six-pivot bridge/vibrato unit.

NASHVILLE B-BENDER TELE 1998–current
Additional center pickup, B-Bender string-bending device installed.
Similar to AMERICAN STANDARD B-BENDER TELECASTER (see 1995 listing) except:
- **Electronics:** one plain metal-cover pickup with visible height-adjustment screws (at neck), one white six-polepiece pickup (in center) and one black six-polepiece pickup (angled in bridgeplate); two controls (volume, tone) and five-way selector, all on metal plate adjoining pickguard.
- **Hardware:** eight-screw white pearloid laminated plastic pickguard.
Known as AMERICAN NASHVILLE B-BENDER TELE (see 2000 listing).

N.O.S. STRAT 1998
Replica of 1965-period original (see STRATOCASTER CBS SIXTIES 1965 listing). Custom Shop production.

RELIC FLOYD ROSE STRATOCASTER 1998
Two-pivot locking vibrato system, two white single-coils and one black humbucker, large headstock.
- **Neck:** fretted maple, or maple with rosewood fingerboard; truss-rod adjuster at body end; single-bar string-guide; locking nut; large headstock.
- **Body:** black or white, distressed finish.
- **Electronics:** two white six-polepiece pickups and one black coverless humbucker (at bridge); three controls (volume, two tone) and five-way selector, all on pickguard; jack in body face.
- **Hardware:** 11-screw white laminated plastic

pickguard; two-pivot locking bridge/vibrato unit.
Custom Shop production.

SHOWMASTER FMT 1998–2005
Model name on headstock, 22 frets, figured carved body top, two single-coils and one humbucker.
- **Neck:** fretted maple, or maple with rosewood fingerboard; 22 frets; truss-rod adjuster at headstock end; staggered height locking tuners; roller nut.
- **Body:** with figured carved top; sunburst or colors.
- **Electronics:** two black six-polepiece pickups and one black coverless humbucker (at bridge); two controls (volume, tone) and five-way selector, all on body; side-mounted jack.
- **Hardware:** no pickguard; two-pivot bridge/vibrato unit (or two-pivot locking bridge/vibrato unit 1998–99).
Custom Shop production.

STANDARD ROLAND READY STRAT (MIM) 1998–current
Six-pivot vibrato, one string-guide, extra slim white pickup at bridge.
Similar to STANDARD STRATOCASTER (see 1991 listing) except:
- **Neck:** maple with rosewood fingerboard only.
- **Electronics:** additional slim white plain-top Roland synthesizer pickup (at bridge); three controls (volume, tone, synth volume), five-way selector, two push-buttons and mini-switch, all on pickguard; jack in body face; side-mounted multi-pin synth output.

TELE-SONIC 1998–2004
Model name on headstock.
- **Neck:** maple with rosewood fingerboard; 24.75-inch scale, 22 frets; truss-rod adjuster at headstock end; one string-guide; black-face headstock.
- **Body:** semi-solid slab single-cutaway; sunburst or red.
- **Electronics:** two black-top six-polepiece pickups;

four controls (two volume, two tone) and three-way selector, all on body; side-mounted jack.

- **Hardware:** six-screw black laminated plastic pickguard; two-section wrapover bridge/tailpiece (six-saddle wrapover bridge/tailpiece from 2003).

TORONADO (MIM) 1998–2004

Model name on headstock, four controls, two metal-cover humbuckers.

- **Neck:** maple with rosewood fingerboard; 24.75-inch scale, 22 frets; truss-rod adjuster at headstock end; one string-guide.
- **Body:** contoured offset-waist; sunburst or colors.
- **Electronics:** two metal-cover humbuckers; four controls (two volume, two tone) on body; three-way selector on pickguard; side-mounted jack.
- **Hardware:** ten-screw tortoiseshell or white pearl laminated plastic pickguard; six-saddle bridge with through-body stringing.

U.S. FAT TELE 1998–2000

One humbucker and one single-coil, five-way selector.

Similar to AMERICAN STANDARD TELECASTER (see 1988 listing) except:

- **Electronics:** one metal-cover humbucker (at neck) and one black six-polepiece pickup (angled in bridgeplate); two controls (volume, tone) and four-way selector, all on metal plate adjoining pickguard.

Known as AMERICAN FAT TELE (see 2001 listing).

VOODOO STRATOCASTER 1998–2000

Large inverted headstock, reverse-angled bridge pickup, Jimi Hendrix image engraved neckplate.

- **Neck:** maple with maple or rosewood fingerboard; truss-rod adjuster at body end; one string-guide; Jimi Hendrix image engraved neckplate; large reverse headstock.
- **Body:** sunburst, black, or white.
- **Electronics:** three white six-polepiece pickups (bridge pickup reverse-angled); three controls (volume, two tone) and five-way selector, all on pickguard; jack in body face.

- **Hardware:** 11-screw white laminated plastic pickguard; six-pivot bridge/vibrato unit.

WILL RAY TELECASTER 1998–2001

Signature on headstock, skull markers.

- **Neck:** maple with rosewood fingerboard, skull markers; 22 frets; truss-rod adjuster at headstock end; one string-guide; locking tuners; Will Ray signature on small Stratocaster-style headstock.
- **Body:** slab single-cutaway; gold foil leaf on various colors.
- **Electronics:** two large rectangular white six-polepiece pickups (bridge pickup angled); three controls (volume, two tone) and three-way selector, all on metal plate adjoining pickguard; side-mounted jack.
- **Hardware:** eight-screw white pearl laminated plastic re-styled pickguard; modified three-saddle bridge with through-body stringing; optional Hipshot bending device on second string.

Custom Shop production.

YNGWIE MALMSTEEN STRATOCASTER (second version) 1998–2006

Signature on large headstock, six-pivot vibrato.

Similar to YNGWIE MALMSTEEN STRATOCASTER FIRST VERSION (see 1988 listing) except:

- **Neck:** Yngwie Malmsteen signature on large headstock.
- **Electronics:** three controls (volume, two tone) and three-way selector, all on pickguard.
- **Hardware:** six-pivot bridge/vibrato unit.

1998 COLLECTORS EDITION TELECASTER 1998

Commemorative fingerboard inlay and neckplate.

Similar to 50s TELECASTER (see 1996 listing) except:

- **Neck:** fretted maple with commemorative inlay at 12th fret; commemorative neckplate.
- **Body:** sunburst only.
- **Hardware:** gold-plated; five-screw white plastic pickguard.

Numbered factory production run of 1,998.

1999

GUITARS

AMERICAN CLASSIC TELECASTER (second version) 1999–2000

Two single-coils, inverted control plate, three-way selector.

Similar to AMERICAN CLASSIC TELECASTER FIRST VERSION (see 1995 listing) except:

- **Electronics:** one plain metal-cover pickup with visible height-adjustment screws (at neck) and one black six-polepiece pickup (angled in bridgeplate); two controls (volume, tone) and three-way selector, all on inverted metal plate adjoining pickguard.
- **Hardware:** eight-screw white laminated plastic pickguard.

Custom Shop production.

AMERICAN DELUXE POWER TELE 1999–2001

Contoured bound body, two dual-concentric controls.

Similar to AMERICAN DELUXE TELECASTER SECOND VERSION (see next listing) except:

- **Electronics:** two dual-concentric controls (volume, tone for magnetic and piezo pickups), three-way selector and mini-switch, all on metal plate adjoining pickguard.
- **Hardware:** Fishman Power Bridge with six piezo-pickup saddles.

AMERICAN DELUXE TELECASTER (second version) 1999–2003

Contoured bound body, 22 frets, two single-coils.

Similar to AMERICAN DELUXE TELECASTER FIRST VERSION (see 1998 listing) except:

- **Electronics:** one plain metal-cover pickup with visible height-adjustment screws (at neck) and one black six-polepiece pickup (angled in bridgeplate); two controls (volume, tone) and three-way selector, all on metal plate adjoining pickguard.

AMERICAN VINTAGE '52 TELE SPECIAL 1999–2001

Replica of 1952-period original (see TELECASTER 1951 listing). Body sunburst only, gold-plated hardware.

AMERICAN VINTAGE '62 CUSTOM TELECASTER 1999–current

Replica of 1962-period original with bound body (see TELECASTER 1951 listing).

AMERICAN VINTAGE '62 JAGUAR 1999–current

Replica of 1962-period original (see 1962 listing).

AMERICAN VINTAGE '62 JAZZMASTER 1999–current

Replica of 1962-period original (see 1958 listing).

CHRIS REA CLASSIC STRATOCASTER (MIM) 1999

Signature on headstock.

Similar to CLASSIC 60S STRATOCASTER (see below) but:

- **Neck:** Chris Rea signature on headstock.
- **Body:** red only.

CLASSIC 50s STRATOCASTER (MIM) 1999–current

Replica of 1950s-period original (see STRATOCASTER PRE CBS 1954 listing).

CLASSIC 50s TELECASTER (MIM) 1999–2006

Replica of 1950s-period original (see TELECASTER 1951 listing).

CLASSIC 60s STRATOCASTER (MIM) 1999–current

Replica of 1960s-period original (see STRATOCASTER PRE CBS 1954 listing).

CLASSIC 70s STRATOCASTER (MIM) 1999–current

Replica of 1970s-period original (see STRATOCASTER CBS SEVENTIES 1971 listing).

CLASSIC '72 TELECASTER CUSTOM (MIM) 1999–current

Replica of 1972-period original (see entry in 1972 listing).

CLASSIC '72 TELECASTER THINLINE (MIM) 1999–current

Replica of 1972-period original (see entry in 1971 listing).

CUSTOM CLASSIC STRAT 1999–current

22 frets, Custom Shop headstock logo, two-pivot vibrato, three white single-coils.
Similar to AMERICAN STANDARD STRATOCASTER (see 1986 listing) except:
• **Neck:** Custom Shop logo on headstock.
Custom Shop production.

DELUXE DOUBLE FAT STRAT (MIM) 1999–2004

Two-pivot vibrato, two black humbuckers, black pickguard, large headstock.
Similar to DELUXE FAT STRAT (see next listing) except:
• **Electronics:** two black coverless humbuckers.
Known as DELUXE DOUBLE FAT STRAT HH (see 2002 listing).
Known as DELUXE STRAT HH (see 2004 listing).

DELUXE FAT STRAT (MIM) 1999–2006

Two-pivot vibrato, two black single-coils and one black humbucker, black pickguard, large headstock.
• **Neck:** maple with rosewood fingerboard; truss-rod adjuster at headstock end; one string-guide; large headstock.
• **Body:** black or white.
• **Electronics:** two black six-polepiece pickups and one black coverless humbucker (at bridge); three controls (volume, two tone) and five-way selector, all on pickguard; jack in body face.
• **Hardware:** 11-screw black laminated plastic pickguard; six-pivot bridge/vibrato unit.
Known as DELUXE FAT STRAT HSS (see 2002 listing).
Known as DELUXE STRAT HSS (see 2004 listing).

DELUXE NASHVILLE POWER TELE (MIM) 1999–current

White six-polepiece pickup in center position, one dual-concentric control.
Similar to DELUXE NASHVILLE TELE (see 1997 listing) except:
• **Electronics:** one dual-concentric control (volume, tone for magnetic pickups), one regular control (volume for piezo pickups) plus one five-way selector.
• **Hardware:** Fishman Power Bridge with six piezo-pickup saddles.

RICHIE SAMBORA STRATOCASTER (second version) 1999–2002

Star position markers, three Noiseless logo white pickups.
• **Neck:** fretted maple, star position markers; 22 frets; truss-rod adjuster at headstock end.
• **Body:** sunburst, red, or white.
• **Electronics:** three Noiseless logo white six-polepiece pickups (bridge pickup angled); three controls (volume, two tone), five-way selector and push-switch, all on pickguard; jack in body face; active circuit.
• **Hardware:** 11-screw white laminated plastic pickguard; six-pivot bridge/vibrato unit.

RITCHIE BLACKMORE STRATOCASTER 1999–2005

Signature on headstock, two white plain-top pickups.
• **Neck:** maple glued-in, with rosewood fingerboard, with scalloping between frets; 22 frets; 'bullet' truss-rod adjuster at headstock end; locking tuners; Ritchie Blackmore signature on large headstock.
• **Body:** white only.
• **Electronics:** two white plain-top Lace Sensor pickups (bridge pickup angled); three controls (volume, two tone) and five-way selector, all on pickguard; jack in body face.
• **Hardware:** 11-screw white laminated plastic or anodized metal pickguard; two-pivot

bridge/vibrato unit.
Roland GK-2 synth pickup system option.
Custom Shop production.

SHOWMASTER SET NECK FMT 1999–2005

Model name on headstock, 22 frets, glued-in neck, two single-soils and one humbucker.
Similar to SHOWMASTER FMT (see previous listing) except:
- **Neck:** maple glued-in, with rosewood fingerboard only.
- **Hardware:** two-pivot locking bridge/vibrato unit only.
Custom Shop production.

SHOWMASTER SET NECK FMT HARD-TAIL 1999–2005

Model name on headstock, 22-frets, glued-in neck, two-section wrapover bridge/tailpiece.
Similar to SHOWMASTER SET NECK FMT (see previous listing) except:
- **Hardware:** no roller nut; two-section wrapover bridge/tailpiece.
Custom Shop production.

SHOWMASTER STANDARD 1999–2005

Model name on headstock, 22 frets, carved body top.
Similar to SHOWMASTER FMT (see 1998 listing) except:
- **Body:** with carved top; various colors.
- **Hardware:** two-pivot bridge/vibrato unit only.
Custom Shop production.

STANDARD FAT STRAT (MIM) 1999–current

Modern-style 'thick' Fender headstock logo in silver, two single-coils and one humbucker, six-pivot vibrato.
Similar to STANDARD STRATOCASTER (see 1991 listing) except:
- **Electronics:** two white six-polepiece pickups and one white coverless humbucker (at bridge).
Known as STANDARD STRATOCASTER HSS (see 2004 listing).

STANDARD FAT STRAT FLOYD ROSE (MIM) 1999–current

Two-pivot locking vibrato system, two white single-coils and one white humbucker, white pickguard, small headstock, three controls.
Similar to STANDARD STRATOCASTER (see 1991 listing) except:
- **Neck:** maple with rosewood fingerboard only; single-bar string-guide; locking nut.
- **Electronics:** two white six-polepiece pickups and one white coverless humbucker (at bridge); two-pivot locking bridge/vibrato unit.
Known as STANDARD FAT STRAT WITH LOCKING TREMOLO (see 2002 listing).
Known as STANDARD STRATOCASTER HSS WITH LOCKING TREMOLO (see 2004 listing).

'51 NOCASTER 1999–current

Replica of 1951-period original with no model name on headstock (see TELECASTER 1951 listing). Offered with three finish distress degrees: N.O.S., Closet Classic and Relic. Custom Shop production.

'56 STRATOCASTER 1999–current

Replica of 1956-period original (see STRATOCASTER PRE-CBS 1954 listing). Available with three finish distress degrees: N.O.S., Closet Classic, and Relic. Gold-plated hardware option. Custom Shop production.

'60 STRATOCASTER (second version) 1999–current

Revised replica of 1960-period original (see STRATOCASTER PRE-CBS 1954 listing). Available with three finish distress degrees: N.O.S., Closet Classic, and Relic. Gold-plated hardware option. Custom Shop production.

'63 TELECASTER 1999–current

Replica of 1963-period original (see TELECASTER 1951 listing). Offered with three finish distress degrees: N.O.S., Closet Classic, and Relic. Custom Shop production.

'69 STRATOCASTER (second version) 1999–current

Revised replica of 1969-period original (see STRATOCASTER CBS SIXTIES 1965 listing). Available with three finish distress degrees: N.O.S., Closet Classic, and Relic. Custom Shop production.

AMPLIFIERS

CHAMPION 30 (MII) 1999–current

Smallest amp in Dyna-Touch solid-state line, in 2004 graduated to Dyna-Touch III as the CHAMPION 300.
- **Cabinet:** black Tolex.
- **Controls:** volume; gain, volume; treble, mid, bass, fx level, fx select (for digital effects); black control panel.
- **Speakers:** 1x10 special design.
- **Output:** 30 watts.

DELUXE 90 (MII) 1999–current

Mid-sized member of the Dyna-Touch solid-state line, in 2004 graduated to Dyna-Touch III as the DELUXE 900.
- **Cabinet:** black Tolex.
- **Controls:** ch 1: volume, treble, mid, bass; ch 2: drive 1, volume 1, drive 2, volume 2, treble, mid, bass; tuner and fx select (for digital effects); black control panel.
- **Speakers:** 1x12 special design Celestion.
- **Output:** 90 watts.

PRINCETON 65 (MII) 1999–current

Mid-sized member of the Dyna-Touch solid-state line, in 2004 graduated to Dyna-Touch III as the PRINCETON 650.
- **Cabinet:** black Tolex.
- **Controls:** ch 1: volume, treble, bass; ch 2: drive, volume, treble, mid, bass; tuner and fx select (for digital effects); black control panel.
- **Speakers:** 1x12 special design Celestion.
- **Output:** 65 watts.

STAGE 100 (MII) 1999–current

Larger member of the Dyna-Touch solid-state line, in 2004 graduated to Dyna-Touch III as the STAGE 1000.
- **Cabinet:** black Tolex.
- **Controls:** ch 1: volume, treble, mid, bass; ch 2: drive 1, volume 1, drive 2, volume 2, treble, mid, bass; tuner and fx select (for digital effects); black control panel.
- **Speakers:** 1x12 special design Celestion.
- **Output:** 100 watts (160 watts with extension speaker cab).

STAGE 160 (MII) 1999–current

Larger member of the Dyna-Touch solid-state line, in 2004 graduated to Dyna-Touch III as the STAGE 1000.
- **Cabinet:** black Tolex.
- **Controls:** ch 1: volume, treble, mid, bass; ch 2: drive 1, volume 1, drive 2, volume 2, treble, mid, bass; tuner and fx select (for digital effects); black control panel.
- **Speakers:** 2x12 special design Celestion.
- **Output:** 160 watts.

WOODY JUNIOR 1999–2001

Also available as WOODY JUNIOR ASH and WOODY JUNIOR EXOTIC. Custom Shop version of BLUES JUNIOR (see 1995 listing) using same electronics except:
- **Cabinet:** custom finished hardwood cabinet.

WOODY PRO 1999–2001

Also available as WOODY JUNIOR ASH and WOODY JUNIOR EXOTIC. Custom Shop version of PRO JUNIOR (see entry in 1994 listing) using same electronics except:
- **Cabinet:** custom finished hardwood cabinet.

2000

GUITARS

AMERICAN DOUBLE FAT STRAT 2000–03

White pearl or tortoiseshell pickguard, two Seymour Duncan-logo white humbuckers.

Similar to AMERICAN STRATOCASTER (see 2000 listing) except:

- **Electronics:** two Seymour Duncan-logo white coverless humbuckers.
- **Hardware:** 11-screw white pearl or tortoiseshell laminated plastic pickguard.

AMERICAN DOUBLE FAT STRAT HARD-TAIL 2000–03

One string-guide, white pearl or tortoiseshell pickguard, two Seymour Duncan-logo white humbuckers, six-saddle bridge with through-body stringing.

Similar to AMERICAN STRATOCASTER (see 2000 listing) except:

- **Electronics:** two Seymour Duncan-logo white coverless humbuckers.
- **Hardware:** 11-screw white pearl or tortoiseshell laminated plastic pickguard; six-saddle small bridge with through-body stringing.

AMERICAN FAT STRAT TEXAS SPECIAL 2000–03

White pearl or tortoiseshell pickguard, two white single-coils and one Seymour Duncan-logo white humbucker.

Similar to AMERICAN STRATOCASTER (see 2000 listing) except:

- **Electronics:** two white six-polepiece pickups and one Seymour Duncan-logo white coverless humbucker (at bridge).
- **Hardware:** 11-screw white pearl or tortoiseshell laminated plastic pickguard.

AMERICAN NASHVILLE B-BENDER TELE 2000–current

Another Name For NASHVILLE B-BENDER TELE (see 1998 listing).

AMERICAN STRAT TEXAS SPECIAL 2000–03

White pearl or tortoiseshell pickguard, three white single-coils.

Similar to AMERICAN STRATOCASTER (see 2000 listing) except:

- **Hardware:** 11-screw white pearl or tortoiseshell laminated plastic pickguard.

Fitted with different-specification but visually similar pickups.

AMERICAN STRATOCASTER 2000–current

22 frets, small headstock, one string-guide, four-screw neckplate, three controls.

- **Neck:** fretted maple, or maple with rosewood fingerboard; 22 frets; truss-rod adjuster at headstock end; staggered height tuners; one string-guide.
- **Body:** sunburst or colors.
- **Electronics:** three white six-polepiece pickups (bridge pickup angled); three controls (volume, two tone) and five-way selector, all on pickguard; jack in body face.
- **Hardware:** 11-screw white laminated plastic pickguard; two-pivot bridge/vibrato unit.

AMERICAN STRATOCASTER HARD-TAIL 2000–06

22 frets, small headstock, one string-guide, four-screw neckplate, three controls, six-saddle bridge with through-body stringing.

Similar to AMERICAN STRATOCASTER (see previous listing) except:

- **Hardware:** six-saddle small bridge with through-body stringing.

AMERICAN TELECASTER 2000–current

Succeeded AMERICAN STANDARD TELECASTER (see 1988 listing).

CLASSIC ROCKER 2000–02

Hollow single-cutaway body, two pickups, Bigsby vibrato tailpiece.

- **Neck:** maple glued-in, with bound rosewood fingerboard, diamond markers; truss-rod adjuster at headstock end; three-tuners-per-side headstock.
- **Body:** hollow single-cutaway bound, with bound f-holes; black or red.

- **Electronics:** two white-top six-polepiece pickups; four controls (three volume, one tone) and three-way selector, all on body; side-mounted jack.
- **Hardware:** white plastic pickguard; six-saddle metal-top bridge, Bigsby vibrato tailpiece.

Custom Shop production.

CUSTOM CLASSIC TELECASTER 2000–06

Two single-coils, inverted control plate, four-way selector.

Similar to AMERICAN CLASSIC TELECASTER SECOND VERSION (see 1999 listing) except:

- **Electronics:** two controls (volume, tone) and four-way selector, all on inverted metal plate adjoining pickguard.

Custom Shop production.

HANK MARVIN CLASSIC STRATOCASTER (MIM) 2000

Signature on headstock.

Similar to CLASSIC 50S STRATOCASTER (see 1999 listing) except:

- **Neck:** Hank Marvin signature on headstock.
- **Body:** red only.
- **Hardware:** six-pivot bridge/vibrato unit with special design vibrato arm.

Limited edition of 250.

SHOWMASTER 7-STRING 2000–01

Model name on seven-string headstock.

Similar to SHOWMASTER FMT (see 1998 listing) except:

- **Neck:** maple with rosewood fingerboard only; no roller nut; seven-string headstock.
- **Body:** with carved top; various colors.
- **Hardware:** two-pivot bridge/vibrato unit only.

SHOWMASTER 7-STRING HARD-TAIL 2000–01

Model name on seven-string headstock, six-saddle bridge.

Similar to SHOWMASTER FMT (see 1998 listing) except:

- **Hardware:** two-section wrapover bridge/tailpiece.

SUB-SONIC STRATOCASTER HH baritone 2000–01

Sub-Sonic on headstock, long-scale neck, white pearl pickguard, two humbuckers.

Similar to SUB-SONIC STRATOCASTER HSS BARITONE FIRST VERSION (see next listing) except:

- **Electronics:** two white coverless humbuckers.

Custom Shop production.

SUB-SONIC STRATOCASTER HSS baritone (first version) 2000–01

'Sub-Sonic' on headstock, long-scale neck, white pearl pickguard, two Noiseless logo single-coils and one humbucker.

- **Neck:** fretted maple, or maple with rosewood fingerboard; 27-inch scale, 22 frets; truss-rod adjuster at body end; one string-guide; 'Sub-Sonic' on headstock.
- **Body:** sunburst or colors.
- **Electronics:** two Noiseless logo white six-polepiece pickups and one white coverless humbucker (at bridge); three controls (volume, two tone) and five-way selector, all on pickguard; jack in body face.
- **Hardware:** 11-screw white pearl laminated plastic pickguard; six-saddle small bridge with through-body stringing.

Custom Shop production.

2001

GUITARS

AMERICAN FAT TELE 2001–03

Another name for U.S. FAT TELE (see 1998 listing).

CLASSIC 60s TELECASTER (MIM) 2001–current

Replica of 1960s-period original (see TELECASTER 1951 listing).

ERIC CLAPTON STRATOCASTER (second version) 2001–current

Signature on headstock, three Noiseless logo white

pickups, active circuit.

Similar to ERIC CLAPTON STRATOCASTER FIRST VERSION (see 1988 listing) except:

- **Electronics:** three Noiseless logo white six-polepiece pickups.

IRON MAIDEN SIGNATURE STRATOCASTER (MIJ) 2001–02

Iron Maiden on headstock.

- **Neck:** fretted maple only; 22 frets; truss-rod adjuster at headstock end; single-bar string-guide; locking nut; Iron Maiden on headstock.
- **Body:** black only.
- **Electronics:** two black twin-blade humbuckers and one small black 12-polepiece humbucker (angled at bridge); three controls (volume, two tone) and five-way selector, all on pickguard; jack in body face.
- **Hardware:** 11-screw mirror plastic pickguard; two-pivot locking bridge/vibrato unit.

JEFF BECK STRATOCASTER (second version) 2001–current

Signature on headstock, three Noiseless logo white pickups.

Similar to JEFF BECK STRATOCASTER FIRST VERSION (see 1991 listing) except:

- **Body:** green or white.
- **Electronics:** three Noiseless logo white six-polepiece pickups (bridge pickup angled); three controls (volume, two tone), five-way selector and push-switch, all on pickguard; jack in body face.

MUDDY WATERS TELECASTER (MIM) 2001–current

Custom Telecaster on headstock, amplifier-type black plastic control knobs.

Similar to CLASSIC 60s TELECASTER (see 1999 listing) except:

- **Neck:** Custom Telecaster on headstock.
- **Body:** red only.
- **Hardware:** nine-screw white plastic pickguard; amplifier-type black plastic control knobs.

SUB-SONIC STRATOCASTER HSS baritone (second version) 2001

'Sub-Sonic' on headstock, long-scale neck, white pickguard, two single-coils and one humbucker.

- **Neck:** fretted maple, or maple with rosewood fingerboard; 27-inch scale, 22 frets; truss-rod adjuster at body end; one string-guide.
- **Body:** sunburst or colors.
- **Electronics:** two white six-polepiece pickups and one white coverless humbucker (at bridge); three controls (volume, two tone) and five-way selector, all on pickguard; jack in body face.
- **Hardware:** 11-screw white laminated plastic pickguard; six-saddle small bridge with through-body stringing.

SUB-SONIC TELE baritone 2001–05

Sub-Sonic on headstock, long-scale neck.

- **Neck:** fretted maple; 27-inch scale, 22 frets; truss-rod adjuster at body end; one string-guide; Sub-Sonic on headstock.
- **Body:** slab single-cutaway; sunburst or colors.
- **Electronics:** one plain metal cover pickup (at neck) and one black six-polepiece pickup (angled in bridgeplate); two controls (volume, tone) and four-way selector, all on metal plate adjoining pickguard; side-mounted jack.
- **Hardware:** eight-screw white laminated plastic pickguard; six-saddle bridge with through-body stringing.

Custom Shop production.

TOM DELONGE STRATOCASTER (MIM) 2001–03

One humbucker, one control.

- **Neck:** maple with rosewood fingerboard; truss-rod adjuster at headstock end; one string-guide; large headstock; Tom Delonge engraved neckplate.
- **Body:** various colors.
- **Electronics:** one white coverless humbucker (at bridge); one control (volume) on pickguard; jack in body face.
- **Hardware:** 11-screw white or white pearl

laminated plastic pickguard; six-saddle small bridge with through-body stringing.

AMPLIFIERS

CYBER-TWIN (MIM) 2001–current

Having had its classic amps featured on so many other digital amp makers' simulation menus, Fender entered the modeling amp arena in its own right. This is the original model; it was followed by the later SE.
- **Cabinet:** black Tolex.
- **Controls:** trim, gain, volume, treble, middle, bass, presence, reverb, master, Dynamic Data Wheel for amp menu selection, assorted pushbuttons; double-height black control panel.
- **Speakers:** 2x12 Celestion G12T-100.
- **Hybrid design:** 2x12AX7 in preamp, digital amp emulations and effects, solid-state output stage.
- **Output:** 2x65 watts stereo.

'65 SUPER REVERB 2001–current

Replica of the original blackface SUPER REVERB circa 1963–65 (see 1963 listing). A printed circuit board is used rather than the original hand-wired eyelet board.

2002

GUITARS

BUDDY GUY POLKA DOT STRAT (MIM) 2002–current

Signature on headstock, black/white polka dot body finish.
Similar to STANDARD STRATOCASTER (see 1991 listing) except:
- **Neck:** Buddy Guy signature on headstock.
- **Body:** black/white polka dot finish only.
- **Electronics:** three black six-polepiece pickups.
- **Hardware:** eight-screw black laminated plastic pickguard.

COMPETITION MUSTANG (MIJ) 2002–03

Reproduction of 24-inch scale MUSTANG (see 1964 listing) except:

- **Body:** stripes on body.

CYCLONE II (MIM) 2002–2006

Name on headstock, three angled single-coils.
Similar to CYCLONE (see 1998 listing) except:
- **Body:** blue or red, with stripes.
- **Electronics:** three rectangular white six-polepiece pickups, each with metal 'sawtooth' sides, all angled; two controls (volume, tone) and jack, all on metal plate adjoining pickguard; three slide-switches on metal plate inset into pickguard.

DELUXE DOUBLE FAT STRAT HH (MIM) 2002–03

Another name for DELUXE DOUBLE FAT STRAT (see 1999 listing).

DELUXE DOUBLE FAT STRAT HH WITH LOCKING TREMOLO (MIM) 2002–03

Another name for DELUXE DOUBLE FAT STRAT FLOYD ROSE (see 1998 listing).

DELUXE FAT STRAT HSS (MIM) 2002–03

Another name for DELUXE FAT STRAT HSS (see 1999 listing).

DELUXE FAT STRAT HSS WITH LOCKING TREMOLO (MIM) 2002–03

Another name for DELUXE FAT STRAT HSS FLOYD ROSE (see 1998 listing).

HIGHWAY ONE STRATOCASTER (first version) 2002–06

Satin body finish, white pickguard, three white single-coils, small headstock.
- **Neck:** fretted maple, or maple with rosewood fingerboard; 22 frets; truss-rod adjuster at headstock end; two string-guides.
- **Body:** various colors, satin finish.
- **Electronics:** three white six-polepiece pickups (bridge pickup angled); three controls (volume, two tone) and five-way selector, all on pickguard; jack in body face.

- **Hardware:** 11-screw white laminated plastic pickguard; six-pivot bridge/vibrato unit.

HIGHWAY ONE TELECASTER (first version) 2002–06

Satin finish, 22 frets, five-screw pickguard.

- **Neck:** fretted maple, or maple with rosewood fingerboard; 22 frets; truss-rod adjuster at headstock end; one string-guide.
- **Body:** slab single-cutaway; sunburst or colors, satin finish.
- **Electronics:** one plain metal-cover pickup (at neck) and one black six-polepiece pickup (angled in bridgeplate); two controls (volume, tone) and three-way selector, all of which are situated on the metal plate that adjoins the pickguard; side-mounted jack.
- **Hardware:** five-screw white plastic pickguard; three-saddle raised-sides bridge with through-body stringing.

STANDARD FAT STRAT WITH LOCKING TREMOLO (MIM) 2002–03

Another name for STANDARD FAT STRAT FLOYD ROSE (see 1999 listing).

STRAT SPECIAL WITH LOCKING TREMOLO HH 2002

Another name for FLOYD ROSE CLASSIC STRAT HH (see 1998 listing).

STRAT SPECIAL WITH LOCKING TREMOLO HSS 2002

Another name for FLOYD ROSE CLASSIC STRAT HSS (see 1998 listing).

TORONADO DVII 2002–04

Model name on black-face headstock, four controls, two black six-polepiece pickups.

- **Neck:** maple with rosewood fingerboard; 24-inch scale, 22 frets; truss-rod adjuster at headstock end; one string-guide; black-face headstock.
- **Body:** contoured offset-waist; blonde or red.

- **Electronics:** two large black six-polepiece pickups; four controls (two volume, two tone) and three-way selector, all on body; side-mounted jack.
- **Hardware:** seven-screw black laminated plastic pickguard; six-saddle bridge, bar tailpiece.

TORONADO HH 2002–04

Model name on black-face headstock, four controls, two black coverless humbuckers.
Similar to TORONADO DVII (see previous listing) except:

- **Electronics:** two black coverless humbuckers.

'68 REVERSE STRAT SPECIAL 2002

Large inverted headstock, reverse-angled bridge pickup.

- **Neck:** maple with maple fingerboard; truss-rod adjuster at body end; one string-guide; large reverse headstock.
- **Body:** sunburst, black, or white.
- **Electronics:** three white six-polepiece pickups (bridge pickup reverse-angled); three controls (volume, two tone) and five-way selector, all on pickguard; jack in body face.
- **Hardware:** 11-screw white laminated plastic pickguard; six-pivot bridge/vibrato unit.

AMPLIFIERS

CYBER-DELUXE (MIM) 2002–2006

Smaller sibling to Fender's flagship modeling amp, the CYBER-TWIN.

- **Cabinet:** black Tolex.
- **Controls:** trim, gain, volume, treble, middle, bass, presence, reverb, master; three two-knob segments for reverb, mod f/x, delay; amp type; Dynamic Data Wheel for amp menu selection, assorted pushbuttons; double-height black control panel.
- **Speakers:** 1x12 Celestion G12T-100.
- **Solid state** incorporating digital models and effects.
- **Output:** 65 watts.

2003

GUITARS

AMERICAN ASH TELECASTER 2003–current
Five-screw pickguard, 22 frets.
Similar to AMERICAN TELECASTER (see 2000 listing) except:
- **Neck:** fretted maple only.
- **Body:** sunburst or blonde.
- **Hardware:** five-screw white or black plastic pickguard.

AMERICAN STRATOCASTER HH 2003–06
One string-guide, black pickguard, two black humbuckers.
Similar to AMERICAN STRATOCASTER (see 2000 listing) except:
- **Electronics:** two black coverless humbuckers; three controls (volume with push switch, two tone) and five-way selector, all on pickguard.
- **Hardware:** 11-screw black laminated plastic pickguard.

AMERICAN STRATOCASTER HH HARD-TAIL 2003–05
One string-guide, black pickguard, two black humbuckers, six-saddle bridge with through-body stringing.
Similar to AMERICAN STRATOCASTER (see 2000 listing) except:
- **Electronics:** two black coverless humbuckers; three controls (volume with push switch, two tone) and five-way selector, all on pickguard.
- **Hardware:** 11-screw black laminated plastic pickguard; six-saddle small bridge with through-body stringing.

AMERICAN STRATOCASTER HSS 2003–current
One string-guide, black pickguard, two black single-coils and one black humbucker.
Similar to AMERICAN STRATOCASTER (see 2000 listing) except:

- **Electronics:** two black six-polepiece pickups and one black coverless humbucker (at bridge); three controls (volume with push switch, two tone) and five-way selector, all on pickguard.
- **Hardware:** 11-screw black laminated plastic pickguard.

AMERICAN TELECASTER HH (first version) 2003–04
Two black coverless humbuckers, no pickguard.
Similar to AMERICAN TELECASTER HS (see following listing) except:
- **Electronics:** two black coverless humbuckers.
- **Hardware:** six-saddle small bridge with through-body stringing.

AMERICAN TELECASTER HS (first version) 2003–04
Coverless black humbucker at neck, no pickguard.
- **Neck:** fretted maple , or maple with rosewood fingerboard; 22 frets; truss-rod adjuster at headstock end; one string-guide.
- **Body:** slab single-cutaway; various colors.
- **Electronics:** one black coverless humbucker (at neck) and one black six-polepiece pickup (angled in bridgeplate); two controls (volume, tone) and three-way selector, all on metal plate; side-mounted jack.
- **Hardware:** no pickguard; six-saddle flat bridge with through-body stringing.

BLUE FLOWER STRATOCASTER (second version) (MIJ) 2003
Blue floral-pattern body finish, small headstock.
Similar to BLUE FLOWER STRATOCASTER FIRST VERSION (see 1988 listing) except:
- **Neck:** small headstock; truss-rod adjuster at body end.

CUSTOM TELECASTER FMT HH (MIK) 2003–04
Glued-in neck, bound body with figured top.
- **Neck:** maple glued-in, with bound rosewood

fingerboard; 22 frets; truss-rod adjuster at headstock end; two string-guides.
- **Body:** single-cutaway bound; figured top; various colors.
- **Electronics:** two black coverless humbuckers; two controls (volume, tone with pull switch) and three-way selector, all on body; side-mounted jack.
- **Hardware:** smoked-chrome-plated; no pickguard; six-saddle small bridge with through-body stringing.

CYCLONE HH (MIM) 2003–05
Name on headstock, two humbuckers.
Similar to CYCLONE (see 1998 listing) except:
- **Electronics:** two black coverless humbuckers.
- **Hardware:** nine-screw white pearl or black laminated plastic pickguard.

ESQUIRE CUSTOM CELTIC (MIK) 2003
Celtic design inlay at 12th fret, single-cutaway body.
- **Neck:** mahogany glued-in, with rosewood fingerboard; 22 frets; truss-rod adjuster at headstock end; two string-guides; no front markers except Celtic design inlay at 12th fret.
- **Body:** single-cutaway, contoured; silver only, satin finish.
- **Electronics:** one black coverless humbucker (at bridge); one control (volume) on body; side-mounted jack.
- **Hardware:** black-plated; no pickguard; six-saddle small bridge with through-body stringing.

ESQUIRE CUSTOM GT (MIK) 2003
Center striped single cutaway body.
- **Neck:** mahogany glued-in, with bound rosewood fingerboard; 22 frets; truss-rod adjuster at headstock end; two string-guides.
- **Body:** single-cutaway, contoured, bound; blue, red, or silver, with center stripes.
- **Electronics:** one black coverless humbucker (at bridge); one control (volume) on body; side-mounted jack.

- **Hardware:** black-plated; no pickguard; six-saddle small bridge with through-body stringing.

ESQUIRE CUSTOM SCORPION (MIK) 2003
Scorpion inlay at 12th fret, single-cutaway body.
- **Neck:** mahogany glued-in, with bound rosewood fingerboard; 22 frets; truss-rod adjuster at headstock end; two string-guides; no front markers except Scorpion inlay at 12th fret.
- **Body:** single-cutaway, contoured, bound; black only.
- **Electronics:** one black coverless humbucker (at bridge); one control (volume) on body; side-mounted jack.
- **Hardware:** black-plated; no pickguard; six-saddle small bridge with through-body stringing.

FLAT HEAD SHOWMASTER 2003–04
Name on headstock, 22 frets, one humbucker.
- **Neck:** maple with ebony fingerboard; 22 frets; truss-rod adjuster at headstock end; staggered height locking tuners; no position markers except 'crossed pistons' inlay at 12th fret; Flat Head on headstock.
- **Body:** various colors.
- **Electronics:** one black coverless humbucker; one control (volume) on body; side-mounted jack.
- **Hardware:** black-plated; no pickguard; six-saddle small bridge with through-body stringing.
Custom Shop production.

FLAT HEAD TELECASTER 2003–04
Name on headstock, 22 frets, one humbucker, single-cutaway body.
- **Neck:** maple with ebony fingerboard; 22 frets; truss-rod adjuster at headstock end; staggered height locking tuners; no position markers except 'crossed pistons' inlay at 12th fret; Flat Head on headstock.
- **Body:** single-cutaway slab; various colors.
- **Electronics:** one black coverless humbucker; one control (volume) on body; side-mounted jack.

- **Hardware:** black-plated; no pickguard; six-saddle small bridge that incorporates through-body stringing.

Custom Shop production.

FRANCIS ROSSI SIGNATURE TELECASTER 2003–04

Signature on headstock.

- **Neck:** fretted maple; truss-rod adjuster at body end; one string-guide; Francis Rossi signature on headstock.
- **Body:** slab single-cutaway, with circular hole; black with green front only, satin finish.
- **Electronics:** three white plain-top pickups (bridge pickup angled in cut-down bridgeplate); two controls (volume, tone) and five-way selector, all on metal plate adjoining pickguard; side-mounted jack.
- **Hardware:** eight-screw white laminated plastic pickguard; six-saddle small bridge with through-body stringing.

HIGHWAY ONE SHOWMASTER HH 2003–04

Name on headstock, 24 frets, two humbuckers.

- **Neck:** maple with rosewood fingerboard; 24 frets; truss-rod adjuster at headstock end; single-bar string-guide; locking nut.
- **Body:** black, pewter, or silver, satin finish.
- **Electronics:** two black coverless humbuckers; two controls (volume, tone) and three-way selector, all situated on the guitar's body; side-mounted jack.
- **Hardware:** No pickguard; two-pivot locking bridge/vibrato unit.

HIGHWAY ONE SHOWMASTER HSS 2003–04

Name on headstock, 24 frets, two single-coils and one humbucker.

Similar to HIGHWAY ONE SHOWMASTER HH (see previous listing) except:

- **Electronics:** two black six-polepiece pickups and one black coverless humbucker; two controls (volume, tone) and five-way selector, all on body.

HIGHWAY ONE STRATOCASTER HSS (first version) 2003–06

Satin body finish, large headstock, white pickguard, two white single-coils and one black humbucker.

Similar to HIGHWAY ONE STRATOCASTER FIRST VERSION (see 2002 listing) except:

- **Neck:** maple with rosewood fingerboard only; large headstock.
- **Electronics:** two white six-polepiece pickups and one black coverless humbucker (at bridge).

HIGHWAY ONE TEXAS TELECASTER 2003–current

Satin finish, 21 frets.

Similar to HIGHWAY ONE TELECASTER FIRST VERSION (see 2002 listing) except:

- **Neck:** fretted maple only; 21 frets.
- **Body:** sunburst or blonde, satin finish.

HIGHWAY ONE TORONADO 2003–04

Model name on headstock, two controls, two black coverless humbuckers.

- **Neck:** maple with rosewood fingerboard; 24.75-inch scale, 22 frets; truss-rod adjuster at headstock end; one string-guide.
- **Body:** contoured offset-waist; black, pewter or silver, satin finish.
- **Electronics:** two black coverless humbuckers; two controls (volume, tone) and three-way selector, all on body; side-mounted jack.
- **Hardware:** seven-screw black plastic pickguard; six-saddle bridge, bar tailpiece.

JIMMY BRYANT TELECASTER 2003–05

Decorative tooled leather pickguard overlay.

- **Neck:** fretted maple; truss-rod adjuster at body end; one string-guide.
- **Body:** slab, single-cutaway; blonde only.
- **Electronics:** one plain metal-cover pickup (at neck) and one black six-polepiece pickup (angled in bridgeplate); two controls (volume, tone) and three-way selector, all on metal plate adjoining pickguard; side-mounted jack.

03

- **Hardware:** five-screw black plastic pickguard with decorative tooled leather overlay; three-saddle raised sides bridge with through-body stringing. *Custom Shop production.*

J5:BIGSBY 2003–current
Headstock with three tuners each side, Bigsby vibrato tailpiece.
Similar to J5:HB TELECASTER (see following listing) except:
- **Electronics:** one plain metal-cover pickup with visible height-adjustment screws (at neck) and one black six-polepiece pickup (angled in bridgeplate); two controls (volume, tone) on metal plate adjoining pickguard.
- **Hardware:** six-saddle bridge, 'F' logo Bigsby vibrato tailpiece.

J5:HB TELECASTER 2003–current
Headstock with three tuners each side, humbucker at bridge.
- **Neck:** maple with rosewood fingerboard; 22 frets; truss-rod adjuster at headstock end; no string-guide; black-face three tuners-per-side headstock.
- **Body:** slab, single-cutaway; bound; black only.
- **Electronics:** one plain metal-cover pickup with visible height adjustment screws (at neck) and one black coverless humbucker (in bridgeplate); two controls (both volume) on metal plate adjoining pickguard, three-way selector on body; side-mounted jack.
- **Hardware:** eight-screw chrome plastic pickguard; six-saddle flat bridge with through-body stringing.
Custom Shop production.

MARK KNOPFLER STRATOCASTER 2003–current
Signature on headstock.
- **Neck:** maple with rosewood fingerboard; truss-rod adjuster at body end; one string-guide; Mark Knopfler signature on headstock.
- **Body:** red only.
- **Electronics:** three white six-polepiece pickups

(bridge pickup angled); three controls (volume, two tone) and five-way selector, all on pickguard; jack in body face.
- **Hardware:** 11-screw white laminated plastic pickguard; six-pivot bridge/vibrato unit.

RICK PARFITT SIGNATURE TELECASTER 2003–04
Signature on headstock.
- **Neck:** maple with rosewood fingerboard: truss-rod adjuster at body end; one string-guide; Rick Parfitt signature on headstock.
- **Body:** slab single-cutaway; white only, satin finish.
- **Electronics:** one plain metal-cover pickup (at neck) and one black six-polepiece pickup (angled in cut down bridgeplate); two controls (volume, tone) and three-way selector, all on metal plate adjoining pickguard; side-mounted jack.
- **Hardware:** some of it gold-plated; eight-screw black plastic pickguard; four-saddle wrapover bridge/tailpiece with through-body stringing.

ROBERT CRAY STRATOCASTER (MIM) 2003–current
Signature on headstock.
Similar to CLASSIC 60S STRATOCASTER (see 1999 listing) except:
- **Neck:** Robert Cray signature on headstock.
- **Body:** sunburst, silver, or violet.
- **Hardware:** six-saddle bridge with through-body stringing.

SEYMOUR DUNCAN SIGNATURE ESQUIRE 2003–current
See other Esquire listings.

SHOWMASTER CELTIC H (MIK) 2003
Celtic design inlay at 12th fret, offset cutaway body.
- **Neck:** maple glued-in, with rosewood fingerboard; 24 frets; truss-rod adjuster at headstock end; two string-guides; locking tuners; no front markers except Celtic design inlay at 12th fret.
- **Body:** silver only, satin finish.

- **Electronics:** one black coverless humbucker (at bridge); one control (volume) on body; side-mounted jack.
- **Hardware:** black-plated; no pickguard; six-saddle small bridge with through-body stringing.

SHOWMASTER DELUXE HH WITH TREMOLO (MIK) 2003

Glued-in neck, no front markers, bound gold body.
Similar to SHOWMASTER HH WITH TREMOLO (see later listing this year) except:
- **Body:** bound; gold only.
- **Electronics:** chrome-plated; two white coverless humbuckers.

SHOWMASTER H WITH TREMOLO (MIK) 2003

Glued-in neck, no fingerboard front markers, one black humbucker.
- **Neck:** maple glued-in, with rosewood fingerboard, no front markers; 24 frets; truss-rod adjuster at headstock end; two string-guides; locking tuners.
- **Body:** silver only, satin finish.
- **Electronics:** one black coverless humbucker (at bridge); one control (volume) on body; side-mounted jack.
- **Hardware:** black-plated; no pickguard; two-pivot bridge/vibrato unit.

SHOWMASTER HH WITH TREMOLO (MIK) 2003

Glued-in neck, no fingerboard front markers, two black humbuckers.
Similar to SHOWMASTER H (see previous listing) except:
- **Neck:** maple glued-in, with bound rosewood fingerboard.
- **Body:** bound; black only.
- **Electronics:** two black coverless humbuckers; two controls (volume, tone) and five-way selector, all on body.

SHOWMASTER SCORPION HH (MIK) 2003

Scorpion inlay at 12th fret, offset cutaway body.

- **Neck:** maple glued-in with bound rosewood fingerboard; 24 frets; truss-rod adjuster at headstock end; two string-guides; locking tuners; no fingerboard front markers except Scorpion inlay at 12th fret.
- **Body:** bound; black only.
- **Electronics:** two black coverless humbuckers; two controls (volume, tone) and five-way selector, all on body; side-mounted jack.
- **Hardware:** black-plated; no pickguard; six-saddle small bridge with through-body stringing.

SPLATTER STRATOCASTER (MIM) 2003

Colored splatter finish on body and pickguard.
Similar to STANDARD STRATOCASTER (see 1991 listing) except:
- **Body:** various colors, splatter finish.
- **Hardware:** 11-screw plastic pickguard in splatter finish matching body color.

STANDARD SATIN STRATOCASTER (MIM) 2003–06

Satin body finish, small headstock, white black pickguard, three black single-coils.
Similar to STANDARD STRATOCASTER (see 1991 listing) except:
- **Body:** various colors, satin finish.
- **Electronics:** three black six-polepiece pickups.
- **Hardware:** 11-screw black laminated plastic pickguard.

STRAT-O-SONIC DVI 2003–04

Model name on headstock, one large black six-polepiece pickup.
- **Neck:** maple with rosewood fingerboard; 22 frets; truss-rod adjuster at headstock end; staggered height locking tuners; black-face headstock.
- **Body:** semi-solid; sunburst, blonde, or red.
- **Electronics:** one large black six-polepiece pickup (at bridge); two controls (volume, tone) on body; side-mounted jack.
- **Hardware:** six-screw black laminated plastic pickguard; six-saddle wrapover bridge/tailpiece.

'03

STRAT-O-SONIC DVII 2003–06

Model name on headstock, two large black six-polepiece pickups.

Similar to STRAT-O-SONIC DVI (see previous listing) except:

- **Electronics:** two large black six-polepiece pickups; two controls (volume, tone) and three-way selector, all on body.

'59 ESQUIRE 2003–06

Replica of 1959-period original (see ESQUIRE 1950 listing).

'60 TELECASTER CUSTOM 2003–04

Replica of 1960-period original with bound body (see TELECASTER 1951 listing). Offered with three finish distress degrees: N.O.S., Closet Classic and Relic. Custom Shop production.

'65 STRATOCASTER 2003–06

Replica of 1965-period original (see STRATOCASTER CBS SIXTIES 1965 listing). Available with three finish distress degrees: N.O.S., Closet Classic and Relic. Custom Shop production.

AMPLIFIERS

CYBER-CHAMP (MIM) 2003–06

Baby brother of the modeling line.

- **Cabinet:** black Tolex.
- **Controls:** gain, volume, treble, middle, bass, master; reverb, mod f/x, delay; seven pushbuttons for amp type; double-height black control panel.
- **Speakers:** 1x12 Celestion G12P-80.
- **Solid state** with digital models and effects.
- **Output:** 65 watts.

'64 VIBROVERB CUSTOM 2003–current

Replica of original VIBROVERB circa 1964 (see 1963 listing), with modifications as suggested by amp technician Cesar Diaz and changes including:

- **Controls:** rear panel switches for mod (to change preamp tube biasing) and rectifier (tube/solid-state).
- **Speakers:** 1x15 Eminence.

2004

GUITARS

AERODYNE STRATOCASTER (first version) (MIJ) 2004

Aerodyne Series on headstock, three pickups, black pickguard.

- **Neck:** maple with rosewood fingerboard; 22 frets; truss-rod adjuster at headstock end; one string-guide; Aerodyne Series on black-face headstock.
- **Body:** bound with carved top; black only.
- **Electronics:** three black six-polepiece pickups (bridge pickup angled); three controls (volume, two tone) and five-way selector, all on pickguard; jack in body face.
- **Hardware:** 11-screw black laminated plastic pickguard; six-pivot bridge/vibrato unit.

AERODYNE TELE (MIJ) 2004–06

Aerodyne Series on headstock, two pickups.

- **Neck:** maple with rosewood fingerboard; 22 frets; truss-rod adjuster at headstock end; one string guide; Aerodyne Series on black-face headstock.
- **Body:** single-cutaway bound with carved top; black only.
- **Electronics:** one large black rectangular six-polepiece pickup (at neck) and one black six-polepiece pickup (angled in bridgeplate); two controls (volume, tone) and three-way selector, all on body; side-mounted jack.
- **Hardware:** no pickguard; six-saddle flat bridge with through-body stringing.

AMERICAN DELUXE ASH STRATOCASTER 2004–current

Three white six-polepiece pickups, staggered height locking tuners, two-pivot vibrato, ash body.

Similar to AMERICAN DELUXE STRATOCASTER SECOND VERSION (see later listing this year) except:

- **Body:** ash body.
- **Hardware:** 11-screw white or black laminated plastic pickguard.

AMERICAN DELUXE ASH TELECASTER 2004-current

Ash body, 22 frets, volume control with push-switch.
Similar to AMERICAN DELUXE TELECASTER THIRD VERSION (see later listing this year) except:
- **Neck:** fretted maple only.
- **Body:** unbound ash; sunburst or blonde.
- **Hardware:** eight-screw black plastic pickguard.

AMERICAN DELUXE STRATOCASTER (second version) 2004-current

Three white or black six-polepiece pickups, staggered height locking tuners, two-pivot vibrato.
Similar to AMERICAN DELUXE STRATOCASTER FIRST VERSION (see 1998 listing) except:
- **Electronics:** three white or black six-polepiece pickups (bridge pickup angled); three controls (volume with push-switch, two tone) and five-way selector, all on pickguard.
- **Hardware:** 11-screw white, tortoiseshell or black pearl laminated plastic pickguard, or gold plastic pickguard.

AMERICAN DELUXE STRATOCASTER FMT HSS 2004-current

Figured-top body, no pickguard, two black six-polepiece pickups and one black humbucker.
- **Neck:** maple with ebony fingerboard; 22 frets; truss-rod adjuster at headstock end; staggered height locking tuners; roller nut.
- **Body:** figured top; sunburst or colors.
- **Electronics:** two black six-polepiece pickups and one black coverless humbucker (at bridge); two controls (volume with push-switch, tone) and five-way selector, all on body; jack in body face.
- **Hardware:** no pickguard; two-pivot bridge/vibrato unit.

AMERICAN DELUXE STRATOCASTER HSS 2004-current

Two white or black six-polepiece pickups and one white or black humbucker, staggered height locking tuners, two-pivot vibrato.

Similar to AMERICAN DELUXE STRATOCASTER SECOND VERSION (see earlier listing this year) except:
- **Neck:** no string-guide; roller nut.
- **Electronics:** two white or black six-polepiece pickups and one white or black coverless humbucker (at bridge).

AMERICAN DELUXE STRATOCASTER HSS LT 2004–06

Two white or black six-polepiece pickups and one white or black humbucker, staggered height locking tuners, two-pivot locking vibrato.
Similar to AMERICAN DELUXE STRATOCASTER SECOND VERSION (see earlier listing this year) except:
- **Neck:** no string-guide; roller nut.
- **Electronics:** two white or black six-polepiece pickups and one white or black coverless humbucker (at bridge).
- **Hardware:** two-pivot locking bridge/vibrato unit

AMERICAN DELUXE STRATOCASTER QMT HSS 2004-current

Similar to AMERICAN DELUXE STRATOCASTER QMT HSS (see earlier listing this year) except figured-top body.

AMERICAN DELUXE STRATOCASTER 'V' NECK 2004-current

Three white six-polepiece pickups, staggered height locking tuners, two-pivot vibrato, fretted maple neck with 'V' profile (a.k.a. 'boat neck').
Similar to AMERICAN DELUXE STRATOCASTER SECOND VERSION (see earlier listing this year) except:
- **Neck:** fretted maple only, 1950s-style 'V'-shaping.
- **Hardware:** 11-screw white, gold, or copper plastic pickguard.

AMERICAN DELUXE TELECASTER (third version) 2004-current

Contoured bound body, 22 frets, volume control with push-switch.
Similar to AMERICAN DELUXE TELECASTER SECOND VERSION (see 1999 listing) except:
- **Electronics:** one plain metal-cover pickup with

visible height-adjustment screws (at neck) and one black six-polepiece pickup (angled in bridgeplate); two controls (volume with push-switch, tone) and three-way selector, all on metal plate adjoining pickguard.

- **Hardware:** eight-screw white or tortoiseshell laminated plastic pickguard, or gold plastic pickguard.

AMERICAN DELUXE TELECASTER FMT 2004–06

Figured top body, two humbuckers, no pickguard.

- **Neck:** maple with ebony fingerboard; 22 frets; truss-rod adjuster at headstock end; one string-guide.
- **Body:** single-cutaway with figured top; sunburst or colors.
- **Electronics:** two black coverless humbuckers; two controls (volume with push-switch, tone) and three-way selector, all on body; side-mounted jack.
- **Hardware:** no pickguard; six-saddle small bridge with through-body stringing.

AMERICAN DELUXE TELECASTER QMT 2004–06

Similar to AMERICAN DELUXE TELECASTER FMT (see previous listing) but with quilted maple top.

AMERICAN DELUXE 50th ANNIVERSARY STRATOCASTER 2004

Commemorative neckplate, staggered-height locking tuners, gold-plated hardware.

Similar to AMERICAN DELUXE STRATOCASTER SECOND VERSION (see earlier listing this year) except:

- **Neck:** fretted maple only; commemorative neckplate.
- **Body:** sunburst only.
- **Hardware:** gold-plated; 11-screw white plastic pickguard.

AMERICAN TELECASTER HH (second version) 2004–06

Two black coverless humbuckers, black pickguard.

Similar to AMERICAN TELECASTER HS SECOND VERSION (see next listing) except:

- **Electronics:** two black coverless humbuckers.
- **Hardware:** six-saddle small bridge with through-body stringing.

AMERICAN TELECASTER HS (second version) 2004–06

Coverless black humbucker at neck, black pickguard.

Similar to AMERICAN TELECASTER HS FIRST VERSION (see 2003 listing) except:

- **Electronics:** two controls (volume with push-switch, tone), three-way selector, all on metal plate.
- **Hardware:** eight-screw black plastic pickguard.

AMERICAN 50th ANNIVERSARY STRATOCASTER 2004

Commemorative neckplate, locking tuners'

Similar to AMERICAN STRATOCASTER (see 2000 listing) except:

- **Neck:** fretted maple only; commemorative neckplate.

ANTIGUA JAGUAR (MIJ) 2004

Replica of early 1960s-period U.S. original (see 1962 listing), with white/brown shaded body finish and matching pickguard.

ANTIGUA STRATOCASTER (MIJ) 2004

Replica of 1977-period U.S. original with white/brown shaded body finish and matching pickguard (see STRATOCASTER CBS SEVENTIES 1971 listing).

ANTIGUA TELECASTER (MIJ) 2004

Replica of 1977-period U.S. original with white/brown shaded body finish and matching pickguard (see TELECASTER 1951 listing).

BLACKOUT TELECASTER HH (MIK) 2004

Glued-in neck, no front markers, two Seymour Duncan humbuckers.

- **Neck:** maple glued-in, with rosewood fingerboard, no front markers; 22 frets; truss-rod adjuster at headstock end; two string-guides.
- **Body:** single-cutaway; black or blue.
- **Electronics:** two Seymour Duncan-logo black coverless humbuckers; two controls (volume, tone) and three-way selector, all on body; side-mounted jack.
- **Hardware:** black-plated; no pickguard; six-saddle small bridge that incorporates through-body stringing.

CLASSIC '72 TELECASTER DELUXE (MIJ) 2004–current

Replica of 1972-period original (see 1972 listing).

DELUXE PLAYER'S STRAT (MIM) 2004–current

Gold-plated hardware, push-switch, three Noiseless logo white pickups.
Similar to STANDARD STRATOCASTER (see 1991 listing) except:

- **Electronics:** three Noiseless logo white six-polepiece pickups; three controls (volume, two tone), five-way switch and push-switch, all on pickguard.
- **Hardware:** gold-plated; 11-screw tortoiseshell pickguard.

DELUXE STRAT HH (MIM) 2004

Another name for DELUXE FAT STRAT (see 1999 listing).

DELUXE STRAT HH WITH LOCKING TREMOLO (MIM) 2004

Another name for DELUXE DOUBLE FAT STRAT FLOYD ROSE (see 1998 listing).

DELUXE STRAT HSS (MIM) 2004–06

Another name for DELUXE FAT STRAT (see 1999 listing).

DELUXE STRAT HSS WITH LOCKING TREMOLO (MIM) 2004–05

Another name for DELUXE FAT STRAT HSS FLOYD ROSE (see 1998 listing).

ERIC CLAPTON STRATOCASTER (third version) 2004–current

Signature on headstock rear, three Noiseless logo white pickups, Custom Shop headstock logo.
Similar to ERIC CLAPTON STRATOCASTER FIRST VERSION (see 1988 listing) except:

- **Neck:** Eric Clapton signature and Custom Shop logo on back of headstock.
- **Electronics:** three Noiseless logo white six-polepiece pickups; no active circuit.
Custom Shop production.

FLAT HEAD SHOWMASTER HH 2004–06

Name on headstock, 22 frets, two black plain-top humbuckers.
Similar to FLAT HEAD SHOWMASTER (see 2003 listing) except:

- **Electronics:** two black plain top active humbuckers; one control (volume) and three-way selector, both on body.
Custom Shop production.

FLAT HEAD TELECASTER HH 2004–06

Name on headstock, 22 frets, two black plain-top humbuckers, single-cutaway body.
Similar to FLAT HEAD TELECASTER (see 2003 listing) except:

- **Electronics:** two black plain top active humbuckers; one control (volume) and three-way selector, both on body.
Custom Shop production.

JAGUAR BARITONE CUSTOM (MIJ) 2004–06

Model name on headstock, long-scale neck.
Similar to JAGUAR (see 1986 listing) except:

- **Neck:** 21 frets, 28.5-inch scale; truss-rod adjuster at headstock end.
- **Body:** sunburst only.
- **Hardware:** nine-screw tortoiseshell laminated plastic pickguard; six-saddle bridge, bar tailpiece.
Known as JAGUAR BASS VI CUSTOM (see 2006 listing).

'04

JEFF BECK SIGNATURE STRATOCASTER
2004–current
Signature on headstock rear, Custom Shop logo on headstock.
Similar to JEFF BECK STRATOCASTER SECOND VERSION (see 2001 listing) except:
- **Neck:** Jeff Beck signature and Custom Shop logo on back of headstock.
Custom Shop production.

JOHN 5 TELECASTER (MIM) 2004–current
Headstock with three tuners each side, humbucker at bridge.
- **Neck:** maple with rosewood fingerboard; 22 frets; truss-rod adjuster at headstock end; no string-guide; black-face, three-tuners-per-side headstock.
- **Body:** slab single-cutaway bound; black only.
- **Electronics:** one plain metal-cover pickup with visible height adjustment screws (at neck) and one black coverless humbucker (in bridgeplate); two controls (volume, tone) on metal plate adjoining pickguard; three-way selector on body; side-mounted jack.
- **Hardware:** eight-screw chrome plastic pickguard; six-saddle flat bridge with through-body stringing.

LITE ASH STRATOCASTER (MIK)
2004–current
Maple neck with maple fingerboard, three Seymour Duncan-logo black single-coils, black pickguard.
- **Neck:** maple with maple fingerboard; 22 frets; truss-rod adjuster at headstock end; two string-guides.
- **Body:** natural, black, or white.
- **Electronics:** three Seymour Duncan-logo black six-polepiece pickups (bridge pickup angled); three controls (volume, two tone) and five-way selector, all on pickguard; jack in body face.
- **Hardware:** 11-screw black plastic pickguard; two-pivot bridge/vibrato unit.

LITE ASH TELECASTER (MIK) 2004–current
Maple neck with maple fingerboard, black pickguard.

- **Neck:** maple with maple fingerboard; 22 frets; truss-rod adjuster at headstock end; two string-guides.
- **Body:** slab single-cutaway; natural, black or white.
- **Electronics:** one plain metal-cover pickup (at neck) and one Seymour Duncan-logo black six-polepiece pickup (angled in bridgeplate); two controls (volume, tone) and three-way selector, all on metal plate adjoining pickguard; side-mounted jack.
- **Hardware:** eight-screw black plastic pickguard; three-saddle raised-sides bridge/tailpiece with no through-body stringing.

RORY GALLAGHER STRATOCASTER
2004–current
Ultra-distressed finished, one mismatching tuner.
- **Neck:** maple with rosewood fingerboard; truss-rod adjuster at body end; one mismatching tuner; two string-guides.
- **Body:** sunburst, ultra-distressed finish.
- **Electronics:** three white six-polepiece pickups (bridge pickup angled); three controls (volume, two tone) and five-way selector, all on pickguard; jack in body face.
- **Hardware:** 11-screw white laminated plastic pickguard; six-pivot bridge/vibrato unit.
Custom Shop production.

SHOWMASTER BLACKOUT (MIK) 2004–05
Glued-in neck, no front markers, two Seymour Duncan humbuckers.
Similar to SHOWMASTER H (see 2003 listing) except:
- **Body:** black or blue.
- **Electronics:** two Seymour Duncan-logo black coverless humbuckers; two controls (volume, tone) and five-way selector, all on body.

SHOWMASTER ELITE 2004–current
Model name on headstock, 22 frets, glued-in neck, two humbuckers, two-pivot vibrato.
Similar to SHOWMASTER FMT (see 1998 listing) except:
- **Neck:** mahogany glued-in, with ebony

fingerboard, ornate markers; pearl tuner buttons; black-face Telecaster-style headstock.
- **Body:** brown or sunbursts.
- **Electronics:** two Seymour Duncan-logo black coverless humbuckers.
- **Hardware:** two-pivot bridge/vibrato unit.

Body with figured carved top in various woods (FMT, LWT, QMT, SMT).
Custom Shop production.

SHOWMASTER ELITE HARD-TAIL 2004–current

Model name on headstock, 22 frets, glued-in neck, two humbuckers, six-saddle wrapover bridge/tailpiece.
Similar to SHOWMASTER ELITE (see previous listing) except:
- **Neck:** no roller nut.
- **Hardware:** six-saddle wrapover bridge/tailpiece.

Custom Shop production.

SHOWMASTER FAT-HH (MIK) 2004–05

Glued-in neck, front markers, figured ash-top body, two Seymour Duncan humbuckers.
Similar to SHOWMASTER H (see 2003 listing) except:
- **Neck:** fretboard position markers.
- **Body:** with figured ash top; sunburst only.
- **Electronics:** two Seymour Duncan-logo black coverless humbuckers; two controls (volume, tone) and five-way selector, all on body.
- **Hardware:** chrome-plated.

SHOWMASTER FAT-SSS (MIK) 2004–05

Glued-in neck, fingerboard front markers, figured ash-top body, three Seymour Duncan single-coils.
Similar to SHOWMASTER FAT-HH (see previous listing) except:
- **Electronics:** three Seymour Duncan-logo black six-polepiece pickups (bridge pickup angled).

SHOWMASTER QBT-HH (MIK) 2004–current

Glued-in neck, fingerboard front markers, figured bubinga-top body, two Seymour Duncan humbuckers.
Similar to SHOWMASTER H (see 2003 listing) except:
- **Neck:** fretboard position markers.
- **Body:** with figured bubinga top; brown only.
- **Electronics:** two Seymour Duncan-logo black coverless humbuckers; two controls (volume, tone) and five-way selector, all on body.
- **Hardware:** chrome-plated.

SHOWMASTER QBT-SSS (MIK) 2004–05

Glued-in neck, fingerboard front markers, figured bubinga-yop body, three Seymour Duncan single-coils.
Similar to SHOWMASTER QBT-HH (see previous listing) except:
- **Electronics:** three Seymour Duncan-logo single-coils.

STANDARD STRATOCASTER HH (MIM) 2004–06

Two-pivot vibrato, two black humbuckers, black pickguard, small headstock.
Similar to STANDARD STRATOCASTER (see 1991 listing) except:
- **Neck:** maple with rosewood fingerboard only.
- **Electronics:** two black coverless humbuckers.
- **Hardware:** 11-screw black laminated plastic pickguard.

STANDARD STRATOCASTER HSS (MIM) 2004–current

Another name for STANDARD FAT STRAT (see 1999 listing).

STANDARD STRATOCASTER HSS WITH LOCKING TREMOLO (MIM) 2004–current

Another name for STANDARD FAT STRAT FLOYD ROSE (see 1999 listing).

TC-90 THINLINE (MIK) 2004–current

Twin-cutaway body with f-hole.
- **Neck:** maple glued-in, with rosewood fingerboard; 22 frets; truss-rod adjuster at headstock end; two string-guides; Telecaster style headstock with matching color face.

- **Body:** semi-solid slab twin-cutaway; f-hole; redburst or white.
- **Electronics:** two large black six-polepiece pickups; two controls (volume, tone) and three-way selector, all on body; side-mounted jack.
- **Hardware:** six-screw black laminated plastic pickguard; six-saddle bridge, bar tailpiece.

50th ANNIVERSARY GOLDEN STRATOCASTER (MIM) 2004

Gold-finish body.
Similar to CLASSIC 50S STRATOCASTER (see 1999 listing) except:
- **Body:** gold only.

'66 STRATOCASTER 2004–current

Replica of 1966-period original (see STRATOCASTER CBS SIXTIES 1965 listing). Available with three finish distress degrees: N.O.S., Closet Classic, and Relic. Custom Shop production.

AMPLIFIERS

CHAMPION 300 (MII) 2004–current

See CHAMPION 30 (1999 listing).

DELUXE 900 (MII) 2004–current

See DELUXE 90 (1999 listing).

PRINCETON 650 (MII) 2004–current

See PRINCETON 65 (1999 listing).

STAGE 1000 (MII) 2004–current

See STAGE 100 (1999 listing).

STAGE 1600 (MII) 2004–current

See STAGE 160 (1999 listing).

STEEL KING (MIM) 2004–current

Solid-state combo designed specifically for pedal-steel players.
- **Cabinet:** black Tolex.
- **Controls:** input pad, gain, EQ tilt, treble, mid level, mid frequency, bass, mute switch, master, limiter

on/off switch.
- **Speakers:** 1x15 Eminence.
- **Output:** 200 watts.

'57 TWIN-AMP 2004–current

Replica of the tweed TWIN circa 1957 (see 1953 listing). Custom Shop production.

'59 BASSMAN LTD 2004–current

Updated replica of the original tweed BASSMAN (see 1954 listing), with improved cabinet construction and tweed covering and stock 5AR4 tube rectifier (as compared to '59 BASSMAN VINTAGE REISSUE; see 1990 listing). A printed circuit board is used rather than the original hand-wired eyelet board.

'65 TWIN CUSTOM 15 2004–current

Replica of the TWIN REVERB circa 1964–65. Identical to '65 TWIN REVERB VINTAGE REISSUE (see 1992 listing) except:
- **Speakers:** 1x15 Eminence.

2005

GUITARS

AERODYNE STRATOCASTER second version (MIJ) 2005–06

Aerodyne Series on headstock, three pickups, no pickguard.
Similar to AERODYNE STRATOCASTER FIRST VERSION (see 2004 listing) except:
- **Electronics:** three controls (volume, two tone) and five-way selector, all on body; side-mounted jack.
- **Hardware:** no pickguard.

CLASSIC 50s ESQUIRE (MIM) 2005–current

Replica of 1950s-period original (see ESQUIRE 1950 listing).

DELUXE BIG BLOCK STRATOCASTER (MIM) 2005–06.

Block markers, black headstock face, chrome pickguard.

- **Neck:** maple with rosewood fingerboard, block markers; truss-rod adjuster at headstock end; one string-guide; black-face headstock.
- **Body:** black only.
- **Electronics:** two black six-polepiece pickups and one black coverless humbucker (at bridge); two controls (volume, tone) and five-way selector, all on pickguard; jack in body face.
- **Hardware:** 11-screw chrome plastic pickguard; six-pivot bridge/vibrato unit.

DELUXE BIG BLOCK TELECASTER (MIM) 2005–06

Block markers, black headstock face, chrome pickguard.

- **Neck:** maple with rosewood fingerboard, block markers; truss-rod adjuster at headstock end; one string-guide; black-face headstock.
- **Body:** black only.
- **Electronics:** two plain metal-cover pickups with visible height adjustment screws (at neck and in center) and one black six-polepiece pickup (angled in bridgeplate); two controls (volume, tone) and five-way selector, all on metal plate adjoining pickguard; side-mounted jack.
- **Hardware:** eight-screw chrome plastic pickguard; six-saddle flat bridge with through-body stringing.

ERIC JOHNSON STRATOCASTER 2005–current

Engraved neckplate.

- **Neck:** fretted maple; truss-rod adjuster at body end; staggered height tuners; engraved neckplate.
- **Body:** sunburst or colors.
- **Electronics:** three white six-polepiece pickups (bridge pickup angled); three controls (volume, two tone) and five-way selector, all on pickguard; jack in body face.
- **Hardware:** eight-screw white plastic pickguard; six-pivot bridge/vibrato unit.

JAGUAR BARITONE HH (MIJ) 2005–current

Black-face headstock, long-scale neck, two metal-cover humbuckers, one metal control plate.
Similar to JAGUAR BARITONE CUSTOM (see 2004 listing) except:

- **Neck:** black-face headstock.
- **Body:** black only.
- **Electronics:** two metal-cover humbuckers; two controls (volume, tone) and jack, all on metal plate adjoining pickguard; three-way selector on pickguard.
- **Hardware:** 11-screw black laminated plastic pickguard.

JAGUAR HH (MIJ) 2005–current

Special on black-face headstock, two metal-cover humbuckers, three metal control plates.
Similar to JAGUAR (see 1986 listing) except:

- **Neck:** truss-tod adjuster at headstock end; black-face headstock.
- **Body:** black only.
- **Electronics:** two metal-cover humbuckers.
- **Hardware:** nine-screw black plastic pickguard.

JOHN MAYER STRATOCASTER 2005–current

Signature on back of headstock.

- **Neck:** maple with rosewood fingerboard; truss-rod adjuster at body end; one string-guide (further up headstock); John Mayer signature on back of headstock.
- **Body:** sunburst, gold with stripes, or white.
- **Electronics:** three white six-polepiece pickups (bridge pickup angled); three controls (volume, two tone) and five-way selector, all on pickguard; jack in body face.
- **Hardware:** 11-screw white or tortoiseshell laminated plastic pickguard; six-pivot bridge/vibrato unit.

RICHIE KOTZEN SIGNATURE TELECASTER (MIJ) 2005–06

Signature on headstock.

- **Neck:** fretted maple; truss-rod adjuster at headstock end; one string-guide; Richie Kotzen signature on headstock.

- **Body:** contoured single-cutaway; bound; sunburst or green.
- **Electronics:** one plain metal-cover pickup with visible height-adjustment screws (at neck) and one black twin-blade humbucker (angled in bridgeplate); one control (volume), pickup mode rotary switch and three-way selector, all on metal plate adjoining pickguard; side-mounted jack.
- **Hardware:** gold-plated; eight-screw white plastic or white pearl laminated plastic pickguard; six-saddle flat bridge with through-body stringing.

ROBIN TROWER STRATOCASTER
2005–current
Signature on back of large headstock.
- **Neck:** fretted maple only; bullet truss-rod adjuster at headstock end; one string-guide; Robin Trower signature on back of large headstock.
- **Body:** various colors.
- **Electronics:** three white six-polepiece pickups (bridge pickup angled); three controls (volume, two tone) and five-way selector, all on pickguard; jack in body face.
- **Hardware:** 11-screw white laminated plastic pickguard; six-pivot bridge/vibrato unit.
Custom Shop production.

SHOWMASTER FMT-HH (MIK) 2005–current
Glued-in neck, fingerboard front markers, figured maple-top body, two Seymour Duncan humbuckers.
Similar to SHOWMASTER H (see 2003 listing) except:
- **Neck:** dot position markers on fretboard.
- **Body:** with figured maple top; sunburst or natural.
- **Electronics:** two Seymour Duncan-logo black coverless humbuckers; two controls (volume, tone) and five-way selector, all on body.
- **Hardware:** chrome-plated.

SHOWMASTER QMT-HH (MIK) 2005–current
Glued-in neck, fingerboard front markers, figured maple-top body, two Seymour Duncan humbuckers.
Similar to SHOWMASTER QBT-HH (see 2004 listing) except:
- **Body:** with figured maple top; sunbursts only.

SO-CAL SPEED SHOP (MIK) 2005
So-Cal logo on body, red/white graphic finish.
- **Neck:** maple with rosewood fingerboard; 22 frets; truss-rod adjuster at headstock end; two string-guides; matching color headstock, neck and fingerboard.
- **Body:** red/white graphic finish only.
- **Electronics:** one black coverless humbucker (at bridge); one control (volume) on body; side-mounted jack.
- **Hardware:** no pickguard; six-saddle small bridge with through-body stringing.

STANDARD STRATOCASTER FMT (MIM) 2005–06
Figured-top body, no pickguard, three black six-polepiece pickups.
- **Neck:** maple with rosewood fingerboard; truss-rod adjuster at headstock end; one string guide.
- **Body:** with figured top; cherry sunburst or tobacco sunburst.
- **Electronics:** three black six-polepiece pickups (bridge pickup angled); two controls (volume, tone) and five-way selector, all on body; side-mounted jack.
- **Hardware:** no pickguard; six-pivot bridge/vibrato unit.

STRAT-O-SONIC HH 2005–06
Model name on headstock, two black humbuckers.
Similar to STRAT-O-SONIC DVII (see 2003 listing) except:
- **Electronics:** two black coverless humbucker pickups.

TIE-DYE STRAT HS (MIK) 2005
Multi-colored body front, matching headstock face.
- **Neck:** maple with rosewood fingerboard, no front markers; 22 frets; truss-rod adjuster at headstock end; two string-guides; multi-color headstock face.
- **Body:** black, multi-color front, two color combinations only.
- **Electronics:** one black six-polepiece pickup (at neck) and one black coverless humbucker (at

bridge); two controls (volume, tone) and three-way selector, all on body; side-mounted jack.
- **Hardware:** black-plated; no pickguard; two-pivot bridge/vibrato unit.

TORONADO GT HH (MIK) 2005–06
Striped body, four controls, two Seymour Duncan black humbuckers.
- **Neck:** maple with rosewood fingerboard; 24.75-inch scale, 22 frets; truss-rod adjuster at headstock end; two string-guides; matching color headstock face.
- **Body:** contoured offset-waist; various colors, with stripes.
- **Electronics:** two Seymour Duncan-logo black coverless humbuckers; four controls (two volume, two tone) and three-way selector, all on body.
- **Hardware:** no pickguard; six-saddle bridge, bar tailpiece.

TORONADO HH (MIM) 2005–06
Model name on headstock, four controls, two black coverless humbuckers.
Similar to TORONADO (see 1998 listing) except:
- **Body:** various colors.
- **Electronics:** two black coverless humbuckers; four controls (two volume, two tone) and three-way selector, all on body.
- **Hardware:** seven-screw black laminated plastic pickguard; six-saddle bridge, bar tailpiece.

50s TELECASTER WITH BIGSBY (MIJ) 2005–06
Fretted maple neck, 'F' logo Bigsby vibrato tailpiece.
Similar to 50s TELECASTER (see 1951 listing) except:
- **Body:** natural or blonde.
- **Hardware:** six-saddle bridge, 'F' logo Bigsby vibrato tailpiece.

60s TELECASTER WITH BIGSBY (MIJ) 2005–current
Bound body, rosewood fingerboard, 'F' logo Bigsby vibrato tailpiece.

Similar to 60s TELECASTER (see 1951 listing) except:
- **Body:** bound; sunburst or red.
- **Hardware:** six-saddle bridge, 'F' logo Bigsby vibrato tailpiece.

'67 TELECASTER 2005–current
Replica of 1967-period original (see 1951 listing). Offered with three finish distress degrees: N.O.S., Closet Classic, and Relic. Custom Shop production.

AMPLIFIERS

G-DEC (MII) 2005–current
Fender's new concept in practice amps, the solid-state G-DEC (Guitar Digital Entertainment Center) boasts 17 amp simulations, 29 effects, backing tracks, Internal Phrase Sampler, and input for CD or MP3 player.
- **Cabinet:** black Tolex.
- **Controls:** rotary and pushbutton amp and effects selectors; volume, tone.
- **Speakers:** 1x8.
- **Output:** 15 watts.

G-DEC 30 (MII) 2005–current
Similar to G-DEC (see previous listing) except:
- **Controls:** includes separate guitar volume and backing volume.
- **Speakers:** 1x10.
- **Output:** 30 watts.

JAZZ KING (MIM) 2005–current
Adaptation of Steel King (see 2004 listing) for use with jazz guitar, similar other than softer preamp and output stage and:
- **Output:** 140 watts.

METALHEAD (MIM) 2005–current
Super-duper high-powered solid-state amp head designed for heavy metal stylings.
- **Cabinet:** black Tolex with steel 'flight-case style' edge and corner protectors.
- **Controls:** clean: volume, treble, mid, bass; tight drive: gain, volume, presence, treble, mid, bass;

loose drive: drive, volume, presence, treble, mid, bass, boost; fx select.
- **Speakers:** separate 4x12 straight and slant speaker cabs.
- **Output:** 550 watts.

2006

GUITARS

AERODYNE CLASSIC STRATOCASTER (MIJ)
2006–current

Aerodyne Series on headstock, figured carved body top.
Similar to AERODYNE STRATOCASTER FIRST VERSION (see 2004 listing) except:
- **Neck:** Aerodyne Series on matching color headstock face.
- **Body:** bound; figured carved top; various colors.
- **Electronics:** three white six-polepiece pickups (bridge pickup angled).
- **Hardware:** 11-screw white laminated plastic pickguard.

AMERICAN VINTAGE 70s STRATOCASTER
2006–current

Replica of 1970s-period original (see STRATOCASTER CBS SEVENTIES 1971 listing).

AMERICAN 60th ANNIVERSARY STRATOCASTER 2006

Commemorative neckplate, maple neck with rosewood fingerboard.
Similar to AMERICAN STRATOCASTER (see 2000 listing) except:
- **Neck:** maple with rosewood fingerboard only; commemorative headstock logo with jewel inlay; commemorative neckplate.

AMERICAN 60th ANNIVERSARY TELECASTER 2006

Commemorative neckplate, maple neck with rosewood fingerboard.
Similar to AMERICAN TELECASTER (see 2000 listing) except:

- **Neck:** maple with rosewood fingerboard only; commemorative headstock logo with jewel inlay; commemorative neckplate.

CLASSIC PLAYER BAJA TELECASTER (MIM)
2006–current

Similar to CLASSIC 50s TELECASTER (see 1999 listing) except:
- **Neck:** neckplate with 'Custom Shop designed' logo.
- **Body:** blonde or sand.
- **Electronics:** two controls (volume with push-switch, tone) and four-way selector, all on metal plate adjoining pickguard.

CLASSIC PLAYER 50s STRATOCASTER (MIM)
2006–current

Maple fingerboard, locking tuners, two-pivot vibrato.
Similar to CLASSIC 50s STRATOCASTER (see 1999 listing) except:
- **Neck:** locking tuners; neckplate with 'Custom Shop designed' logo.
- **Body:** sunburst or gold.
- **Hardware:** two-pivot bridge/vibrato unit.

CLASSIC PLAYER 60s STRATOCASTER (MIM)
2006–current

Rosewood fingerboard, locking tuners, two-pivot vibrato.
Similar to CLASSIC 60s STRATOCASTER (see 1999 listing) except:
- **Neck:** locking tuners; neckplate with 'Custom Shop designed' logo.
- **Body:** sunburst or blue.
- **Hardware:** two-pivot bridge/vibrato unit.

DELUXE POWER STRATOCASTER (MIM)
2006–current

Fishman Powerbridge vibrato, two volume controls, one tone control.
Similar to STANDARD STRATOCASTER (see 1991 listing) except:
- **Electronics:** two white six-polepiece pickups and

one white coverless humbucker (at bridge); three controls (volume, tone, piezo volume) and five-way switch, all on pickguard.

- **Hardware:** 11-screw tortoiseshell pickguard; six-pivot Fishman Powerbridge vibrato with six piezo pickup bridge saddles.

HIGHWAY ONE STRATOCASTER (second version) 2006–current

Satin body finish, white pickguard, three white single-coils, large headstock.

Similar to HIGHWAY ONE STRATOCASTER FIRST VERSION (see 2002 listing) except:

- **Neck:** large headstock.

HIGHWAY ONE STRATOCASTER HSS (second version) 2006–current

Satin body finish, large headstock, white pickguard, two black single-coils and one black humbucker.

Similar to HIGHWAY ONE STRATOCASTER HSS FIRST VERSION (see 2003 listing) except:

- **Electronics:** two black six-polepiece pickups and one black coverless humbucker (at bridge); black plastic knobs.

HIGHWAY ONE TELECASTER (second version) 2006–current

Satin finish, 22 frets, eight-screw pickguard.

Similar to HIGHWAY ONE TELECASTER FIRST VERSION (see 2002 listing) except:

- **Hardware:** eight-screw white laminate plastic pickguard.

JAGUAR BASS VI CUSTOM (MIJ) 2006

Another name for JAGUAR BARITONE CUSTOM (see 2004 listing).

JAMES BURTON TELECASTER (second version) 2006–current

Similar to JAMES BURTON TELECASTER FIRST VERSION (see 1990 listing) except:

- **Body:** black with blue or red paisley flame pattern, white.

- **Electronics:** three black plain-top pickups.

KOA STRATOCASTER (MIK) 2006–current

Rosewood fingerboard, white pearl pickguard.

- **Neck:** maple with rosewood fingerboard; 22 frets; truss-rod adjuster at headstock end; two string-guides.
- **Body:** with Koa veneer top; sunburst only.
- **Electronics:** three white six polepiece pickups (bridge pickup angled); three controls (volume, two tone) and five-way selector, all on pickguard; jack in body face.
- **Hardware:** 11-screw white pearl laminated plastic pickguard; two-pivot bridge/vibrato unit.

KOA TELECASTER (MIK) 2006–current

Rosewood fingerboard, white pearl pickguard.

- **Neck:** maple with rosewood fingerboard; 22 frets; truss-rod adjuster at headstock end; two string-guides.
- **Body:** with koa veneer top; sunburst only.
- **Electronics:** one plain metal-cover pickup (at neck) and one Seymour Duncan-logo black six-polepiece pickup (angled in bridgeplate); two controls (volume, tone) and three-way selector, all on metal plate adjoining pickguard; side-mounted jack.
- **Hardware:** eight-screw white pearl laminated plastic pickguard; three-saddle raised-sides bridge/tailpiece with through-body stringing.

STANDARD 60th ANNIVERSARY STRATOCASTER (MIM) 2006

Commemorative neckplate, fretted maple neck.

Similar to STANDARD STRATOCASTER (see 1991 listing) except:

- **Neck:** fretted maple only; commemorative neckplate.
- **Body:** silver grey only.

STRAT PRO 2006–current

Large headstock, roller nut, two-pivot vibrato.

- **Neck:** fretted maple, or maple with rosewood

fingerboard; 22 frets (from 2007); truss-rod adjuster at body end; roller nut; large headstock.
- **Body:** black or white, distressed finish.
- **Electronics:** three white six-polepiece pickups (bridge pickup angled); three controls (volume, two tone) and five-way selector, all on pickguard; jack in body face.
- **Hardware:** 11-screw white laminated plastic pickguard; two-pivot bridge/vibrato unit.

Custom Shop production.

TELE THINLINE 2006–current
F-hole body, two single-coils, 12-screw white or black pickguard.
- **Neck:** fretted maple; truss-rod adjuster at body end; one string-guide.
- **Body:** semi-solid slab single-cutaway; f-hole; black or blonde, offered with three finish distress degrees: N.O.S., Closet Classic, and Relic.
- **Electronics:** one plain metal-cover pickup (at neck) and one black six-polepiece pickup (angled in bridgeplate); two controls (volume, tone) and three-way selector, all on pickguard; side-mounted jack.
- **Hardware:** 12-screw white or black plastic pickguard; three-saddle raised-sides bridge with through-body stringing.

Custom Shop production.

'65 MUSTANG REISSUE (MIJ) 2006–current
Replica of 1965-period original with 24-inch scale (see MUSTANG 1964 listing).

AMPLIFIERS

G-DEC EXEC (MII) 2006–current
Similar to G-DEC (see 2005 listing) except:
- **Cabinet:** maple finished in three-tone sunburst.

G-DEC JUNIOR (MII) 2006–current
Champ-shaped version of solid-state G-DEC (see 2005 listing) with:
- **Cabinet:** narrow panel style, black Tolex covering.
- **Controls:** gain, volume, tone, amp select, fx select, loop volume, tempo, key select, loop.
- **Speakers:** 1x8.
- **Output:** 15 watts.

PRINCETON RECORDING-AMP 2006–current
Replica of original blackface tube PRINCETON REVERB circa 1965 (see 1963 listing) except:
- **Cabinet:** modified to hold extra rack-mount style effects and attenuator.
- **Controls:** added controls for rack-mounted effects: compressor: sensitivity and level; overdrive: overdrive, tone, level; attenuation control for Trans-Impedance Power Attenuator; headphone output.

SUPER-SONIC 2006–current
Channel-switching amp designed to capture sounds of '65 Vibrolux, blackface '66 Bassman, plus modern high-gain tones.
- **Cabinet:** blonde or black Tolex.
- **Controls:** vintage: volume, treble, bass, voicing switch; burn: gain 1, gain 2, treble, bass, middle, volume; master reverb; brown control panel.
- **Speakers:** 1x12 Celestion Vintage 30; also available as amp head and separate speaker cabinet.
- **Tubes:** 6x12AX7, 2x12AT7, 2x6L6GC, (solid-state rectifier).
- **Output:** 60 watts.

TWIN-AMP 2006–current
Latest incarnation of the long-time cornerstone of the Fender amp line, now with channel switching and high-gain sounds.
- **Cabinet:** black Tolex.
- **Controls:** normal: volume, treble, bass, middle, bright switch; drive: gain, treble, bass, middle, volume; channel switch; reverb, speed, intensity, presence.
- **Speakers:** 2x12 Eminence.
- **Tubes:** 7x12AX7, 12AT7, 4x6L6GC, (solid-state rectifier).
- **Output:** 100 watts; switchable to 25 watts.

90s

VIRTUAL TONE

The advent of viable 'virtual' instruments, made possible by continuing advances in digital technology, spurred Fender to release the VG Stratocaster in 2007. This guitar was capable of hopping from standard Strat to acoustic guitar to humbucker-loaded rock machine at the flick of a couple of switches.

Unlike models from some rival makers, which displayed no traditional pickups at all and relied entirely on a digital pickup linked to internal emulation circuitry to simulate guitar sounds, Fender packaged the VG Stratocaster within an otherwise standard American Series Stratocaster, wedded to onboard Roland VG technology. Rather than overcomplicating matters and packing in all the potential that digital sound emulation can provide, Fender made a conscious decision to keep the instrument simple and functional, so that players can easily make changes on the fly in live performance without the danger of slipping into an undesired soundscape.

In addition to its three traditional magnetic single-coil pickups, the single master Volume and Tone controls, and five-way pickup selector, the VG Stratocaster carries a slim Roland GK pickup near the bridge, a rotary Mode control to select either Normal (non-digital mode), Stratocaster, Telecaster, Humbucking, or Acoustic sounds, and a rotary Tuning control to select Normal, Dropped D, Open G, D Modal, Baritone, or 12-string sounds. In all, between the Mode control and five-way pickup selector, the VG Stratocaster offers 37 pickup sounds.

Of course, Fender is no newcomer to digital technology. Fender's Cyber series of digital emulation amps was launched in 2001 with the original Cyber-Twin, which was joined for a time by the smaller Cyber-Deluxe, now discontinued. Fender's modeling flagship evolved into the Cyber-Twin SE (Second Edition), a 2x65-watt stereo combo with two 12-inch Celestion speakers, two 12AX7 preamp tubes, and digital amp emulation circuitry. It offered 69 preset sounds, 36 'Your Amp Collection' sounds (with the tones of classic Fender amps alongside the sounds of amps from other makers), and a bevy of digital effects.

Out of the virtual and back into the actual realm, Fender's genuine all-tube amp offerings of 2006 and 2007 included a handful of 'new' models inspired by another lingering glance backward: the Princeton Recording-Amp is a reproduction of the 'blackface' mid-'60s Princeton Reverb with added rack-style compressor, overdrive, and power attenuator; the '57 Deluxe Amp is a faithful replica (many players would say long overdue) of the popular 5E3 model tweed Deluxe circa 1957 (the '57 Amp is the same in a custom piano-lacquered maple cabinet); and the Champion 600 is a partial reproduction of the like-named model launched almost 60 years before, but with a hotrod preamp stage.

The Super-Sonic of 2006 is a blend of looking both backward and forward: it's a channel-switching tube amp with two different voices in its Vintage channel, inspired by the blackface '65 Vibrolux and blackface '66 Bassman, and contemporary rock sounds in its high-gain Burn channel. The 60-watt amplifier is offered either as a 1x12 combo with Celestion Vintage 60 speaker or as an amp head and separate speaker cabinet.

2007

GUITARS

AMERICAN VG STRATOCASTER 2007–current

Extra slim white pickup at bridge, two large and two small controls.

Similar to AMERICAN STRATOCASTER (see 2000 listing) except:

- **Electronics:** extra slim white plain-top Roland synthesizer pickup (at bridge); four controls (two large: Volume, Tone; two small: Roland Mode, Tuning), five-way selector and LED, all on pickguard; jack in body face; side-mounted multi-pin synth output.

G.E. SMITH TELECASTER 2007–current

Differing black position markers, cut down bridge, body-mounted bridge pickup.

- **Neck:** fretted maple, differing-pattern black position markers; truss-rod adjuster at body end; one string-guide.
- **Body:** slab single-cutaway body; red or blonde.
- **Electronics:** one plain metal-cover pickup (at neck) and one black six-polepiece pickup (angled at bridge); two controls (volume, tone) and three-way selector, all on metal plate adjoining pickguard; side-mounted jack.
- **Hardware:** five-screw white or black plastic pickguard; three-saddle raised-sides cut-down bridge with through-body stringing.

J5 TRIPLE TELE DELUXE (MIM) 2007–current

Three split-polepiece humbuckers.

- **Neck:** maple with rosewood fingerboard; 22 frets; truss-rod adjuster at headstock end; no string-guide; black-face large Stratocaster-style headstock.
- **Body:** contoured single-cutaway, bound; black only.
- **Electronics:** three metal-cover split-polepiece humbuckers; two controls (volume, tone) and three-way selector, all on pickguard; side-mounted jack.

- **Hardware:** 13-screw chrome plastic pickguard; six-pivot bridge/vibrato unit.

TELE PRO 2007–current

Five-screw pickguard, 22 frets, four-way selector.

- **Neck:** fretted maple, or maple with rosewood fingerboard; 22 frets; truss-rod adjuster at headstock end; one string-guide.
- **Body:** slab single-cutaway; black or blonde.
- **Electronics:** one plain metal-cover pickup (at neck) and one black six-polepiece pickup (angled in bridgeplate); two controls (volume, tone) and four-way selector, all on metal plate adjoining pickguard; side-mounted jack.
- **Hardware:** five-screw white plastic pickguard; three-saddle raised-sides bridge with through-body stringing.

VINTAGE HOT ROD '52 TELE 2007–current

Metal-cover small humbucker at neck.

Similar to AMERICAN VINTAGE '52 TELECASTER (see 1998 listing) except:

- **Electronics:** one plain metal-cover small humbucker (at neck) and one black six-polepiece pickup (angled in bridgeplate).

VINTAGE HOT ROD '57 STRAT 2007–current

Two white six-polepiece pickups and one twin-blade pickup.

- **Neck:** fretted maple; truss-rod adjuster at body end; one string guide.
- **Body:** sunburst, black, or red.
- **Electronics:** two white six-polepiece pickups and one twin-blade pickup (angled at bridge); three controls (volume, two tone) and five-way selector, all on pickguard; jack in body face.
- **Hardware:** eight-screw white plastic pickguard; six-pivot bridge/vibrato unit.

VINTAGE HOT ROD '62 STRAT 2007–current

Circuitry modifications.

- **Neck:** maple with rosewood fingerboard; truss-rod adjuster at body end; one string guide.

- **Body:** sunburst, white, or green.
- **Electronics:** three white six-polepiece pickups (bridge pickup angled); three controls (volume, two tone) and five-way selector, all on pickguard; jack in body face.
- **Hardware:** 11-screw white laminated plastic pickguard; six-pivot bridge/vibrato unit.
Circuitry modifications as standard.

YNGWIE MALMSTEEN STRATOCASTER (third version) 2007–current
Signature on large headstock, six-pivot vibrato, 'bullet' truss-rod adjuster.
Similar to YNGWIE MALMSTEEN STRATOCASTER SECOND VERSION (see 1998 listing) except:
- **Neck:** 'bullet' truss-rod adjuster at headstock end.

AMPLIFIERS

CHAMPION 600 2007–current
From Vintage Modified line: replica of original CHAMPION 600 (see Amplifiers Of The 1940s listing) but with higher-gain preamp.

'57 AMP 2007
Limited Edition (300) identical to '57 DELUXE AMP (see next listing) except:
- **Cabinet:** black piano-lacquered solid maple with retro split-grille design.
- **Speakers:** 1x12 Celestion Alnico Blue.
Custom Shop production.

'57 DELUXE AMP 2007–current
Replica of tweed DELUXE circa 1957 (see Amplifiers Of The 1940s listing). Custom Shop production.

This index is divided into two A-to-Z listings, one for amplifiers; the other for guitars.

index

index

index

index

The publishers would like to thank the following for their contributions to this project.

Fender Facts:
Paul Day; Dave Hunter.

DVD:
Dave Hunter and Carl Verheyen; Brian Fischer, whose fine collection provided the wonderful instruments seen throughout the DVD, and also Stephanie Fischer; Colin Mottram and Kathy Plaskitt at Lenzflare Creative Production for shooting, lighting, and authoring the DVD.

Trademarks. The Fender logos used on the jacket of this package are registered trademarks of Fender Musical Instruments Corporation, used with permission. Also, throughout the book we have mentioned a number of registered trademark names. Rather than put a trademark or registered symbol next to every occurrence of a trademarked name, we state here that we are using the names only in an editorial fashion and that we do not intend to infringe any trademarks.

Updates? The author and publisher welcome any new information for future editions. Write to: Interactive Fender, Jawbone, 2A Union Court, 20-22 Union Road, London SW4 6JP, England. Or you can email: interfender@jawbonepress.com.